COMPLETE SCREENWRITING COURSE

Charles Harris

Teach Yourself®

Complete Screenwriting Course

Charles Harris

First published in Great Britain in 2014 by John Murray Learning. An Hachette UK company.

First published in US in 2014 by The McGraw-Hill Companies, Inc.

British Library Cataloguing in Publication Data: a catalogue record for this title is available from the British Library.

Library of Congress Catalog Card Number: on file.

Paperback ISBN 978 1 47 180176 1

eBook ISBN 978 1 47 180551 6

10 9 8 7 6 5 4 3 2 1

The publisher has used its best endeavours to ensure that any Website addresses referred to in this book are correct and active at the time of going to press. However, the publisher and the author have no responsibility for the Websites and can make no guarantee that a site will remain live or that the content will remain relevant, decent or appropriate.

The publisher has made every effort to mark as such all words which it believes to be trademarks. The publisher should also like to make it clear that the presence of a word in the book, whether marked or unmarked, in no way affects its legal status as a trademark.

Every reasonable effort has been made by the publisher to trace the copyright holders of material in this book. Any errors or omissions should be notified in writing to the publisher, who will endeavour to rectify the situation for any reprints and future editions.

Typeset by Cenveo® Publisher Services.

Printed and bound in Great Britain by CPI Group (UK) Ltd, Croydon CR0 4YY.

John Murray Learning policy is to use papers that are natural, renewable and recyclable products and made from wood grown in sustainable forests. The logging and manufacturing processes are expected to conform to the environmental regulations of the country of origin.

John Murray Learning
338 Euston Road
London NW1 3BH

www.hodder.co.uk

Also available in ebook

For Elaine

'There's nothing more important in making movies
than the screenplay.'
Richard Attenborough

'Do something for me – that idea you have, that script you want
to start, that film you want to make, go and do it. Whatever you
do, do it. Now.'
Elliot Grove, Raindance Film Festival

Acknowledgements

This book would have been impossible without the help of many people, far too many to name all of them here. First must come Bernard Miller, who originally taught me that writing could be fun. Then, the innumerable directors, producers, script editors and fellow writers who have helped, nudged and pushed me over the years. Linda Aronson, who kept telling me to write down what I knew. The many industry players and teachers who generously donated their time to give me the view from their part of the industry – in particular Tim Bevan, Naomi de Pear, Farah Abushwesha, Richard Holmes, Kate Leys, Chris Rice, Skip Press, Jane Wittekind, Kevin Dolan, Simon Williamson, Paul Ashton, Brian Dunnigan, Jude Holland, Anita Lewton and Elliot Grove. I am also enormously grateful to: Richard Moxon, for his advice on the legal sections; Jan Woolf, Eve Richings and Charlie Hopkinson in my own writers' group, for their constant encouragement and feedback; Penny Macleod, Mark Hill, Gianpiero Cognoli and Afia Nkrumah for their detailed comments; my fellow directors and screenwriters at Euroscript, who keep challenging me to rethink what I thought I knew; my agent Julian Friedmann for providing necessary reality checks; Chris Jones and the London Screenwriters' Festival, for their support of this book, and of screenwriting in general; Chris Sykes, who suggested to John Murray Learning that I write this in the first place; Victoria Roddam, for welcoming me in; and Jamie Joseph and Sarah Bauer, for making this book a reality. Finally, I would like to thank my wife, Elaine, for her astute comments and for putting up with this mad career over the years.

Contents

About the author

Charles Harris is an award-winning writer-director and a highly regarded script consultant. He has written and directed for cinema, TV drama and documentary and directed theatre. In 1983 he co-founded the London Screenwriters Workshop, the first screenwriters' workshop in the world, now Euroscript, where he still teaches. He has lectured and run workshops at London University, the London Film School and internationally, and continues to direct and write, with a first novel due out next year. He lives in north London with his wife and has two sons.

List of figures

1

How to use this book

In 1981 only 24 films were made in the UK and almost all TV drama was produced in-house. Now, over 250 movies are made in the UK each year, an increase of over 1,000 per cent. Over 5,000 are produced worldwide, and independent TV production is also blossoming. Yet how many of those movies, dramas and series do you remember? How many did you see? How many more screenplays were written yet never made?

At their most powerful, cinema and television have the ability to move us, to change us, to reflect the world back to us or take us to new worlds. They draw us in, engage us deeply for two hours, or two minutes, or many years. At the heart of all these experiences lies a screenplay. Except for a few (very few) entirely improvised dramas, every great movie and TV programme was born as words on a page.

If you're like me, one day you decided to write a story for the screen, whether that screen was in a cinema, on TV or DVD, or even a computer or mobile phone. Perhaps you started by loving and admiring certain films or TV programmes. You thought, this doesn't seem too difficult: 90 or so pages equal 90 or so minutes of screen time and (compared to a novel or play) relatively few words.

Then you found it wasn't so easy. The blank page glared back at you. Those few words felt inadequate, weak. When you did manage to complete a script, it was rejected with hardly a word of explanation. You began to look for rules to help you; a template to follow; a path through the wilderness; a way to beat the competition.

When I was starting, I had the luck to make friends with a group of other wannabes, and we formed what turned out to be the first scriptwriters' workshop in the world, London Screenwriters' Workshop. At that time we had no books expounding ideas about the three acts or heroes' journeys. We had to find our own way and teach ourselves. We still exist, as Euroscript, and are still made up of people who work in the industry, helping writers improve. I, myself, have continued to write, direct and produce for TV, cinema and theatre, and have won international awards. I have worked with hundreds, if not thousands, of writers, directors and producers, learning from some and guiding others, including screenwriters from all over the world. In the process, I have developed a range of very practical techniques and exercises for helping writers find their stories, and their individual voice, many of which are in this book.

 Tim Bevan, co-director, Working Title Films

'One of the beauties of what I do is that there are very few businesses where you've been in it for 25–30 years, and at the top of your game, where you're still properly learning something new, every time.'

What this book gives you

I'm guessing you picked this book up because you, too, want to learn to write better screen stories. Maybe you have never written anything before. Or you tried and now you want to improve. Or you have tasted success and realize, as we did, that you never stop learning and improving. Or it could be that you love watching cinema and TV and simply want to learn more about the strange and wonderful craft on which it all relies.

You can use this book in many ways – as a primer to get you started; as a road map that you can work through step by step, ending up with a completed, marketable script; as a reference work to dip into when you have specific problems to address. You will also learn methods for breaking the rules and getting away with it, because you will need to do that, too.

This book will give you professional techniques that work in real-life writing situations, time and time again, and can be relied on. These are methods which can release your imagination, not lock it in.

Here is an outline of what you can expect:

 Snapshot – a short exercise to draw your attention to some concept or technique

 Write – a longer exercise where you are invited to write a page or two related to the topic of the chapter

 Edit – a chance to rework and strengthen a piece of your own work

 Workshop – see below for a detailed explanation of this end-of-chapter exercise

 Key quote – what screenwriters and others have had to say about a topic

 Key idea – the most important element to grasp

 Focus point – advice to take forward and apply to what you write

Where to next? – outlines what we're going to cover in the next chapter.

What this book doesn't give you

What this book will not give you is a one-size-fits-all formula that you can apply without using your brain. Nor does it get you out of the job of doing the writing.

I won't tell you to write a particular kind or script. To write well you should be true to your writer's voice. But first you need to discover what that voice is. It may grow out of the kinds of films and TV programmes you like to watch – or it may be surprisingly different.

The way to find your voice is to write – to develop an idea, create a script and edit it. And then to do it a second time, and a third. Write until a pattern begins to emerge, a style, something that is different, original and yet truthful. You.

> ## Key idea
>
> An artist needs luck, skill and effort.

Any good artist needs luck – whether you call it inspiration, the Muse, or simply ideas. There is an element of something magical and unpredictable that can't be reduced to rules. No book can give you that magic. However, to develop the magic (often to find the magic in the first place) takes skill and effort. You need to master a number of important tools and techniques. Indeed, you need to become so skilled that you can use them without thinking.

A carpenter becomes unconsciously adept at using his tools in order to focus on the wood. A composer becomes instinctively able to manipulate sound in order to concentrate on making music. In the same way, you need to become unconsciously adept at structure, character, dialogue and the other tools of the screenwriter's trade.

The way to become instinctively adept at a skill is to use it, frequently and energetically. Preferably with good guidance and feedback.

 Key idea

The way to become adept at a skill is to use it again and again with good guidance, so that it becomes instinctive.

The screenwriting road map

Writers work in many different ways. Some like to start with a central idea, maybe a single sentence, and build on it, writing a treatment or synopsis, and then a first draft script. Others start writing without any idea of where they are going and discover the shape when they edit the results. Yet others will mix and match – planning roughly but not in so much detail as to cramp their imagination.

If you read this book from start to end, it will lead you step by step through the process of writing for cinema or TV, single drama or series, from planning to selling. However, maps are just maps, and all journeys have variations, so I'll also be showing you how to vary the route to suit your individual needs.

You can also use this book to dive in and start writing by the seat of your pants, or even to jump to a chapter that covers a particular problem you want to solve.

 Focus point

You can use this book to write a script from start to finish, or vary the route to suit your needs.

There is much energy devoted to structure in screenwriting literature, and probably rather more heat than light. There are fierce supporters of three-act structure, who trace the ideas back to classical Greek tragedy and Aristotle, and they include many producers and script executives who will judge your work by three-act standards. And there are equally fierce opponents, who insist that writing in three acts will destroy your talent. I examine both sides and show you how to get the best of both worlds (later we'll look at how you can abandon three acts altogether if you so wish).

Great screenplays vary from the Hollywood rollercoasters of a Joe Eszterhas to the intelligent humour of a Tom Stoppard or the indie thoughtfulness of a John Sayles, from the edgy crime satire of Vince Gilligan's *Breaking Bad* to the offbeat horror of Fabrice Gobert's series *Les Revenants* (*The Returned*), from the emotional fizz of Bollywood to the contemplative stillness of the Japanese master Ozu.

You'll learn how to work within the rules, if that's what you wish. You'll learn how to use GOATS to strengthen every aspect of your script, how to develop an involving Character Constellation and a powerful Obstacle Chain to underpin your storytelling. And if you wish, you'll also learn how to write unconventional scripts, with unusual characters, scenes, dialogue and visuals.

Then, I'll show you what you need to get your script to market. How to find producers for film and for TV. How to pitch effectively. How to build your career and what you can look forward to when you succeed.

The book ends with appendices of useful information, including a glossary of technical terms you'll come across, a list of useful books and websites to help you take your skills to the next level, and some suggested organizations and places to help you network.

Making it stick

Just as going to the gym gets you fit only if you do the workouts, so your writing muscles will develop only if you practise the skills. To this end, you'll find a range of exercises you can use if you wish, to help you bed in the core ideas. Some are relatively short one-off exercises and others are a little more demanding. These are designed to allow you to build on what you've learned.

A useful method for speeding up your development is to keep a writer's journal. Begin it when you start a new project, and record each day that you work on it. Use it to note down your initial ideas, thoughts, feelings, hopes and fears. Don't hold back. Share (with yourself) all your doubts and difficulties as they arise – and the solutions that you find. Be brave and share, too, your immodest dreams of glorious success and the people who will be changed, challenged or amused by your story. In the dark days, when nothing seems to be working, you can turn to it to remind yourself why you started and how far you've come. And, at the end, you can look back to see what you have learned.

Writers don't reward themselves enough for the hard work they do. It may be a long time before anyone else rewards you. Give yourself rewards along the way, large or small, to keep your energy high and focused.

Focus point

Reward yourself as you go.

In particular, reward good habits – completing a tough scene, writing on a day when you didn't feel like it, or simply getting up early and facing a blank screen.

One word of warning: all writers crave certainty. We want to be sure that what we're writing is good, effective, worth while. Some books make the process seem clear and certain. This is attractive, but misleading. From the inside, the journey often feels anything but clear. Indeed, I have come to believe that uncertainty is a valuable part of writing. Too much certainty can lead to a very dull, if slick, screenplay. A living screenplay comes from a process of discovery. A good writer learns to live with, indeed to welcome, uncertainty – to welcome the chance to explore.

The same applies to exercises. You may be uncertain as to whether they are taking you anywhere. Live with the uncertainty and go where the exercises take you. That way you will discover what you don't expect.

We've all had the experience of going to a workshop, or reading a book, and rediscovering a tip or technique we'd forgotten. Wouldn't it be better to remember it the first time?

If you want to retain new techniques or ideas, use them, preferably as soon as possible. One excellent method is to create a 'Three ways' list: each time you come to a new understanding, turn to the 'Three ways' pages at the end of this book and write down what you've just learned, in a sentence. Underneath add three simple, concrete actions that you can take, based on this new learning. (You can, of course, add more.)

For example, if 'The way to find your voice is to write' struck home, you might put down:

1 Schedule a fixed time to write every morning, starting Monday.

2 Practise at least one exercise a day, starting tomorrow lunchtime.

3 Mark the number of pages I complete each day on my calendar.

To be most effective, the three actions should be specific and should include the time or date that you're going to perform them. At least one should be easy enough that you can be sure that you'll do it. And if you reward yourself afterwards, that makes it even more likely that you'll remember next time.

Technical terms will generally be defined the first time they appear. If you miss that definition or want to be reminded, most will be found in the glossary at the back of the book (and in the index of the paperback format).

Since writers (and directors, producers and agents) can be male or female, I've varied the pronouns I've used in a totally arbitrary manner. To try to combine them always as *he or she* or, worse, *s/he* would be too distracting. So I use *he, she, they* and *you* more or less at random. Blame the English language.

Using a workshop

Each chapter ends with a workshop exercise, which you can work through alone or in a group. I highly recommend joining a screenwriters' workshop, if you want to progress rapidly. A good group will provide you with a support network and a source of helpful feedback to allow you to grow.

There are two kinds of screenwriters' workshop: informal collections of equals, and more formal groups with an experienced writer or consultant in charge. In both, you each read one an other's work (either beforehand or aloud during the workshop) or perform an exercise, and then comment in turn. If there's a professional convenor, they will normally be the last to give their feedback before throwing the issues out for general discussion.

Most groups will meet regularly, sending out reading material in advance, and sharing any costs. A professional consultant will normally expect to be paid, although it's rarely a great amount and often less than covers their time. A well-run group will also have clear rules as to how the time is divided and how much material can be submitted at a time, as well as rules about the importance of maintaining a constructive, supportive atmosphere.

Key idea

A workshop, formal or informal, is an ideal way of combining a support network with a constructive focus group that helps everyone to grow.

Look for a local group on the Internet, or through local film clubs and arts or adult education centres. If there isn't one close to where you live, consider setting one up yourself. Send out a call for fellow screenwriters via Twitter, Facebook or LinkedIn, through local arts organizations or, in the UK, your nearest regional screen development agency.

In addition, Euroscript runs a regular development workshop in London and will also assist with advice on how to set up a group of your own, wherever you are. They also have consultants who can come out to groups in the UK or abroad, to help get things started and run a feedback session.

Alan Parker: Urban Warrior

'Many are prepared to suffer for their art, few are prepared to learn how to draw.'

Where to next?

The world is filled with people who talk about writing, and never do anything about it. You've done something. At the very least, you've picked up this book.
Now turn the page and we can get started.

2

Getting into gear

To write your script and allow your creative juices to flow, you will need four fundamental skills – skills which will form the basis of everything that follows. Think of them as four gears – as in driving a car. Most writing problems, such as writer's block, come from using one of these skills at the wrong time, and most writing solutions start with choosing the right skill at the right time.

First gear: look in – imagine

Ideas can come from anywhere and everywhere. They surface unexpectedly and partly formed, born out of your feelings, memories, concerns, experiences, to make themselves available for use. And one of the primary jobs of a creative artist is to nourish the process and encourage it to bring us its unpredictable gifts.

Look in. Look inside yourself and see what there is to be seen. At times, this will be nothing. This doesn't mean you give up. An amateur can afford to do nothing and wait for those golden moments. A professional sets about preparing the soil so that inspiration can grow.

THE 'SEED IMAGE'

You may find it useful to start with the 'seed' of a picture, an image that somehow both stimulates your imagination further and sums up an idea that may become a script one day.

> ## Key idea
>
> Writers start with pictures in their minds.

The novelist Paul Scott tells of how an image once came to him: a woman was running down a road in India. This was his start. He became curious; he asked himself who she was, who she was running away from so urgently, where she might be running to. From this single image grew four books, the acclaimed series of novels known as the 'Raj Quartet', and a fourteen-part award-winning TV series, *The Jewel in the Crown*.

Seed images can also help when you take over an idea that comes from outside.

When I was commissioned to rewrite the script of a Portuguese epic, I found a vivid story based on a true-life struggle by a group of farmers against poverty and injustice. The events were dramatic and yet, initially, rather formless. I needed to find my way into the script.

The story opened in the dead of night. A young farmer was walking home, finding his way by the light of a small lantern along a mountain railway track. The image of that single lantern became my seed image. With its help, the screenplay followed a continuous movement, from fighting alone to strength in numbers – from a single lantern, to two lamps, to a burning warehouse, all the way to the climactic rising of the entire region.

Ethan Coen, on *Inside Llewyn Davis*

'One day Joel just said, "What about this? Here's the beginning of a movie: Wouldn't it be interesting, to start with a folk singer, specifically Dave Van Ronk, getting beaten up in the alleyway behind Gerde's Folk City?" We thought about the scene, and then we thought, "Why would anyone beat up a folk singer?" So it became a matter of trying to come up with a screenplay, a movie that could fit around that and explain the incident.'

LOOKING IN

Find a quiet place where you won't be disturbed. It may help to close your eyes. Imagine that there is a screen in your mind and that you can put any image you like there – black and white or colour, still or movie, silent or sound.

Now think about the script you want to write. What pictures appear on the screen? If there are none, then invent some. Feel free to borrow from other films, from your own memories or from any other source.

When you have one or more pictures that satisfy and excite you, start to ask questions: where, what, who, why, how, when? What came before? What might come next? Do other pictures start to appear?

Try out other possible seed images until you have one you feel works best as the seed of your story. (Don't worry if you're not sure yet; you'll be able to improve and enrich your pictures as you develop your ideas.)

 ## Focus point

Keep a notebook with you at all times – whether paper or electronic – to write down seed ideas, lines of dialogue that come to mind, intuitions. Refer to it later when looking for inspiration or guidance.

RUNNING THE FILM IN YOUR HEAD

During the process of developing your ideas, you should constantly be adding new images.

See how movies often open with an appropriate mood shot – light glinting on water at night (*The Usual Suspects*), an actor applying a false moustache (*Tootsie*) – if you can find a strong mood image early on, you have your opening fixed and never have to face the terror of the blank first page. It is equally useful to have a rough image for the end – though you probably don't as yet know how you are going to get there. You may have a sense of a picture: the two lovers parting; the young child finding his way home (you'll work out the how and when later).

One useful habit is to run the film in your mind as it grows. The joy of 'looking in' is that your imagination can be fluid and flexible. Once your story is written down in more detail, it becomes more difficult to rearrange. When you are still in your mind, you can jump, shift and edit at will.

'The way you write a screenplay is that you close your eyes and run the movie in your head and then you write it down.'

Run your story in your head...

Run your story in your imagination. Note those places where you already know many details and other points where your imagination goes fuzzy, maybe even leaps over important parts. That's fine. You can go back over it later and see what's missing.

You'll use the skill of 'looking in' throughout the writing process. If you find that you're stuck with a scene, you can ask yourself the following questions:

• Have you imagined it fully yet?

• What could be added?

• What could be subtracted?

As you develop your ideas, you'll create notes, start to write down fragments of action and dialogue that come to you, perhaps even whole scenes.

However, you will find that there is a limit to what you can create through imagination alone. Some gaps can't be filled. Some pictures just don't come.

What you need now is to 'look out' …

Second gear: look out – observe

The well of your imagination constantly needs refreshing – and that refreshment comes from outside.

It's a myth that great creative geniuses work by plucking ideas from nowhere. The images that come to you, however bizarre and strange, grew out of your life, your memories, your hopes and fears. Even Shakespeare invented the plots of only two of his plays. The rest were adaptations. His characters, his language and his ideas were deeply rooted in the world he lived in.

Key idea

Writers observe.

Start by watching how people really behave – as opposed to how they do it in books and films. Fill your notebook with what you see around you, describing:

- interesting characters
- actions
- patterns of speech
- locations
- anything and anyone that may help fuel ideas as your scripts progress.

For example, note actions and gestures that betray what people are really thinking and feeling – these will be valuable in developing character and freshening descriptions of action. And listen to how people really speak: the way they express themselves, their rhythms and their verbal tics.

RESEARCHING YOUR STORY

Whatever your subject, your script will gain from research into the world of your story, the characters, their jobs, beliefs and so on. It doesn't have to be heavy or boring – keep it light and fun to do. Obviously, you'll want to research a story that's set in a period or social world that is far from your own. However, don't underestimate the value of careful observation, even of a world you know well, to bring out freshness and avoid easy clichés. And sometimes the smallest detail can stimulate your imagination or add a sense of credibility to a scene.

In our modern society, there is little excuse for not researching – we can draw on bookshops, libraries, TV, cinema, radio, plays, museums, galleries, newspapers, magazines and, of course, the Internet. Nowadays there are also powerful programs and apps that will help you quickly clip and store a wide range of material on your computer, tablet or phone (see the Resources section for useful software).

 Looking out

Consider the world of your story. What do you already know and what more might you need?

List areas you wish to explore (such as locations, social forces, beliefs, characters) and possible sources of information (experts, websites, Facebook, Twitter, books, newspaper archives).

Begin your research. As you read/watch/listen, jot down any thoughts that come to you – not solely the substance of the research but also any ideas that spark scenes, characters, lines of dialogue. Keep it light and enjoyable.

When you've finished, write a very rough draft scene. Try not to refer to your research directly in the scene, but allow it to add a flavour or subtext to what happens between the characters.

RESEARCHING WITH PEOPLE

Nothing is quite as powerful as talking to real people … from police officers and nurses to footballers, divorced couples, stage magicians or astronauts.

This may sound daunting, but most people, if approached in a friendly and open manner, are more than happy to talk about their area of expertise. Lawyers and police can provide valuable insights into the minds of the criminals they deal with. Universities contain experts in all kinds of fields. Other experts can be found through their blogs, newspaper articles or books.

Approach sources with care and politeness. If it is a large organization, use the press office to help you make contact with the right person. Stress that you are looking for deep background. Explain that you don't want to expose personal matters, but to ensure that your story is accurately based.

Some people will not want to be involved. Accept their wishes politely and move on. Others will go beyond the call of duty to help you. I have visited a secret weapons factory, been offered a 100-mph ambulance drive with lights and sirens, shadowed a prosecution lawyer, discussed the ins and outs of life in a rock band, and toured a gangland front-line with a policeman who pointed out all the local hoods. Many of my sources have been remarkably open and generous in helping me solve plot problems and suggesting new twists.

This leads to another benefit of research meetings – you'll find yourself running your early plot ideas past a number of people who know your story world, and gaining from their feedback.

ENJOY

Looking out doesn't only mean conventional research. It includes everything that will add to your skillset, from studying how other screenwriters work, perhaps by reading and listening to their interviews and biographies, to reading books on screenwriting (such as this one).

In the early stages, follow anything that stimulates your writer's mind. Learn about visual storytelling from art galleries; structure and character from football matches; dialogue from sitting in a coffee shop and eavesdropping.

It can be good to follow your instincts. An apparent detour into Arctic plant life or African music may turn up later as a line of dialogue or an unexpected character insight. Or maybe it's a sign that you need to give yourself a break.

But beware! Don't let the joys of research become a way of putting off the inevitable. Because at some point you have to sit down and write …

Nora Ephron, screenwriter

'I don't care who you are. When you sit down to write the first page of your screenplay, in your head, you're also writing your Oscar acceptance speech.'

Third gear: look forward – create

All the imagination and observation in the world ultimately mean nothing for your script without words on a page.

Writers write … frequently, voraciously, quickly, slowly, when inspired, and when not in the mood at all. An amateur waits for inspiration; a professional gets on with the job and writes.

Key idea

Writers write. Amateurs wait. Professionals get on with it.

Don't confuse writing with the next skill – editing. Most books about 'writing' aren't actually about the act of writing at all, but about editing, about getting it right.

However, putting the words on the page is *not* the time for getting it right. If you try to judge your work as you write it, you will wrestle yourself to a halt. It is the quickest way to give yourself writer's block. And the quickest way to solve writer's block is to write … anything, good, bad, indifferent … without judgement.

Focus point

Don't get it right – get it written!

This is *first draft* writing – and there is no good or bad in a first draft. The sole job of a first draft is to give you something to edit in the second.

The novelist Stephen King talks about how he creates his first drafts 'with the study door closed' – that is, with his critical mind deliberately left outside – and his second draft 'with the study door open'.

In fact, it is impossible to judge whether something is right or wrong while you are in the process of writing it. Your inner writer and your inner critic simply can't work properly at the same time. That passage that you are sure is brilliant when you write it may well look terrible the next day. Conversely, the scene you are convinced is terrible may turn out to be one of the best you've ever written.

The inner critic is the part of you that deals with abstract ideas. It is good at analysing problems, but not so good at coming up with creative solutions. Writers who focus too much on analysis are great at editing, but tend to create dry and flat scripts without the energy and detail that bring good writing to life.

By contrast, your creative mind has little interest in abstract thoughts. It loves to get lost in the moment and to relish the words for their own sake. If you have ever come out of a session of writing (or any other activity) with a slightly woozy sense of waking up and 'coming back' to the world, then you were sunk in creative mind work.

The best way to strengthen your creative mind is speed-writing.

Jack London, novelist

'You can't wait for inspiration. You have to go after it with a club.'

Speed-write

To develop your creative fluency, set aside a regular period of time every day. It doesn't have to be long – ten minutes a day is ideal. Ensure that you won't be interrupted. Turn off your phone. Now take a notepad or open a file on your computer and write non-stop … no editing, no going back, no rereading. Just keep putting down words.

During that ten minutes it doesn't matter what you write. Describe what you can see and hear, write down what you had for breakfast, boast, complain … anything. If you can't think of anything to write, then write 'I can't think of anything to write' over and over again, until something else comes.

The point is to practise ignoring that little critical voice in your head. At first this may not seem easy, but after a while you'll find that you can. Your inner critic won't understand what you're doing. It may even tell you that this exercise is stupid, a waste of time. It will try anything it can to distract you, but soon you'll get so engrossed in some detail of the shape of a rose or the sound of a train stopping that it will fade away for a few moments.

If it comes back before the set period is up, then politely ask it to step aside again until the ten minutes is over.

Seamus Heaney, poet

'The gift of writing is to be self-forgetful … to get a surge of inner life or inner supply or unexpected sense of empowerment, to be afloat, to be out of yourself.'

Practice is the key to trusting your writing mind. With experience, you'll grow to recognize the moments when your inner critic returns. You might, for example, find yourself doubting that you are any good, or that you have chosen the right scene to work on, or that you are writing fast enough, or slowly enough, or a myriad other concerns that your analytical inner critic may come up with. It likes to think that it should always be in charge, but you will learn to trust your creative mind and gently ask the critical voice to withdraw for a while, so that you can continue to create.

The good thing is that the louder and more insistent your inner critic, the more you can relax and create, confident that it will be there when you need it. For that's when you open the study door, and look at what you've got …

Fourth gear: look back – edit

That critical voice, which you asked to step back earlier, now takes centre stage. However, it must be a constructive critic if it's to be of use.

Most developing writers are their own strongest critics. Some criticism, however, can be negative and destructive. Constructive criticism is different. A constructive critic starts from the position of wanting to help. You need to work constructively with your inner critic to make your screenplay the best it can be. Finding a flaw in your writing is painful, but essential if you want to make it better. It's easy to feel a failure when something doesn't work, but almost all problems can be solved with time and patience. The experienced writer learns to welcome the feedback and turn the painful feeling into a positive determination to improve.

READ, READ, READ

The first way to sharpen your editing skills is to read. Just as a novelist needs to read novels and a painter needs to study paintings, if you want to improve, you absolutely must read as many scripts as you possibly can.

 Key idea

Writers read – voraciously.

Read screenplays of movies and TV programmes you've seen and of those you haven't seen, especially those you haven't. Because this is what you will be doing with your own work: you will need to read and analyse it before you see a single frame on screen.

Scripts can be found in a number of ways. They are published in book form, sold as original scripts and available (often for free) on the Internet (see Resources). You can also join online sites where you read unproduced scripts. Often you can give feedback in exchange for feedback on your own – this is an invaluable way to strengthen your critical muscles.

It's easier to find movie scripts than TV scripts, but the situation is improving, and some genres are more widely featured than others. Also, many screenplays will not be laid out correctly (see Appendix 2) and some are 'post-production' scripts, transcribed by fans or academics after the film was made. Nevertheless, any script you read will teach you something.

Howard Jacobson, novelist

'To teach them how to write, teach them how to read.'

STRENGTHENING YOUR EDITING MUSCLES

Other ways to sharpen your critical mind include reading biographies of writers and film-makers, as well as interviews, articles, reviews and essays. Books on other kinds of writing will also bring new perspectives. A good writer can make you more sharply aware of possibilities and pitfalls that may not be immediately obvious on the page.

Feedback on your work is essential. Paying a reputable script reader, or using a script-reading service, for reports on your scripts will be a wise investment. You will also gain enormously from joining a writers' group, either face to face or online. You will learn not only from comments on your own work, but just as much from reading and commenting on the work of others.

What you are developing all this time is a gut feeling, a trust in your instinct that, combined with good technical knowledge, good feedback and good practice, will enable you to turn the rough diamond of a first draft into a polished gem.

However, ultimately there is no substitute for learning by doing. This is where you will really welcome having a strong inner critic. Most people tinker when they edit. They trim a little here, polish a little there, but never pluck up the courage to make serious changes. Don't tinker – be bold.

You will learn to become a better editor by editing – by seeing what happens when you remove a page of dialogue, halve the length of a scene, add a character, find a better location, cut an entire subplot. All the advice in the world cannot replace the feeling you get when you remove a piece of writing you've been hanging on to, and the whole script suddenly works better. Learn from experience.

Key idea

Writers edit, and edit, and edit again ...

Using the four gears

With practice, you'll become adept at shifting smoothly and neatly from one gear to another, so quickly and instinctively that you hardly notice the change.

As you start to develop your ideas, spend time visualizing your story and characters. Alternate that with a little research, as much as you feel comfortable with. Read up on the setting and background.

Keep speed-writing on a regular basis. Create a pile of fragments that might lead somewhere or might not. Jot down lines of dialogue and action as they come to you.

Start describing characters, locations and situations. Dive into a few scenes that feel 'hot' and improvise, like an actor or jazz musician in rehearsal.

Workshop

Read the script of a film or TV programme that you haven't seen. Read it through from start to finish without stopping.

1 Discuss it in the workshop. What strikes you? What works and what doesn't work? Why do you think that is?

2 Jot down a brief synopsis, say a half-page to a page. How does it start? What is the main story? How does it end? Why did the writer make those decisions and not others? Could you see it in your mind as you read?

3 Finally, ask how you might have written it differently. (Note that I said 'differently', which is not necessarily 'better'. This is your chance to develop your individual voice. Maybe you'd have focused more on the woman in the story, or would never have thought of the twist at the end.)

If you can get hold of the finished movie/programme, watch it now. How has it changed? How much is it the same? What have you learned? How can you put what you've learned into your own writing?

Where to next?

If you have an idea and want to dive straight in and write a first draft without rules or preconceptions, jump straight to Chapter 15 now, and come back afterwards to edit. Otherwise, in the next chapter, it will be time to begin creating the premise – deciding which of the many images and ideas might make a good starting point for your first, or next, screen story.

3

Finding your spark – the premise

I'm going to assume, for simplicity, that you are starting from scratch. Maybe you're searching for ideas. Or you already have a few ideas and want to know how best to develop them further. However, this chapter will work equally well if you've already gone away and written a draft.

Wherever you are with your script, at some point you need to be clear on its central dramatic idea – its premise.

The spark

Woody Allen, in *Annie Hall*

'Right now it's only a notion, but I think I can get money to turn it into a concept, and then later turn it into an idea.'

The best premise contains what writer and script consultant Linda Aronson calls the 'spark'. It's almost impossible to define, but you can see it in other people's reactions. When you tell them your premise, their eyes light up. If their eyes don't light up, you haven't got a spark yet, or else you haven't articulated it well enough to your listener. Be prepared for the fact that the spark might come to you as a surprise. What excites your listener might be something you've barely noticed. Do, though, be careful to double-check your spark on a number of people.

The spark has nothing to do with money, big stars or special effects. The spark could be there in a low-budget independent road movie about a illiterate boy who befriends a cantankerous Brazilian letter writer (*Central Station*), a TV sitcom about a perennially angry hotel keeper (*Fawlty Towers*) or the true story of a black violinist falsely imprisoned as a slave (*12 Years a Slave*). It's also not a question of high art or low culture, commercial or not commercial. You could find the spark in a pirate adventure story or a dark exploration of the nature of love.

It's an indefinable something that says: *This could work on screen.*

You can't legislate for the spark and there are no formulae. However, there are ways to keep building, playing and experimenting until it catches fire and you get that kick in the gut that says you might be on to something.

This premise will also help form the basis of your pitch, when you come to sell the screenplay later (see Chapter 27).

Naomi De Pear, Head of Development, Kudos TV

'I want to feel the writer can't put down what or who they're writing about. The more unputdownable the better.'

Creating the premise

A good premise gives you a sense of focus and direction. It saves editing time and gives you a certain confidence that your script might eventually work.

A premise can often grow out of the question 'What if?' What if a high-flying businessman fell in love with a prostitute? (*Pretty Woman*). What if the dead began to return to a small French alpine town? (*The Returned*).

- The premise of *Skyfall* is that James Bond has to save MI6 from being destroyed by a lethal and brilliant insider.

- The premise of *Her* is that a man falls in love with his computer's operating system.

- The premise of *Friends* is the lives, loves and personal complications of six young friends struggling to survive in Manhattan.

- The premise of *Borgen* is that the leader of a minority party in Denmark unexpectedly finds herself Prime Minister.

Seeing the spark

Write down the premise for each of your favourite films or TV series. Keep it as short as possible. What's the core idea that makes each come to life? What's the spark?

Anne McCaffrey, writer

'Tell the readers a story! Because without a story, you are merely using words to prove you can string them together in logical sentences.'

GOATS

To help find your spark, let me introduce you to my GOATS.

These adventurous animals will help you in 99.9 per cent of difficult writing situations. They will help you solve questions of plot and character development, dialogue editing and visuals. If you keep using them, you'll learn to work with them naturally and unconsciously. And, of course, they will help you create your premise.

I like them because they are memorable, simple and practical. The acronym may sound simplistic, but if you remember it you are more likely to use it. GOATS stands for the five most important ideas in all story writing:

- Goal
- Obstacle
- Action
- Tactics
- Stakes.

1 GOAL

A story can begin only when a character has a goal. It doesn't matter how big or small that goal is, as long as it's important to her. The goal could be as large as saving the world or as small as getting home, buying a sandwich or crossing the road.

For us, it must also be capable of being filmed. While a novel can take place inside a character's head, a screen story goal must exist in the visible, outside world.

Some stories are very internal. The focus of the main character is on growing up, becoming a better person or dealing with their inner issues. However, even then you have to find a goal that can be seen. For example, in the coming-of-age movie *Stand by Me*, the central character's inner struggle to grow up is dramatized through a visible outer goal – to find a dead body.

As we'll see, this need to develop outer goals comes up constantly. It applies to a whole story, an individual scene or even a moment within a scene, such as a line of dialogue.

 ## Key idea

Every story needs a goal. A screen story needs a visible, outer goal.

In the premise I gave above for *Skyfall*, the outer goal is clearly stated: to save MI6. The outer goal for Theodore Twombly in *Her* is implied rather than spelled out: to spend his life with the object of his love.

A series may have an overall series goal, and also individual goals for each episode.

The series goal for the characters in *Friends* is to find success and happiness in New York, while individual episodes bring secondary goals – to start or end a relationship, get a job, persuade Chandler to give up smoking again … For *Borgen*, the overarching goal of the Prime Minister, Birgitte Nyborg, is to run her government, while an episode sub-goal might be to win a vote in the Danish Parliament, manage a difficult colleague or spend promised time with her family.

 ## Ray Bradbury, novelist

'First, find out what your hero wants, then just follow him!'

 ## Find your character's goal

Write down your protagonist's outer goals, large and small. Which of these is her primary goal, the goal that will drive the film, series or episode?

(Keep any lesser goals to one side. They could be useful later, to add conflict and texture to the story.)

Focus point: Do I have the right goal?

If you find listeners don't respond to your premise, or feel it lacks focus, this may mean you haven't yet found the main goal. Your protagonist's overall goal sharpens the story and gives it direction. You may find that your premise does a lot of setting up, creates a strong sense of the situation your protagonist is in, but not what she sets out to do.

If your goal is too general or vague, we won't be able to see your story in our minds. Make it specific so we can see it.

First attempts at a premise often focus on the set-up rather than the story. Leap over the set-up and go straight to the goal that energizes the piece. Maybe she's short of money. You spend time explaining all her money problems and that she has decided to go and get the money she needs. This is only part of her goal. To focus the story, we need to know how specifically she commits to getting it. Does she set out to rob a bank? Teach school kids to play rock music? Win the local karate competition?

For example, in pitching *Lincoln* you might make the mistake of describing the background to the Civil War, the need to abolish slavery and so on. Instead, you have to jump straight to Abraham Lincoln's goal of forcing his amendment to ban slavery through Congress, before peace comes and it's too late.

Another possible reason for lack of clarity could be that you have more than one protagonist. You need to find the goal that all your protagonists have in common. If they are all fighting for a common cause, this will be easy – in *Seven Samurai*, the seven warriors are united in saving the village from the bandits. However, the common goal may be a thematic one. In Paul Haggis's 2004 movie *Crash* there are 13 protagonists, each with their own individual outer goals. But, if you step back, you see that they are all, in their different ways, trying to survive the racial tensions that divide the city of Los Angeles.

Key idea

To find clarity, jump ahead or stand back to see the goal that runs through the whole story.

2 OBSTACLE

A goal on its own is not enough to create a story. If I want to save MI6 and nothing stops me, my story is both rather short and rather boring. I need obstacles.

Key idea

A story is only as powerful as the obstacles standing in the protagonist's way.

One of the tests of a good writer is her ability not simply to come up with obstacles, but to find the *right* obstacles – obstacles that create the right mood or emotion, obstacles that lead to the most useful action. If you want to improve fast, you must become sophisticated at creating all kinds of obstacles, large and small.

Initially, you'll need large obstacles for the premise of your story. The best premise obstacles are those which seem impossible to overcome.

- In *Skyfall*, the obstacle to saving MI6 is the extraordinarily clever and lethal cyberterrorist Raoul Silva.
- The obstacle for Theodore in *Her* is that Samantha, his operating system, has her own ideas and needs.
- In *Friends*, the issue is even more complicated, as the six main characters become obstacles to one another. This varies from episode to episode, depending on who is dating who. As the series continues, opposing characters become allies, and allies change sides. This is typical of stories involving love, friendship and romance, and is part of the fascination of romantic stories in general.
- In *Borgen*, Birgitte Nyborg must face down the leaders of the larger, more powerful parties.

 ## Key idea

Obstacles are a writer's best friend.

 ## Pinpoint the biggest obstacle

Write down the obstacles that face your central character. Focus on the largest and most consistent. Is it visible (in the outer world) and almost impossible to defeat? If not, can you find an obstacle that is?

 ## Focus point

Do you have a strong enough obstacle? Some premises grab your attention immediately; others need more energy. One way to add energy to an idea is to increase the obstacles and the stakes.

Look again at the main obstacles facing your central character. They may not be large enough. They should be so challenging that overcoming them seems almost impossible (though not so impossible that the story loses credibility). They may also be too unfocused. A series of vague or wide-ranging obstacles can be less effective. In such a case, you should consider concentrating the main obstacles into one antagonist.

If you were developing *Lincoln*, you might have such a problem in the early stages. There were many opponents to abolition, but a hundred or a thousand opponents make for bad drama. You would look to focusing the opposition into a much smaller number of especially formidable politicians.

Key idea

To add energy and pace, ramp up the obstacles.

3 ACTION

The prime energy of a story comes from watching the protagonist take purposeful action to overcome the obstacles that face him. In screenwriting, the word 'action' has this very specific meaning: an attempt to overcome an obstacle. Any action that does not have this purpose behind it is not *action* in the dramatic sense – it is *activity*. (Later, we'll develop this in more depth when we look at the Act Two Project, in Chapter 8.)

This is a mistake many developing screenwriters make. Instead of purposeful action, they give their characters activity. I hear a great many pitches from writers, and far too many of them are based on premises that don't have enough purposeful action in them. The characters are passive. They fail to grasp their own story and make it theirs.

Action is overcoming an obstacle to achieve a goal:

- The overall action in *Skyfall* is to find a way to save MI6.
- The overall action in *Her* is to build a meaningful relationship with Samantha.
- The overall action in *Friends* is to look for, find, try to keep and deal with losing partners.
- The overall action in *Borgen* is to try to govern the country and stay in power.

Note that this in no way describes everything that happens in these stories. It doesn't even begin to touch on the variety, depth and richness of the writing, and does not attempt to. It clarifies the outer story.

The outer story is something you may well be asked about many times during your career. It essentially defines the dramatic pulse that should go through any good screenplay from early in the story all the way to the end. If you stopped a film at any point and asked the audience 'What are you most concerned about here? What is this story about?', the answer should most often relate directly to this.

The outer story is fundamentally the GOA of GOATS: Goal – Obstacle – Action.

Focus point

Story = goal + obstacle + action

Snapshot exercise

Write down the possible actions your protagonist could take to achieve her main goal and overcome the obstacles that face her. Can you find one overarching action that encompasses them all? Is this action visible and concrete, in the outer world?

Focus point

Is your protagonist active enough?

One common cause of a weak story is a protagonist who fails to act enough. A passive/reactive protagonist who allows things to happen to her, or spends too much of the story reacting to what others do, will kill a story stone dead. Some settings and environments make it difficult for the protagonist to make things happen – perhaps because of her personality, age or lack of power. You need to seek these out and, if necessary, change her situation so that she can.

For example, in *House,* Greg House doesn't simply wait for the results of tests or react to strange variations in symptoms. This would be too passive. He makes active decisions, forces things to happen, takes risks with treatments, fights the authorities, makes waves and generally takes charge of his story.

Key idea

Ensure that your protagonist will have the potential to be active and push her story forwards under her own steam.

4 TACTICS

Tactics relate directly to what's going on inside your characters – their inner story. If actions are the things that your characters *actually* do to achieve their goals, tactics cover what they *could* do.

In any given situation, a person has things they habitually do and things they would never contemplate doing. For example, you might be a quiet, contemplative person who tends to be polite and perhaps a little easily pushed around. You would ask nicely but never make a fuss, even if badly dealt with. Your friend may be quite different, noisy and pushy; she won't put up with anyone who tries to boss her, but sometimes speaks before she thinks. Your approach to life is not the same. You have different tactics for dealing with the problems that face you.

A character's tactics comprise all the things she *could* do, all the possible actions at her disposal, her strengths and her flaws. They include actions she generally takes, and exclude those which she believes she would never take.

Most importantly, a character's tactics are always limited by her flaws. And the protagonist's flaws lie at the very heart of the story. Tactics and flaws are important because many writers focus merely on what happens in their story. However, the audience is hooked not only by what happens, but also by what *doesn't* happen, and what they *fear* and *hope may* happen.

In *Her*, Theodore Twombly lives an unreal life. His job entails inventing falsely intimate love letters for others. At home, he plays a 3D video game where he pretends to engage with others. When faced with divorce from his childhood sweetheart, he delays signing the papers. We learn quickly what kind of person he is – what tactics he uses in his life. He's a man who tends to run away from reality. And his primary flaw is that he is afraid to commit.

> ## Key idea
>
> A character's tactics are limited by his flaws.

However, as the story progresses, Theodore starts to deal with his flaw. He begins to include different actions among his available tactics: he grows intimate with Samantha. He opens up with friends. He admits his feelings and risks being rejected. Tragically, all this comes too late to save their relationship.

For the vast majority of stories, this inner character growth is essential. Indeed, if the outer story is what the drama is 'about', this inner journey is what the drama is 'really about'.

> ## Key idea
>
> If a character's tactics grow, then he grows. This is your inner story and your theme.

- The inner story of *Her* is about Theodore learning to face reality and take risks.
- The inner story of *Friends* is about the six friends maturing and growing up.
- The inner story of *Borgen* is about Birgitte growing tougher while trying not to lose her better qualities.

As human beings, we are fascinated by ourselves and other people and most of all by their personal moral choices. We identify with their inner struggles. The inner story is (in most cases) what engages our deepest contact with the script, and you will need to satisfy that need as you develop your idea.

Brian Dunnigan, Head of Screenwriting, London Film School

'I want to be moved at some level. It could be by spectacle, but most often it's by something human.'

If you are still unsure of the central character's primary flaw or journey, work backwards. Look at how the story ends, and in particular how she's changed. What can she now do that she couldn't do before? What change enabled her to achieve her goal? From this you can deduce what must have been the initial flaw and therefore what her journey is going to be.

 Key idea

If you are still unsure of the central character's journey, look at what she can do at the end that she couldn't do before.

There are, however, exceptions to this 'rule'.

There are three kinds of series that offer little or no permanent character growth – adventure, satire and episodic series.

The adventure genre includes film franchises such as *James Bond*, *Indiana Jones* and *Pirates of the Caribbean* and TV series such as *Spooks* and *Heroes*. In an adventure story, we aren't especially concerned about the hero's inner life. No one particularly wants to see Indiana Jones face his personal flaws. We want to see him fight the bad guys and win. Any slight character growth is incidental.

And when the producers of the James Bond franchise tried, a few years ago, to introduce a more thoughtful, emotional inner story for 007, audiences didn't like it. Thus, in *Skyfall* there is little or no inner story. The audience doesn't care whether James fights his inner demons – just as long as he fights Raoul Silva.

The other genre that has little or no character growth is satire. In both the film and TV series of *M*A*S*H*, the army doctors and nurses are fixed from the start. Whether rebellious, God-fearing, inept, insecure, passionate or lazy, each character has his or her fixed identity and the fun comes from watching the characters interact. In a satire, the characters are stuck with their flaws and cannot grow at all.

Finally, in certain kinds of episodic series, the protagonist may grow during the episode, and yet her inner story is reset at the start of the next show. In a sitcom such as *Mrs Brown's Boys* or a police procedural such as *The Mentalist*, any learning or growth is forgotten by the next episode. There is little or no personal change across the series as a whole. (For more on series and serials, see below.)

Snapshot exercise

Write down your central character's inner journey. What flaws is she going to struggle with? If you're not sure, then look at how it's going to end. How different will she be? What will she be able to do at the end that she couldn't do at the start?

Focus point

Your premise must have meaning or resonance. It must enthuse other people and keep you enthused for the time it takes to write.

The outer story holds the attention, but it's the inner story that brings meaning and personal engagement – on the part of the audience and also the writer.

We want stories about people who have flaws. In some stories, they conquer their failings. In others, they are conquered by them. In yet others, their flaws make us laugh – or grow angry. But in almost all cases (barring straight-up adventure movies) it's the flaws that draw us in.

The premise of François Truffaut's début movie *Les Quatre Cents Coups* (*The Four Hundred Blows*) could be expressed as follows: a young boy fails to cope with school and with his dysfunctional home and is drawn into crime. But that dry skeleton could have rapidly faded in interest, if Truffaut hadn't also developed Antoine's inner story: his refusal to knuckle down to a society that seems to be intent on stifling his natural and exuberant love of life.

Naomi De Pear, Head of Development, Kudos TV

'Write from the heart, have something to say, and know why that story needs to be told now, and not before. Not put together like it's a recipe for a cake. Think about stories you like, and why you like them.'

Key idea

Dig deep to find the inner story and develop it. Be honest to yourself about how much your character flaws relate to your own issues. Find ways to bring them out more strongly.

Truffaut could not have written such a strong and moving script if the story hadn't dealt honestly with his own personal issues. (Indeed, the story is largely autobiographical.) But the same would apply to any fiction, from *ET* to *Absolutely*

Fabulous. This is not to say that your central character is the same as you – you have to be able to stand back and see her in perspective. But you will (must) share some of her most important flaws and be prepared to go on a journey of discovery with her.

This applies whether you are creating the lightest romcom or the grittiest social realism, autobiography or fantasy. The greatest screenwriters face their own issues with courage and put them on the page. This is what will keep the script alive for you, during the many months it will take to write. It is also what readers and audiences will respond most strongly to.

 ## John Cusack, actor and screenwriter

'Anything that's interesting in a film, or in a character (all your passion, your sex, your anger, your rage, all that) comes from that part of you that you want to hide and push away, and you want to deny all those things most.'

Workshop

This is possibly the most important exercise in the book. Ask yourself why you want to write this story. Look inside and ask yourself what you care about most at this point in your life. Be honest. Write down the issues that fire your emotions, make you excited, angry, passionate, frustrated …

Now see how these issues relate to your central character's struggle. How much do you share strengths and flaws? Can you see ways to share them more deeply, more honestly?

If you're writing light comedy, seek out ways to laugh about your flaws that draw out your sharpest insights. If writing heavy social drama, seek out the truth and cut out any false dramatic poses.

While you are not the same as your protagonist, are you prepared to take the risk and dig deeper into the reality of what makes you both tick? To dramatize it? To take a journey together and discover what lies at the end of the road?

 ## Jude Holland, senior lecturer, Goldsmith's College, London

'Don't write what anybody else could write – try to write what only you could write.'

5 STAKES

If there is nothing serious at stake in your story, why should we care? Why should we pay for expensive cinema tickets, hire DVDs or even bother to turn on the TV?

Attaining her goal must be the most important thing in the world for your protagonist, whether it's a save-the-galaxy blockbuster or an indie road movie. Nothing could be more important – and not only does she feel that, but we should feel that, too. It should be a matter of life and death, *or more important than that*:

- In *Skyfall*, James Bond risks his life to save the Secret Service.

- In *Her*, Theodore's life is at stake in a very different way. At the start of the movie, his life is a living death. What is at stake is whether he can become fully alive.

- In *Friends*, sorting out the friends' personal lives is more important than life or death.

- In *Borgen*, Birgitte Nyborg stakes everything, career and private life, on trying to build a better Denmark. Living with failure would be much harder than death.

The stakes must be credible not only for the protagonist but also to the audience. We don't need to agree with Birgitte's politics for the script to make us sympathize with her, and we want to see her succeed against the unfair and manipulative intrigues that surround her.

Kevin Dolan, Film London

'*Think of an element in your film that can connect with an audience.*'

Snapshot exercise

Write down what's at stake for your protagonist. Is it a matter of life and death? If not, then what makes it so important? Why should we care? What universal values can you find for us all to identify with?

Focus point

Are the stakes high enough?

Low stakes drain energy from a premise. You'd add energy to the premise of *Lincoln* by showing the personal danger to the President and the awful cost of prolonging the war.

In *Crash*, you could amplify the racial biases of key characters and the fact that navigating the racial tensions in Los Angeles can become a matter of life and death.

Developing a premise for a series or serial

A serial follows a single story across a number of parts. Examples include the five-episode BBC drama *The Fall*, which told the story of the search for a serial killer in Belfast. To confuse matters, a shorter serial, of two to three episodes, is often called a mini-series. (And in the United States, *all* serials are called mini-series.) The premise for a serial is the same as for a single-story film or drama, except that it must show that the story is strong enough to hold an audience over a number of days or weeks.

A series is made up of individual stories, usually one per episode, under an overall umbrella idea. This classically includes detective series, such as *Columbo,* sitcoms such as *The Office,* and soaps such as *EastEnders* and *Emmerdale,* all of which have multiple running storylines and no defined ending. It also includes anthological shows, which feature separate stories but a common theme, such as a location or idea – for example *Number 9,* a series of stand-alone dramas set in houses, flats or rooms all called Number 9.

In recent years, the distinction has become blurred and hybrid series have appeared, such as *West Wing* or *The Good Wife*. In a hybrid series, we follow an overall story across the entire series (or even series of series) while at the same time each episode features a stand-alone episode story. For example, *The Good Wife* develops the overarching story of Alicia Florrick's legal career and complex relationships, while each episode presents a new legal case to be fought and, if possible, won by the end of the TV hour.

For a multi-episode series you'll need an overall series premise as well as a premise for each episode. The series premise needs to reassure you that there is enough juice in the idea to sustain it across a number of separate stories – or, in industry jargon, that it has 'legs.' To do this, you must create enough tension between the characters, or between the characters and their environment, to yield at least a dozen or more varied and different stories, with the potential of more to follow.

 ## Key idea

Tension between the characters, or between them and their environment, lies at the heart of a series premise.

- The series *House* centres on a brilliant but emotionally stunted physician who can cure mysterious and fatal diseases, but whose unorthodox methods constantly bring him into conflict with authority.
- In *The Office*, a needy and inept office manager thinks that he's God's gift to business and sets out each week to prove it.
- The soap *EastEnders* focuses on the strong families living in a community in London's East End and their conflicts at a time of social change.

Note the importance of the protagonist's tactics or personal flaws in seeding the potential for ongoing conflict and future stories. *House* without House would be a far less interesting series idea. *The Office* without David Brent would be impossible. At the heart of *EastEnders* lie the community's dealings with the changing world in which they find themselves.

Premises for short films

Short films are very useful as calling cards for writers, as well as directors and producers. They can be uploaded to the Net and sent to film competitions, where any prizes will do no harm to your CV. However, they present particular challenges depending on how short they are.

THREE MINUTES OR UNDER

A micro-short can run from a few seconds to three minutes. TV ads, for example, tend to run for 30 seconds, while many online competitions ask for three minutes. The best story premises at this length set up a situation, build it quickly and end with a twist.

With so little time for character development, the twist is more or less essential to avoid a sense of 'So what?' when it's all over.

Gregor Jordan's *Swinger*, shot in a single three-minute take, shows what seems at first sight to be a deserted, if messy, room. In the background a series of phone messages reveal that the owner's girlfriend has changed her mind about leaving; that a job refusal was a mistake; that he's in line to win a large cash prize. The twist comes when we see his legs hanging we realize that he's been in the room all the time trying to commit suicide, but now starts increasingly frantic attempts to get out of the noose in time to claim his winnings.

THREE TO TEN MINUTES

At between three and ten minutes, a film is generally too long for such a simple structure but not long enough to develop a full-blown story. It's a very important length, though, because it's controllable, and many film competitions set a ten-minute maximum.

It's a mistake to try to make anything that looks like a conventional movie, and the best ploy is generally to focus on a pivotal, but simple, event, or run two strands of story in parallel. Parallel storylines allow you to cut between the two, jumping over material that otherwise would force you over the ten-minute mark.

The eight-minute short *Bouncer,* written by Geoff Thompson, follows just such parallel storylines. In the present, we see the protagonist at a gym, bigging up his expertise in dealing with trouble to his fellow weight-lifters. At the same time, we intercut with the story he's telling, about a violent incident outside a club. The two lines build in parallel to a denouement, where we discover just what he did, and that the gym is in fact inside a prison.

FIFTEEN TO FORTY MINUTES

Between ten to 15 minutes is rather a no-man's-land, but in a film of over 15 you have space to develop a story that is closer to the kind of premise outlined for a longer drama, with an inner and outer story. (Over 40 minutes and your film is no longer a short but a support feature.)

Again, you'll find it better to focus on a small but significant event, rather than trying to cram a feature-length story into a pint pot. A character in peril, an older person realizing something about their previous life, a child faced with a small but significant decision as part of growing up ... these are the kinds of stories that work well at this length.

A Hero of Our Time centres on an impulsive, if brave, young man who saves a woman from being beaten by her vicious partner, only to find that the other man is tracking them down. In 25 minutes, writer-director Michael Almereyda develops a brief but significant moment in a life, laced with suppressed violence and eroticism.

Short scripts for research are hard to find, but short films of all lengths can be found increasingly, for example on YouTube or Vimeo, and even as compilations on DVD. If you search hard on sites such as www.amazon.co.uk / www.amazon.com or www.bfi. org.uk you can even find the occasional DVD of shorts made by directors who have since become well known, either in compilations or as extras on the DVDs of their later films.

Adding power to any premise

Before you put out to sea, you should check that your boat floats. Before you entrust months of work to your premise, you should ensure that it doesn't leak. Before you finally decide on your premise, there are four key questions to ask:

1 **Will it work on screen?**

2 **Does it bring something different?**

3 **Does it own 'mental real estate'?**

4 **Is it your copyright?**

1 WILL IT WORK ON SCREEN?

A screen story needs to work on screen – it needs to be visual. Some writers misunderstand this, thinking that they have to write copious descriptions of beautiful scenery or clever camerawork. This is not the job of the screenwriter.

What it means is that there should be a strong outer story that can be filmed. Many otherwise good ideas would work better on stage, on radio or as a novel or short story. If your story relies on long static dialogue scenes or takes place mostly inside a character's head, then you may need to have a rethink. Maybe it shouldn't be a screen story at all.

That's not to say that such stories can't work – think, for example, of courtroom thrillers or intense personal dramas – but you have to look for ways to compensate, with the promise of high tension or strong dramatic action.

 Key idea

Screen stories need to work visually, with strong, visible action or high tension.

2 IS IT DIFFERENT?

Be honest with yourself. What makes your story stand out? How does it differ from the other stories in your genre? Many otherwise well-written scripts fail to sell simply because they add nothing new.

Research examples of stories in the same area as yours. Know what it is that you bring that's different. And be prepared to deal with the question, should it come up.

- *The Office* took a standard sitcom format, the workplace comedy, and added one new element: mock documentary.
- *The King's Speech* took the venerable genre of the 'mentor' movie and added royalty and a speech impediment.
- *Side Effects* is a classic thriller; however, the threat comes not from guns or knives but from the world of medicine.

3 DOES IT OWN 'MENTAL REAL ESTATE'?

The Hollywood screenwriter Terry Rossio once asked what would have happened if an unknown writer had pitched a spec script about a boy going to wizard school. It probably would have been sent back unread.

Fast-forward a few years to when the Harry Potter books were an international success, with three bestsellers behind them. By the time the movie was commissioned, the name 'Harry Potter' had taken up residence across the planet. It occupied mental real estate in millions of minds.

The idea of using names, people, places or ideas that are popular is hardly new, and many great artists have drawn on it. Many of Shakespeare's plays featured characters or stories that his audiences would have been familiar with.

Terry Rossio, screenwriter

'You hear Potter, and instantly know what I'm talking about. There have been Time magazine covers and lines of customers around the block and months spent on the bestsellers list and a big movie deal with Chris Columbus … How hard is it going to be to get people to go see that movie?'

Of course, bestselling books are generally in copyright, and if you want to use any such stories or characters you will need to ensure that you obtain the legal rights, which are unlikely to be cheap (see below). However, there are many ideas that are not in copyright. The films *Titanic*, *Elizabeth* and *Shakespeare in Love* drew on popular names in the public domain. The TV series *Homeland* draws on the resonance of 'Homeland security' as well as very topical fears and tensions in US society. *House* is essentially Sherlock Holmes in a hospital (and look how even the name of the character has been chosen to resonate with our lives).

Mental real estate can extend to places (*Casablanca, Sarajevo, The West Wing*), works of art (*Girl with a Pearl Earring*), pieces of music (*Death and the Maiden*), jobs (*The Negotiator*), situations (*In Treatment*) … indeed anything that occupies the attention of your target audience.

Snapshot exercise

Is there an opening for mental real estate in your premise? Not every story will be appropriate, but you may find that changing a setting, or a character name, or adding in a new element, can strengthen the premise and also add to its audience appeal.

Make a list of names and ideas that are trending, or that have been popular for years. Think how you could use these mental real-estate opportunities to help you write the stories you want to write. Write down possible new stories, and potential changes to existing stories and ideas. Can you see any you could use?

4 IS IT YOUR COPYRIGHT?

Copyright normally extends over any material until 70 years after the original author's death. If you're basing any of your script on work still in copyright then you will need a written agreement to use it, for which you may have to pay. After that period, the work is generally considered to be in the public domain and free to use. However, be careful if you're basing part of your research on a newer work (such as a translation, a history book, an article or a documentary), which may have its own rights. Get this clear before you do too much work. There is nothing sadder than a brilliantly written script that can't be used for copyright reasons. It may mean months, if not years, of work wasted.

If you've been told the story in confidence, then you would also be well advised to obtain permission from the individuals concerned.

However, this need not be as daunting as it sounds. Find out who owns the film or TV rights (from the publisher, if it's a book) and establish contact with the rights holder. Money may not be their primary concern. If it's the author, for example, then a friendly approach may instil trust that you share their values and can be relied on to adapt their work sensitively, even though you can't offer much, or any, cash up front. As so often in the industry, it's about relationships.

The American writer-director Frank Darabont discovered that Stephen King had a policy of granting free rights to student film-makers creating short films. He wrote a short from King's story 'The Woman in the Room'. Liking Darabont's work, King later agreed to a 'handshake deal' for the rights to what became Darabont's hit movie *The Shawshank Redemption*.

If the rights holder does agree, then you must, absolutely must, get his permission in writing, and you *must* get the advice of a media lawyer. I know of writers who spent years on their scripts, only to find that they couldn't sell them because the contracts had small but fatal flaws (see the section on using a lawyer in Chapter 28).

The same applies if you're working with a co-writer to develop a script. Even if you are the best of friends, even if you have only a single-page 'Heads of Agreement', agree on your priorities, such as the ownership of rights and allocation of any fees or revenues. It will save heartache later and ensure that you stay friends.

USING REAL PEOPLE AS CHARACTERS

Most writers draw on their experience and memories of the people they know, meet or see in the media, with powerful results. In the majority of the cases, the original model remains hidden. Sometimes, the inspiration is obvious. The presidential couple in the movie *Primary Colors* was immediately recognized as the Clintons. Nora Ephron notoriously drew on her recently broken marriage to write the novel and screenplay of *Heartburn*.

Be careful, though, of the law of libel. Your local newsagent might make a great basis for a Mafia hitman but, if he recognizes himself, he may not find it so funny. Libel suits can be expensive.

If you use any real people as your models for fictional characters, ensure that nothing remains recognizable – change names, combine characteristics. Don't reference officials, such as members of the police or the army, without clearing the name first – particularly if that individual is portrayed in a potentially damaging way. If you have any concerns at all, take legal advice from a lawyer experienced in the field.

Of course, you may want to depict people as themselves, in a fictional or a true story. In that case, you definitely need to take legal advice. If they are alive, you may, in some countries, need to obtain permission to use them in your script. You will certainly need to ensure that you are not defaming them in any way. However, at present, in the UK, the law of defamation doesn't cover the dead.

If you have any doubt about copyright, confidentiality or libel, you must get legal advice.

Workshop

With your group, share the premise for your film, single drama or series in a single sentence (two at the most). Include the protagonist, their goal, main obstacle, action, primary flaw and stakes.

Brainstorm ideas for possible developments, further characters, complications. What dramatic scenes might you see? What climax? What ending?

What would the poster or TV ads look like? Invent an advertising strapline.

Listen for the spark. Learn to tell the difference between politeness and real interest. One day, you will hear it in their voices: this is a project worth pursuing.

A note on giving workshop feedback

Receiving even the smallest criticism can be profoundly painful. We writers can become defensive, even without meaning to be. We may try to explain why we wrote that way, rather than listening to what isn't working. Or we may become over-critical of ourselves and risk throwing away the parts that are working well.

Whenever you give feedback, you should always deliver it in the most helpful and constructive way, and you should ask your friends and colleagues to do the same for you.

The best method to use in your workshop, or indeed anywhere, is called 'sandwich feedback'. Sandwich feedback is delivered in three parts:

1 **Positive comments**

2 **Constructive suggestions**

3 **Final positive comment.**

Always begin by focusing on the good. Accentuate what you like. This ensures that the writer realizes that you're on her side, that there is good in the script and that it's worth continuing with. Your praise at this point must be entirely positive. This is not the time for ifs or buts. Don't say. 'It's very funny except …' Be unequivocal. You must also be truthful. Find something you honestly like about the idea, the aims of the writer and/or the execution, and praise it.

Next, give a brief summary of what needs to be worked on for the next draft. Be constructive. Your job is to help the writer. If possible, find out beforehand what's most important for the writer about her story, and then try to help her achieve it.

Keep each point brief. A sentence or two per point is more than enough. It's possible to waste half an hour making a detailed argument about one issue, only to find that the writer agreed with you after the first 15 seconds. Once you've listed your headline concerns, you can always offer to discuss them. Usually, the writer has already taken your criticism and is more interested in batting around possible solutions with you.

Finish the sandwich with more praise. Single out one or two things you really like about the script and remind the writer of them.

Focus point

Always give feedback in sandwich form.

Ideally, the writer should remain silent throughout the three layers of the sandwich, listening and making notes to ensure that she fully understands what's being said. Once everyone has given their sandwich feedback, the writer is allowed to speak and you can discuss any key issues in a more conversational way.

Where to next?

As you keep rehearsing your premise, you will grow increasingly confident that it will work. But there's still one very important angle to the premise that we haven't yet touched upon: it's time to look at genre.

4

Finding your genre

The word 'genre' comes from the French and it simply means the kind or category of work. What kind of screenplay are you aiming to write? Is it the kind that will make people laugh, cry, scream, watch in awe, cheer from the sidelines or shrink back in dread …?

Genre is a very powerful tool for creating emotions and meaning in your script. Some people think of genre as limiting, the province of lesser writers. But, as we'll see, all writers use genre all the time, and the greatest writers in all media use genre with skill and sophistication in their most powerful works.

John Gardner, *The Art of Fiction*

'The artist's primary unit of thought – his primary basis for selecting and organizing – is genre.'

Snapshot exercise

To warm up, choose three of your favourite films, TV dramas and series, focusing on those which are similar in kind to the scripts you want to write. Find as many answers as possible for each: what kind of film or programme is it? What, in particular, do they have in common? Don't be afraid of the obvious and don't limit yourself to technical 'genre' language.

For example, your three films may all be funny, scary, fictional, low-budget, dark, stylish, set generally in urban areas, have witty dialogue, revolve around issues of identity, concern central characters who have lost touch with the important things in life, often focus on a crime, frequently feature guns, cars, pet animals and expensive or eccentric fashion accessories, and make a pointed comment about modern life.

For the moment, simply list the characteristics that appear regularly in your chosen films or programmes, no matter how small. Their importance will become clear as you work through this chapter. (You may also want to return to this exercise to add more relevant details that come to you as you read on.)

Genre does not equal second-rate

Let me clear up two popular misunderstandings:

First, there are some who say it's not important to know about genre. However, the greatest artists have almost always been the greatest experts at using genre. Shakespeare, like the great classic writers who preceded and followed him, was highly sophisticated in his use of such genres as high comedy, history and so on. *Hamlet* is a sophisticated take on a popular Elizabethan genre – the revenge tragedy – a 'low' genre that he raised using high literary style. He transcended genre, not by ignoring it but by becoming expert in it. The greatest films and TV programmes use genre in similarly sophisticated ways – from *Citizen Kane* (fictional biopic) and *La Règle du jeu* (*The Rules of the Game*) (drama) to *Breaking Bad* (crime/satire) and *The Thick of It* (satire/sitcom). Thus …

Second, genre doesn't imply 'limited'. There's a particularly misguided phrase used in the industry that goes something like 'It's only a genre movie'. The implication is that there are some movies (and TV programmes) outside of, or above, genre. As we'll see, there is no such thing. To repeat, all 'genre' means is 'What kind of story is it?' And all stories fall into one or more genres, and that (as above) includes the work of the greatest writers as much as the lowliest hack.

Key idea

The best writers understand genre profoundly and use it in sophisticated ways.

You can't avoid genre because every word you write raises expectations in the audience. Like it or not, from the first frame – and even before, from the title, the poster, the trailer – the audience is trying to work out what kind of story this is. By the first three or four minutes, the audience will, or should, have a clear idea of what they are in for.

Understanding genre can help you in many ways – providing powerful tools with which to draw your audience in. It will also ensure that you don't disappoint your audience by unwittingly raising expectations that you don't fulfil.

How to prepare for genre

You may already have a clear idea of the genre you're aiming for – epic, sitcom, satire, road movie, soap… On the other hand, you may not. As with everything in screenwriting, developing genre is a mix of planning and discovery.

In any one script, some aims will dominate over others. You don't have time to give equal weight to all the possibilities. While a comedy may have moments of seriousness and a horror may contain a few laughs, you need focus, or the audience will become confused about what you are offering them.

There are four key areas:

• emotion

• pattern

• surprise

• style.

 Frank Cottrell Boyce, screenwriter and actor

'Suspense is the hidden energy that holds a story together. It connects two points and sends a charge between them. But it doesn't have to be all action. Emotions create their own suspense.'

1 EMOTION

No story can work without emotion. This emotion may be intense and visceral or more detached and intellectual, but if the audience is not emotionally engaged as they watch, then they will rapidly stop watching.

Each genre delivers a specific range of emotions. A thriller creates fear. A comedy makes the audience laugh. A horror horrifies us.

One of the most common mistakes made by beginners is that they fail to create emotion. They focus so much on the mechanics of the story that they forget their emotional purpose. Their comedy scripts are so busy setting up what happens next that they entirely fail to make us laugh. Ghost stories spend pages and pages of talk before we see any signs of a haunting.

The emotion should start from the very premise of the story. The premise for a horror story should have something horrifying about it; the premise for a sports story should already make us want to cheer our side to victory.

Amy Poehler, original pitch for the TV sitcom *Parks and Recreation*

'A comedy West Wing, *only with really low stakes.*'

Drama, as a genre, can cause confusion for writers. Classically called 'melodrama', this is a catch-all for the stories that aren't covered by the other genres: stories that don't involve guns, footballs, cowboys, spaceships, ghosts or non-stop laughs.

It's a drama if the story is resolved primarily through personal interaction, such as a court case, a marriage, a separation, finding a cure for a sick child, giving up a romantic dream, coming out as gay, or simply growing up. There are many sub-genres in this genre including political drama, medical drama, therapy drama, historical drama and drama-drama (putting on a play). Other sub-genres include road movie and rite of passage, such as coming of age.

The primary emotion in a drama is one of sympathy. This should not be confused with empathy – which is common to all genres. We feel *empathy* towards the two detectives in *Seven* – we want them to catch the serial killer – but we don't feel *sympathy* for them. It's their job, after all. However, we do feel sympathy for the husband in *Kramer vs. Kramer* (legal drama), for Gilbert in *What's Eating Gilbert Grape* (coming-of-age drama) or for the protagonists of *Cold Feet* (relationship drama). It doesn't seem fair that they're having to endure the pain they're going through. Our sympathy for the protagonists of a drama means that we feel for them and want them to find the happiness we believe they deserve.

Snapshot exercise

What genre or genres is your planned script going to work in? What emotions will you want to evoke as the story runs? Note them down.

Look back at your premise. Does it already offer a flavour of those emotions? If your premise doesn't yet hint at the important emotions that will be there in your script, is there anything you can do to add them in? What new elements would you need?

Alfred Hitchcock

'Give them pleasure. The same pleasure they have when they wake up from a nightmare.'

2 PATTERNS AND MOTIFS

As well as emotion, a genre will suggest certain elements – patterns and motifs. Fail to provide those and once again your audience will probably be very disappointed.

A contemporary crime movie will raise expectations of guns, fast cars, fast women (and men), a career criminal, an urban setting where laws must be defended and violence breeds. There will be chases, fights, investigations, interrogations … all coming to a climactic showdown. These are only a few of the genre expectations, which include flawed detectives (often with profound personal issues) and what is known as the 'obligatory scene' in which criminal and detective finally come face to face and realize what they have in common. The detective may be a professional police officer or not, as long as his goal is to solve the crime. The detective in the movie *In the Valley of Elah* is the retired father of a missing soldier, determined to find out what happened to his son.

However, if the criminal is an amateur, the genre is more likely to be noir. This is a dark genre, both emotionally and pictorially – classic noir territory features dangerous streets at night. We first meet the protagonist when he's almost given up on life, but he is 'saved' by becoming obsessed with (classically) a woman who will entice him to break the law and betray himself. In later versions, the protagonist could be a woman and the obsession could be with drugs, money or anything else that appears to hold the answer to all ills.

 Key idea

Miss any expected patterns or motifs for your genre, and you risk leaving your audience disappointed.

 Brainstorm ideas

Take a piece of paper and in the centre write the core goal of your story – in a word or short phrase, such as 'Find the girl' or 'Win the court case'. Around it, brainstorm any events, scenes, goals, obstacles, actions and locations that could arise – *all* the ideas you can think of, good and bad. You can edit down later.

When you've done this, add any other elements you'd expect to see in your chosen genre or genres: archetypal actions, settings, situations and characters, etc. Use them to spark off new ideas.

3 SURPRISE

Fail to deliver expected emotions and patterns, and the audience will be disappointed. However, if you deliver them precisely as expected, the audience will dismiss your story as predictable! Catch 22.

Key idea

You must deliver what the audience expects, but not in the way that they expect!

- *Fargo* refreshed the film noir genre by taking it out of the city and setting it firmly in the snow-swept wastes of Minnesota. Instead of a disillusioned male detective, the Coen brothers give us a happily married detective with morning sickness. The audience gets the hostile environment and edgy characters it wants, but not in the way they expected.
- *Unforgiven* revitalized the Western by taking the expected conflict between good and evil and adding a dark, moral complexity. The audience gets the moral conflict it anticipated, but in a new and surprising manner.
- *The Sopranos* brought a whole new slant to TV crime series by combining the gangster genre with therapy drama.

Your job is to understand the patterns and motifs and then find fresh and exciting ways of delivering them. Ask yourself: what might happen in real life? What is your own individual take? What might be an unusual twist or reversal?

Snapshot exercise

A romantic comedy demands a moment when the two lovers 'meet cute'. Can you find a fresh and surprising twist on the norm? Perhaps they can meet on the Internet (*You Got Mail*). Or one hears the other on the radio (*Sleepless in Seattle*). How many new variations can you think of?

Julian Friedmann, agent

'*Amadeus was the only composer film ever to make money, because they made it as a murder mystery – opening with Salieri confessing to killing Mozart ... great hook.*'

Another way to bring surprise is to combine genres. Most films nowadays combine two genres. Romcom came originally from the combination of romantic drama and comedy; noir from a fusion of gangster and horror. Few combinations have not been explored: science fiction/screwball (*Galaxy Quest*), sports/satire (*Dodgeball*), coming of age/war (*The Red Badge of Courage*).

Indeed, it is rare nowadays for any film to be firmly in a single genre. Such single-genre films tend to have a deliberately retro feel. Examples include *The Untouchables* – a homage to gangster movies about the capture of Al Capone – and *Far from Heaven* (2002) – made in the style of a classic 1950s melodrama.

The Indian movie *Lagaan*, set in the nineteenth century, broke new ground by combining sports with historical epic. Faced with devastating taxes levied by the British Raj, the farmers of a desperately poor village accept a wager: if they win a cricket match against a British team, their taxes will be cancelled for three years. However, if they lose, their taxes will be doubled, and they will probably starve. The film has all the familiar patterns of historical epic (individuals pitted against large social forces) and sports (the villagers must form a team, learn a difficult game, and play to win against the odds). However, the combination gives a completely fresh twist, adding an extra bite and very high stakes.

As each new film or TV series brings fresh variations, so the genres themselves evolve and shift. What was once fresh and new rapidly becomes cliché in its turn. There is no substitute for deeply researching your chosen genres, so that you know as much as possible about them, past and present.

Snapshot exercise

Look at the patterns and motifs you've listed for your genre and ask yourself how you can find new ways to use them. What twists and shifts could you invent to keep them fresh? What surprises could you spring?

Brainstorm as many as you can. Then go over the list and underline the best.

4 STYLE AND TONE

The style and tone of your script is also a part of 'what kind' of script it is, and underpins the emotional impact.

Thriller is a style. Essentially, a thriller could be seen as a story in any other genre, plus added tension. Most thrillers are high-tension crime, horror or noir, although there are thrillers in other genres including fantasy (*Pan's Labyrinth*), psychological drama and comedy.

Whatever your genre, a writer needs to find a style that suits the effect she is looking to achieve:

- **Thrillers** will generally be realistic, often city-based and modern. The style of writing will be clipped and short, to add to the feeling of pace. Visuals, props and settings will be chosen for their ability to add to the feeling of fear, even on a subliminal level – playing on archetypal fears such as heights, wide open or enclosed spaces, run-down city streets with unsettling characters, guns, drugs, hospitals and so on.

- For **horror**, you must select a setting, events and a writing style that add to the feeling of horrific tension. Most horror stories therefore feature isolated locations, darkness, half-glimpsed movements, strange noises. The style of writing will be less terse than thriller, but may reflect older forms, evoking deeper psychological or spiritual issues.

- **Comedy** is usually set in light, upbeat locations. Brisk and energetic, it is written in a light, upbeat style.

Choosing an appropriate style doesn't mean writing in clichés. You still need to find freshness and surprise in your writing. However, your style must have the appropriate emotional weight.

We've already seen how *Fargo* refreshed noir by being written in a very un-noir bright and breezy style that extends to the plot and dialogue, too. However, Ethan and Joel Coen were careful to build dark undertones into their script.

The original Dutch version of *The Vanishing* took horror out of the night-time and showed that life can be just as horrifying and scary in the broad light of day.

The visual and written style of *Fargo* and *The Vanishing* – the agoraphobic snowy wastes of Minnesota; the harsh, dehumanized motorway service stations and ironically pretty villages of the South of France – are as emotionally powerful as any conventional style would have been.

Snapshot exercise

Create a list of the stylistic elements that would be normal for the genres you are working in. What typical settings, dialogue, tone, style of action, weather, times of day and so forth would be expected? Will they serve your story best or do you need to change them? If you go with the norms, you still need to avoid cliché and keep the elements fresh. And if you do change them, make sure that they still do the job they need to do.

Close your eyes and visualize your story. Does the style feel right? Does it excite you? Can you imagine the effect on an audience? If not, what would need to be added or taken away?

Workshop

Create a scene (not from your planned script) in which a character has a simple goal – say, to catch a train. Put all kinds of obstacles in the way and have the character take action to overcome them. Write it as a horror story. Use all the patterns and styles that you can to create the horror feeling, with freshness and surprise.

Now rewrite the scene as comedy.

Try a third version, in a completely different genre. Choose one of your favourites.

How different can you make the three versions? Edit them to fully bring out the emotional effect. Have the pieces read by the workshop without telling them which genre is which. Can they tell the genres? If not, what else would you need? If they can tell, what were the clues?

Where to next?

With the premise becoming clearer and the genre developing, it's time to turn to the people at the heart of your story – your characters.

5

Engagement and insight – developing your characters

Good characters lie at the heart of all good screen stories. As an audience, we identify with them, love, hate, sympathize, hope and fear for them. Characters are usually human but can be animals, plants, computers, cars, angels, aliens, ghosts … anyone or anything that can take action to achieve a goal. In *Everything You Always Wanted to Know About Sex* (*But Were Afraid to Ask)*, Woody Allen created a character who is a sperm. While, as we'll see, structure is vitally important to a film, TV play or series, it's the characters that bring involvement, individuality, emotional impact, integrity and authorial voice.

Developing your cast of characters is part of the fun of writing. However, if you're the kind of writer who works best when you already have a clear structure in place, you may prefer to jump to Chapter 7 and come back to these chapters later.

Key idea

Interesting characters make interesting stories.

Getting started with character

Where characters come from is often a mystery, especially to the writer. Sometimes they appear fully formed, begging to be written about. This rare but blessed occurrence is to be cherished. More often, characters appear in fragments, tempting glimpses of partially formed roles that must be teased out.

Sometimes characters need to be created for functional reasons – dictated by the needs of the script. The challenge for the writer, in this case, is to bring them fully to life, to make them real and ensure that they never seem to be mere plot devices, pawns to be pushed around in the service of the story.

In all cases, the production of credible, living characters is very intuitive, relying on the writer's instincts, on dark and unknowable processes. And, every time, the writer must dig deeper, asking challenging questions as to who these people are, what they want, what they are hiding from themselves, and why they are doing what they do. For every answer there are further questions: What lies beneath? What really makes this person tick?

The sad thing is how many writers slog away without asking these questions, creating characters that never rise above the functional.

Snapshot exercise

Look at the people around you, people you know, people you meet, people you remember from your past. Can you give your own characters a hundredth of the richness and unpredictability you find in real life? What details or twists can you adapt to enrich your own inventions and make them more real?

Approaching your character from the outside or the inside?

Some writers like to develop their characters through deep psychological analysis, while others prefer to do it by choosing their shoes and working out how they walk. In other words, some like to start inside and work out, while others prefer to start with the outside and work in.

Whichever approach you take, you end up doing both. If you start with the outside, you need to dig inside; and if you start on the inside, you need to express this in ways the camera can see.

WORKING ON THE OUTSIDE

Characters reveal themselves in many ways – how they look, what they own, how they dress, how they speak, their general style (fast, slow, cool, thoughtful, aggressive, etc.). They also reveal themselves through their history, where they grew up, who their friends were, and are, and their past and current jobs.

Snapshot exercise

Cut out shots of people from newspapers and magazines, or print them from the Internet if you have a good-quality printer. The photos can be head and shoulders or full length, of individuals or groups, but remove any captions (who they really are is irrelevant to your needs).

Select one of the people pictured and take their part, answering questions in the first person – from major character issues to tiny details: 'What is your name?' 'Where were you born?' 'Who do you love?' 'What do you hate?' 'What is your favourite item of clothing?' and so on.

You can do this in a group, with each writer taking turns to pick out a picture for themselves, or you can do this by yourself, talking into a recorder or writing the answers down.

It doesn't matter if the person you have selected is like you or totally unlike you (different age, gender, race, etc.). In fact, the more different they are, the more interesting it can become. But you should always answer in character. This means, of course, that there may be some things you know (as the writer) that the character would never say, perhaps because of embarrassment or denial. You may hint at such issues between the lines.

Pay particular attention to how your character feels. Ideally, each answer should suggest a feeling about what you are talking about – what you love, hate, like, shudder over, regret … Questioners can help by prompting when necessary: 'What do you feel about that?'

There is no need to mimic accents. But you will begin to get a sense of the inner pace and tone of the character's thoughts.

This exercise is very powerful. You can do it as a general exercise or use it to 'cast' characters for your script. When preparing a screenplay, or novel, I will often seek out photos for the major characters and pin them to the wall next to my desk while I write.

Justin Zackham, screenwriter

'For me, screenwriting is all about setting characters in motion and as a writer just chasing them. They should tell you what they'll do in any scene you put them in.'

DEVELOPING A CHARACTER CV

Each element on a character's 'CV' can help you get under their skin and make him come alive, initially for you and then for the reader and audience. However, you will need to know much more about your characters than will ever appear in the script: 99 per cent of the information you create about your characters will be best used by giving you the confidence and insight to write the 1 per cent that we are ultimately told.

Write

Write down all the external attributes of your character, whatever comes to mind. You might like to begin with the most immediately visible – name, age, occupation, gender, physical type – the things we most usually notice in others when we first meet.

Continue with more detailed questions about the main aspects of your character's life. Answer in as much detail as you like. A character CV could run to three pages, or 30 if you're enjoying yourself. Key aspects could include:

- **Childhood** – What can they remember? Where did they grow up? Who was in the family? Where did they go to school?
- **Occupation** – What training did they have? Are they are a leader or a follower? How much do they earn? Where do they work and who with?
- **Personal life** – Who are their closest friends? What relationships have they had, and are having now? What relationships would they like? How do they treat people?

- **Physicality** – What do they look like? How do they move, talk, dress, eat, drink and deal with their health?
- **Possessions** – Where do they live? How is it decorated? What do they have next to their bed? What car do they drive? Do they love their possessions or hate them?
- **Pastimes** – Do they have hobbies, or are they workaholic? What do they do for enjoyment and relaxation? What was their favourite holiday, and their worst?
- **General** – What are their politics, religious beliefs, best and worst memories, dreams, nightmares? What special skills do they have? What are their attitudes? How do they approach life? What do they think about death? What's the best thing that's happened to them, and the worst?
- **Surprises** – What would surprise you about them? Where is their electricity? What makes them get up in the morning? What makes them laugh / get angry? Do they strike sparks?

You can do this as an observer, or as if you were the character talking. Try both, and see which you prefer. Whichever you choose, also ensure that you include how your character feels about each answer – how they feel about their age, their job, even about their name. Scripts are all about feelings and this prevents this exercise becoming dry and mechanical. If your feelings are excited from the off, then the reader is more likely to be fully engaged.

 Focus point

Ask how your characters feel about the details of their lives.

You can, of course, combine this with the previous exercise, to research a character in depth.

The advantage of writing this kind of CV is that, if you let your writing flow, fresh ideas can come spontaneously. Sometimes asking an apparently unimportant question can open up a whole side to a character that you didn't suspect, and suggest possible scenes for inclusion in the script. At the same time, the character's voice can begin to emerge, especially if you write in the first person and keep coming back to how they feel.

Some writers find this too mechanical and prefer to allow specifics to emerge as they become necessary in the script. The golden rule is: if it bores you, don't do it.

However, without a background file of some kind, you might introduce inconsistencies – forgetting or inadvertently changing crucial details. To avoid this, keep a file with a page on each character, and update it every time you add a character, or introduce a fact, a description or an attitude. Then you can easily check on your previous decisions as the script develops.

 Focus point

Keep a file on each character for reference, and update it as your idea grows.

WORKING ON THE INSIDE

You can also start from the inside of the character's head and work outwards.

To understand and develop the inner life of your characters, look at their:

- values
- beliefs
- attitudes
- memories
- preferred strategies and tactics
- preferred language.

We are driven first of all by our values – the things we hold dear. Central characters almost invariably find that two or more of their values are in conflict.

Much of what we do is determined by what we believe – whether we believe, for example, that we are capable, brave or a victim.

Different characters may display very different attitudes – aggressive or passive. Our memories – happy and sad – will always colour the way we see the world, past, present and future. As we saw in Chapter 2, characters have distinctive tactics and strategies – one may be devious; another blunt and direct – while the language we use reveals a great deal about what's going on inside. One character may use long-winded, evasive language, while another might prefer to call a spade a spade.

Snapshot exercise

Take the list above and fill it out for your central character. What are her values, beliefs, attitudes and memories? What strategies does she prefer? How does she speak? As before, you might find it most useful to write this in the first person, as if she's speaking directly to you. Be specific and include how she feels about her answers.

Listen to her voice as it begins to emerge.

Key idea

If you allow your character to talk to you in the first person, you can begin to hear her voice as it emerges.

CHARACTER COMPLEXITY

The most interesting characters are the most conflicted. In scripts, as in real life, people are never just one thing. A real person might be friendly towards some people, and aloof towards others. She may be brave in some circumstances, yet cowardly in others. A perfectly pleasant woman, she might suddenly react with vicious sarcasm for reasons that lie deep within her, reasons she may not even understand himself.

 ## Key idea

Conflicted characters are interesting characters.

Alicia Florrick (in the series *The Good Wife*) is a highly successful, astute lawyer, outwardly loyal to her philandering State's Attorney husband. Yet she is torn between him and her suppressed feelings for an old lover, who she now finds herself working for. She can be brave and forthright in court, yet fearful for her children, and over how best to bring them up. She is also deeply conflicted when dealing with a friend and colleague who has had a one-night stand with her husband some time before. Often, she has to deal with issues that force her to confront her own strong moral feelings, and decide between her survival in the cut-throat world of Chicago law and politics and doing the right thing.

A strong character such as Alicia will naturally create ideas for all kinds of potential scenes. Her strengths and weaknesses will suggest many different interesting situations and spark all manner of conflicts.

A lead character, whether for a single story or a series, will need to have a similar level of complexity, depending on the genre – the hero of an adventure story, for example, will not need to display as much inner conflict as the protagonist of a drama, but will still need to show contradictions that make him or her seem alive. Katniss Everdeen, Indiana Jones, Luke Skywalker, James Bond and Jack Sparrow all have their strengths and flaws, fears and moments of denial. However, these are brushed in with a much lighter touch.

Write

Write down as many adjectives as you can to describe your character. Aim for single words, or, at the most, two to three-word phrases in each case. Keep going until you have exhausted all the attributes you can think of.

Now look at the list and notice how many of the words are variations of the same idea. Group them together. For each group, underline or ring the adjective that seems to best sum up the essence of that group.

Ask yourself whether the groups are distinctly different. If you have fewer than four different character traits for a lead character, you should dig for more. If you have more than six, you may be overcomplicating things and should consider cutting down.

Quentin Tarantino, film-maker and screenwriter

'As a writer, I demand the right to write any character in the world that I want to write. I demand the right to be them, I demand the right to think them and I demand the right to tell the truth as I see they are.'

The six primary traits

Good screenwriters will fall in love with their lead characters, which is all to the good, but you can easily forget to include an important aspect of a character that the audience needs so that they can identify with them.

When you look at the groups of character traits you've chosen, you should find that they divide into the following six patterns. If there's a pattern missing, then fill it in:

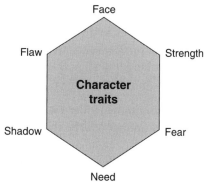

Figure 5.1 The six main traits of a central character

1 FACE

We all try to present a certain face to the world – a face that tries to portray us as someone we like and feel comfortable with. We all know the kind of boss who is weak but likes to put himself forward as strong and purposeful; the child who wants to be thought of as truthful but will sometimes lie to get herself out of trouble. Depending on how self-aware the character is, their *face* may be accurate or deluded.

2 FLAW

A character without flaws insults the audience, who know that every human being is fallible. It also throws away one of your most valuable assets. Audiences love characters *because* of their flaws, not *despite* them. More importantly, as we've seen in Chapter 3 it is the protagonist's flaws that drive the inner story.

3 STRENGTH

A major failing in many scripts, and indeed completed films, is to forget to include something to admire in the central character. You can be so focused on her flaws that you forget that she needs to be good at something as well. It's difficult to care about a character who is so flawed that she has no redeeming features at all.

This is a typical problem in romance stories, where it's essential that the audience sees the strengths that the characters love in each other.

What is your protagonist good at? What can we admire?

 Key idea

In a romantic story, make sure that you show us the positive traits that your characters love in each other.

4 FEAR

We are all afraid of something, even those who profess to be afraid of nothing. And those fears drive us on; often they drive us to do something we know is dangerous or wrong. Fears are at the root of good stories. Fears are not the same as flaws, although they may underlie them. Fear of looking foolish may drive a character's indecisiveness. In another character, that same fear might cause them to be rash.

What is your lead character most afraid of? Is there a deeper fear that lies below? Is this something they would admit to others? Maybe they would not admit it even to themselves?

5 SHADOW

How low are you capable of going, if pushed? What might you do, or have done, that reveals your darker side? Complex characters have a shadow side – a part of them that, if let loose, would harm them or others, possibly very gravely indeed.

Ask yourself how low your central character could go, Would they be likely to self-harm, either their own body or through sabotaging a relationship, say? Might they be capable of violence, emotional or physical? Would they steal or lie? Could they torture or murder? Might they even enjoy it?

 Richard Russo, screenwriter and novelist

'A lot of my characters in all of my books have a self-destructive urge. They'll do precisely the thing that they know is wrong, take a perverse delight in doing the wrong thing.'

6 NEED

The protagonist of a story often wants one thing, but needs another. This is the flipside of the character's main flaw.

Your character may *want* to win a medal at the Olympics, but what she *needs* to do is learn to stand up for herself. Another may *want* to chase the rustlers off his land, but what he *needs* to do is give up violence. Initially unconscious of his need, your lead character will become increasingly aware of it as the story progresses and will grapple with the internal conflict that results.

In a series, that need may be partially filled at the end of an episode, only to be lost again at the start of the next.

Here are a couple of examples showing characters constructed around the six primary traits, the first in a film, the second in a TV series:

- **Jack Sparrow** (in the 'Pirates of the Caribbean' franchise) is a cheeky, warm-hearted pirate (*face*). He is also devious (*flaw*) yet courageous, an independent spirit who survives on his wits (*strengths*). He is afraid of violence (*fears*) and prefers negotiation where possible. However, when pushed, he's happy to steal, fight and kill, with little provocation (*shadow*). Jack Sparrow needs to live an honest, peaceful life (though it is highly unlikely ever to happen) (*need*).

- **David Brent** (*The Office*) believes himself to be an efficient office manager with strong personal skills (*face*). However, in reality, he's insecure and desperate to please (*flaws*). For all his manifest faults, though, he's rarely malicious and honestly wants to succeed (*strengths*). Afraid of failure (*fears*), Brent, however, is totally unaware of his darker side, and always taken by surprise when he clumsily insults or hurts others in the office (*shadow*). What he needs is self-awareness, and many episodes end with him attaining a brief and painful vision of himself, which is rapidly forgotten by the start of the next (*need*).

Give yourself time

Exploring your lead character takes time. Be patient and thorough, but at the same time ensure that you enjoy the work. It shouldn't be mechanical.

The great playwright Henrik Ibsen said that the first time you meet your characters they are like distant acquaintances. When you write the second draft, they become good friends. And by the time of the final draft, they are family.

Start making friends with them. If you start the right way, with the solid foundations you need for creating interesting, intriguing characters who we want to spend more time with, you will find that your characters sustain and continue to intrigue and fascinate you – and your audiences – to the end of the script.

Workshop

Start to get to know your central character. Have each member of the workshop write a letter or leave a voicemail message in the person of their protagonist to someone from whom he or she wants something. Read it out and have the others fire questions. Answer as the character. Next, each member suggests different difficult situations to find out how they react.

Where to next?

Discovering the hidden depths of your characters, starting with the lead character and working outwards, is one of the ongoing tasks – and joys – of dramatic writing. And the next step is to see how the characters interact to add power to your screen story.

6

The character constellation for single stories and series

No screen story can work with only one character. (The only film to have come close to a single-character story with no other human character involved, even on the soundtrack, is *All Is Lost*, written and directed by J.C. Chandor, the story of a sailor stranded at sea. Even then we briefly hear unnamed voices on the boat's radio and occasionally see passing ships; and, of course, there is the constantly present antagonist, albeit non-human, of the sea.)

Whether a single story or a series, your protagonist needs other characters to bounce off, help, argue with, defeat or be defeated by. These other characters create a constellation around her, each with their own outer and inner role in the story.

The worst person to be stuck with

The most interesting characters to write for are those who tread on one another's toes in some way, who strike sparks off one another and who reveal new and surprising facets when they interact. They circle around the central character and have their own flaws. These flaws grate on each other – annoy, irritate, anger or maybe even flatter, inflate or encourage, in ways that threaten to be the downfall of others.

Your job is to create this situation, and then ensure that they can't escape. You design 'handcuffs' – a solid, credible reason why they are stuck together, such as a prison, a storm or money – or an abstract reason, such as a common goal, a common enemy, greed or even love.

And because they push each other to extremes, this forces them to face the possibility of change – so, for some characters, that *worst* person in the world to be stuck with may turn out in the end to have been the *best* person in the world to be stuck with …

 ## Focus point

Create a constellation of characters whose flaws make each of them the worst person in the world for your protagonist to have to deal with.

When creating your character constellation, ask yourself: who would be the worst person for my protagonist to be stuck in her story with, and why? What flaws in others would most effectively make things worse for her?

In the strongest character constellations, each of the lead character's flaws are reflected, mirrored or distorted in some manner by the other characters who surround her. If her primary flaw is lack of courage, you can be sure that she'll find herself dealing with people who are more afraid or more foolhardy, dramatically brave or constantly anxious. There will be people whose flaws make them try to protect her from danger and hold her back. And there will be those whose flaws lead them to push her into danger, fail to support her or fail to warn her of the perils ahead. Each would be the worst person for her to be stuck in a lift with. They tread on her emotional toes, push her emotional buttons or encourage her worst faults.

That is a wonderful place to be, for a writer. It means that you can put any two of your characters in a scene and know that they'll have issues with each other. Sparks will fly. No matter what they are talking about, there will be heat between them.

 ## Leigh Brackett, screenwriter and author

'Plot is people. Human emotions and desires founded on the realities of life, working at cross purposes, getting hotter and fiercer as they strike against each other until finally there's an explosion – that's Plot.'

Snapshot exercise

Choose a flaw for an imaginary protagonist. Who might be the worst people for her to be stuck in a story with?

Write down as many examples as you can. Make sure that you include *their* flaws. Create characters with similar flaws, opposite flaws, variations on the flaw, the same flaw only worse, a hatred for the flaw, and so on. Imagine how these people will tread on each other's corns. How will they relate to the protagonist and to one another? How might they support her in her flaw, or oppose her? How will they make things worse for her?

Key idea

Sometimes the worst person is someone who opposes your flaw, sometimes it is someone who supports it.

Consider the following ways in which your characters can relate through their flaws:

- **Support the flaw** Characters who pander to the protagonist's flaw will be useful. They can push your protagonist into worse situations, by encouraging her vices and helping her avoid facing the truth. Later, they can provide a test – by tempting the lead character, to see whether she has truly grown. She may be strong enough to resist the temptation, or she may fall back.

- **Reflect the flaw** Similarly, characters who have similar flaws can play a powerful part. They can raise the stakes, providing a warning of consequences of failing to grow, or a demonstration of the possibilities of change.

- **Oppose the flaw** You will doubtless also want someone in your story who stands up strongly against the flaw. This person may be sympathetic or unsympathetic but they devote themselves to denouncing your character's flaw at frequent intervals.

- **Reverse the flaw** Some characters should display the reverse flaw. For example, if the protagonist is cowardly, another character could be foolhardy. By demonstrating the dangers of being brave, you add tension and spice to the character's inner struggle. It also stops the character journey becoming predictable and simplistic.

In *What's Eating Gilbert Grape*, Gilbert is faced with the choice between a dead-end life, caring for his learning-disabled younger brother, and abandoning him by leaving home. His flaw is that he's too nice.

His main antagonist in the story is his brother, Arnie, who chains him to the family home. Arnie's learning difficulties, and inability to grow up, are not technically inner flaws as they are not within his control. However, through his childishness he certainly treads on Gilbert's toes.

Grossly obese, Gilbert's mother, Bonnie, is hardly able to care for herself, and even more indulgent than Gilbert of Arnie's whims. The local sheriff has the opposite flaw. He has no truck with Arnie's childish behaviour and threatens to send him into care. Meanwhile, the real 'parent' of the house is Gilbert's elder sister, Amy, whose flaw is her dedication to duty, hardly living at all for herself. She has been forced to grow up too fast.

A younger woman, Becky, who arrives when her grandmother's car breaks down, shows a more independent spirit, signalling perhaps the way that Gilbert could progress, if he allowed himself to.

Conversely, Gilbert's estranged older brother (now no more than a black-and-white photo on the fridge) and father (who hanged himself in the cellar) remind him of the dangers of running away.

By using character to block off all easy answers to his problem, the script forces Gilbert to take the most difficult path.

Write

Create a character constellation for your story. You may well already have ideas for characters who'll strike sparks. List as many characters as possible whose varied flaws relate to those of your protagonist.

Invent new characters who will add texture and dimension in unexpected ways. And give interesting flaws to existing characters who have so far been little more than plot devices.

Using the character constellation in a film or series

Often, in developing the character constellation, you develop a clearer understanding of your protagonist's own flaw. You can also begin to use it to create scenes and plot points. Because they come from character, they will feel much more organic than if you developed the structure intellectually.

Creating a powerful character constellation is of vital importance in developing a series. As we've seen, the dynamics between the main characters give a series 'legs' and ensure a flow of involving episodes with variety and emotional strength. This applies to all series, from comedy to drama, historical to futuristic.

You need core series characters with powerful issues and flaws that bind them into a continuous round of potential conflict.

In the American cop series *The Shield*, Vic Mackey is an out-of-control cop who breaks the law to catch criminals, runs his own drugs deals and thinks nothing of killing people who get in his way. Deeply flawed, egoistical and violent, he nevertheless has strengths. Charismatic and energetic, he believes, despite everything, in bringing bad guys to justice. He is enormously loyal to his men and his family, and hates the sly ambitions of those more political cops above him.

Supporting him, Mackey's main sidekick, Shane, is even more out of control than he is. His flaw is to be even more violent and unpredictable. Without Mackey's cleverness, he is constantly creating problems that Vic has to solve, contrasting with his boss's greater street-smartness and relative restraint.

On the other hand, Curtis, the other close member of the team, is more thoughtful and self-aware. Weaker, and more easily led by his colleagues, he's drawn into criminality against his better judgement.

Meanwhile, Captain David Aceveda is deeply suspicious of Mackey's team. Aceveda is an ambitious cop with an eye on the political main chance. He wants to clean up the station, but his instinct is to be Machiavellian and this weakness leads him into dangerous waters.

Among the other detectives in the precinct, Dutch is one of the straightest. His flaw is the opposite of Mackey's: fastidious to the point of prissiness, he is intellectual and cold.

Danni, a uniformed woman cop, finds herself drawn into Mackey's schemes when they have an affair. Attracted to him, despite her moral uprightness, her loyalties are split.

These – and other – regular characters in the series bring a dark moral edge to every episode. Any two will bring energy and conflict to a scene together. We switch on the TV to watch such series week after week, to see how the character conflicts will work out in new and developing situations.

Key idea

A strong character constellation lies at the heart of any series.

Write

Write a random scene between any two characters.

Give them each an outer goal that is not directly related to the main story (e.g. one of them wants the heating turned up and the other wants to eat). Start them off and allow their inner attitudes to fuel the way they relate to each other.

Don't worry about clever plotting or polished dialogue at this stage. That can come later. Aim to get a feel for how they express themselves in words and action, and ensure that each remains true.

Try different pairings to find how they spark off each other in different ways – some positive, some negative, some mixed.

Outer roles

As well as their inner roles in the story, each character has an outer role. We've focused so far on the central character – the **protagonist**. The protagonist is the character who drives the story forwards. It is her goal that is most important to the story. It is also her character arc that is the most important. If you have any doubt as to who should be the protagonist, look for the character who changes most by the end – this will invariably give you the most potential for development and audience involvement.

(For multiple, awkward and other kinds of 'difficult' protagonists, see Chapter 21.)

THE ANTAGONIST

In most stories, one character leads the conflict against the protagonist. He may act alone or with a large team of followers. He may even appear initially to be on the protagonist's side, but by the end it will be the antagonist who must be faced in the final battle.

The stronger your antagonist, the stronger your script. Many films and series are watched as eagerly for their antagonists as for their lead characters. Take Rhett Butler in *Gone with the Wind*, Darth Vader in the 'Star Wars' series, Albert Steptoe and Mr Mackay in the British sitcoms *Steptoe and Son* and *Porridge* and the cynical and ambitious lawyer Joséphine Karlsson in the dark French TV series *Engrenages* (*Spiral*).

 Key idea

A strong script needs a strong antagonist.

To create a strong antagonist, make sure that you provide him with strengths and flaws, as you would a protagonist. Indeed, give him greater strengths than the lead character. The more invincible the opponent, the more compelling the protagonist's struggle becomes. At the same time, giving the antagonist a number of admirable traits adds complexity and involves the audience at a deeper, personal level.

In *The Silence of the Lambs*, we admire Hannibal Lecter's intellectual abilities. He'd make a far more interesting dinner companion than the rather single-minded heroine, Clarice Starling – as long as we ensured that we weren't the ones being eaten.

In many stories, protagonist and antagonist have more in common with each other than with the characters who are nominally on their own side.

In the BBC TV series *The Fall*, serial killer Paul Spector and Detective Superintendent Stella Gibson have much in common – not least their intelligence, emotional coldness, capacity for using others for sexual gratification, and ability to be personable on the surface and unyielding underneath.

The main differences between the antagonist and protagonist are (a) we side with the protagonist's goals and (b) the antagonist will generally have no inner story. Paul Spector and Hannibal Lecter make no attempt to grapple with their inner flaws – indeed, it would severely weaken the stories if they tried. While we generally see a story from the point of view of the protagonist, we rarely see properly inside the head of the antagonist. While there's no problem occasionally giving the audience a glimpse of what he's feeling, or what drives him on, an antagonist will almost always work best if he retains a large element of mystery and surprise. This makes him all the more frightening and difficult to second-guess.

PROTAGONIST–ANTAGONIST

One exception is a dual-protagonist romance movie, where the two protagonists become each other's antagonist. In this case, each has a character arc.

In Nora Ephron's script for *When Harry Met Sally*, we see most of the movie from the split point of view of Harry Burns and Sally Albright – in some scenes literally, as the screen is split in two. Each is equally protagonist (we want them to achieve their goals – of finding a way to have a romantic relationship and remain friends) and antagonist (they make it difficult for each other to achieve this) – and we follow their inner stories as they learn to grow. Harry's major flaw is a fear of commitment and an insistence on always seeing the dark side of life. Sally is too fastidious and demanding, and naively optimistic. As they grow, she helps him lighten up and learn to commit, while he provides her with the realism that she lacks. (The ending shifts more towards Harry's point of view, as Sally matures a few scenes earlier and he only finally commits at the very finish.)

Key idea

In a romance movie, the two lovers are often each other's antagonist.

Write

List your antagonists and decide who will be the principal antagonist or antagonists in your story. Write a biography for him – using the techniques introduced in the last two chapters. Write it in the first person, ensuring that you include how he feels about the facts in his life.

Note any subtext – what he is not saying (it could even be something of which he himself is not aware). Make him complex and contradictory. Ensure that there are things we like about him, as well as dislike, and that he'll be extremely difficult to defeat.

SUPPORT CHARACTER

Both protagonist and antagonist can be further developed by providing a support character (sometimes known as a 'reflection'). The reason is simple: unlike in a novel, we can only know what a character is thinking when they act or speak. So friends and allies provide invaluable opportunities for your characters to reveal themselves.

The support may be a friend or colleague, a willing or reluctant ally, anyone who shares some of the protagonist's goals. They may well also come into conflict over smaller goals – or on how to achieve the main goal.

Kurt Vonnegut, novelist

'Every character should want something, even if it is only a glass of water.'

A support will not be as fully developed as a protagonist or antagonist, and will have fewer character traits – perhaps two or three distinct primary traits rather than six.

Many writers put all their effort into their leads and skimp on the lesser roles. However, it's worth spending time on your support characters. They give a script texture and depth. An important test of a good film or series is the quality of the supporting cast. You want roles that will strengthen the story, bolster the main cast and attract good support actors. That means examining each character in turn to ensure that they are credible, rounded and bring an element of surprise.

Key idea

Your support characters bring texture and depth.

In Pedro Almodóvar's film *All about My Mother*, Manuela travels to Barcelona to look for the father of her son, who has died. She meets a number of support characters who act variously as advisers, sounding boards and helpers: Agrado, a transvestite; Rosa, a pregnant nun; and Huma, an actress who gives her a job. Each is surprising, freshly observed and has her own inner contradictions. They also help her relearn how to be a mother, by allowing her to help them through their various difficulties.

In *When Harry Met Sally*, Harry Burns and Sally Albright also have their friends – Jess and Marie – who both act as sounding boards and reflect similar issues. They allow the protagonists to discuss their hopes and fears, at times when they would be unable to talk about such things openly with each other. They are also distinctively different and rounded characters in their own right, avoiding the easy clichés of the genre.

ROMANCE SUPPORT

A romance support is a subsidiary character whose role is to be loved by the protagonist, in a romantic subplot.

As with romantic protagonists, they should nonetheless still have strengths and flaws – not least because this allows us to understand what the protagonist loves in them and what they love in the protagonist.

As with other support/reflection characters, they will not be as complex as the protagonist, but will still need to have contradictions, strengths and flaws, to make them credible and interesting.

Key idea

Romance characters also need contradictions, strengths and flaws.

Edit

In one column, write the names of your protagonist, antagonist and their supports. Alongside each, write a few words for their principal character traits, their goals, the obstacles that face them, their strengths and their flaws.

Do you see any parallels or connections? Do their strengths and flaws relate to each other?

List all the support characters, and write a brief paragraph on each.

Character names

Inexperienced writers often fall down when it comes to naming their characters. Character names set the right mood for the reader. Nothing is more depressing than a series of boring character names, while good names can prepare you for an interesting ride.

Charles Dickens laid great stress on the importance of finding the right character names – from Copperfield and Twist to Scrooge, Bumble and Pecksniff. His notebooks are filled with the lists he made as he tried them out. Georges Simenon, who wrote nearly 200 novels, used to spend days solely writing down possible names and combinations, throwing most of them away.

While you don't need to be so offbeat and quirky as Dickens (or as prolific as Simenon), you do need to find names that give the right resonance and yet are memorable and fresh. Here are a few tips:

- **Avoid the bland and the cliché.** Predictable names give no extra energy to a character. Not all Irishmen are called Paddy, nor are all upper-class men called Peregrine. Go wider in your search for names. Remember Gregory House, Hannibal Lecter and Scarlett O'Hara.

- **Hint at what lies beneath** – the 'Scarlett' in Scarlett O'Hara suggests her fiery nature. Taking a word and shifting it slightly can also work. 'Hannibal' is a letter shift from Cannibal. 'Lecter' suggests intellectual. You could create a name for a strong, hard character by taking, say, the name Stone and adding or changing an element: Stonebury, Stoneham or Stine.

- **Internal repetition** can create memorable names, such as J.J. Hunsecker or Bilbo Baggins.

- Make sure that the names are **appropriate for the character's age, ethnicity** and so on. Age is a particular trap as names go rapidly in and out of fashion and it's all too easy to choose a name which is either a cliché or out of date.

- **Keep names distinct.** A script about James, Jane, Jake, John and Joan will leave readers struggling. Use different initial letters. Draw on both short and long names, surnames, nicknames, different ethnicities and so forth.
- **Walk-ons are often best kept as types** – for example 'Angry Photographer'.
- **The Internet is a great resource for names** – you can look up lists of popular baby names for a given year or by ethnicity. There are other kinds of lists that can also help with finding accurate first and last names from different backgrounds or countries, such as sports teams.

Focus point

The name is your character's shop window. Take the time to get each one right.

Edit

Take another look at your characters' names. Can they be improved? Are they resonant and varied? Do they work well together? Are they predictable or do they feel fresh and true?

Make lists of possible names. Research online as well in books and newspapers. Ensure that you have the best possible names.

Workshop

Collect together all the lists, scraps and biographies you've created on your characters.

1 Quick-draft fragments and scenes so that you can see and hear the characters come to life. See how protagonist, antagonist, supports and smaller roles interact. Begin to hear their voices.

2 Workshop these scenes for your colleagues' reactions to the characters as they begin to come into focus.

3 As you go, expand your notes, adding more biographical detail, feelings and snippets of dialogue and action. Keep a file on each character – in a computer file, a notebook or sections of a ring-binder. This will be very useful for reference later as you write.

Where to next?

The characters are growing clearer, and their roles are beginning to come into focus. But no character fully exists without a story. It's time to take your cast of characters and plunge them into the challenges, difficulties and moral problems that will reveal their true natures and move an audience.

It's time to look at structure.

7

Act One – normality and disaster

Important as it is to have strong, credible, living characters, they are nothing without a structure to work within. Hamlet would be a bore without the play – in fact, he wouldn't exist. The structure of the play *Hamlet* is there to bring out the character of Hamlet. In the next three chapters, we are going to work in detail on your story.

Why three acts?

You will, if you haven't already, read many articles and books about three-act structure, some of it sensible, much of it over-heated. The truth is that more hot air is expended on structure than almost any other area of screenwriting.

Structure is most talked about simply because structure is most easily talked about. It can be measured, discussed and argued over more easily than issues of character, theme and genre. Yet, with rare exceptions (the movies *The Usual Suspects* and *Pulp Fiction* are two of the very few), audiences are not consciously aware of a film's structure at all. They want an interesting story, with well-constructed characters, and to be emotionally (and possibly intellectually) engaged.

This isn't to say structure isn't important – quite the reverse. The wrong structure will leave the audience dissatisfied and unmoved. The story will feel flabby or rushed. The plot may meander, and confuse or simply frustrate the viewer. The job of the structure is to ensure that the audience feels that the right things happen at the right time and to keep them watching to the end.

It's also a mistake to think that structure automatically restricts a writer's imagination. Lack of structural constraint is rarely as liberating as writers or theorists expect. Rules can often stimulate the imagination as much as anything; they give you something to push against – as poets find with rhyme and metre, and composers with form such as the sonata or the symphony.

You can plan your structure from the start, or uncover it as you edit the later drafts, but at some point you need to find your story's best shape.

For most screenplays, a three-act shape is the most effective way of achieving that aim, just as four wheels are the strongest shape for most cars and four legs for most tables. In later chapters, I will show you how to recognize when you have a story that breaks those rules. Just it's possible to have a motor vehicle with three wheels, or indeed two wheels or one wheel, so you can have stories in five acts, seven acts or no acts at all. But, even then, you'll need a working understanding of three-act structure to understand how to get away without it.

 ## Noël Coward, playwright, composer, actor and director

'Building a play is like building a house – everything is structure, the rest is just decoration.'

Stories and acts

Three-act structure existed in classical Greek drama before Aristotle, and can be traced through Shakespeare (whose five-act plays nevertheless follow essentially the same form) to the vast majority of the greatest movies and TV dramas.

They present their audiences with a clear beginning, middle and end – from *Oedipus Rex* to *Django Unchained*:

1 **Protagonist finds he has a problem.**

2 **Protagonist sets out to deal with the problem.**

3 **Protagonist defeats, or is defeated by, the problem.**

In his book *Story*, Robert McKee defines an act as a unit of storytelling, at the end of which something crucial has changed. At the end of Act One, the protagonist has been forced to realize he has a problem. By the end of Act Two, he faces imminent defeat.

By contrast, at the end of Act Three something irreversible has changed. The protagonist has either won or lost – or, in some cases, partially won and partially lost (a bittersweet end). Sarah Connor has crushed the Terminator. Michael Dorsey, in *Tootsie*, has revealed his real identity to the world. Manuela, in *All about My Mother*, has found a second chance to be a mother, but on new terms.

Key idea

Stories are all about change – at the end of a story something has changed irreversibly.

Edit

Go back to your premise and clarify the three elements:
1 What is your protagonist's problem?
2 What does he set out to do about it?
3 How does he defeat, or get defeated, by it? (Or will there be a bittersweet ending?)

Billy Wilder, writer-director

'If you have a problem with the third act, the real problem is in the first act.'

Planning Act One[1]

In the first act, we meet your lead character for the first time, living his normal life – but his normal life is flawed because *he* is flawed. He could continue in this way without ever changing, except that that would not be very interesting to an audience, so the writer's job is to throw problems at him until he is forced to see that things have to change. He seizes on a new goal that he thinks will solve all his problems.

---

1   The next three chapters build on analysis developed by (among others) Sam Smiley, Paul Thompson, Frank Daniel and Dara Marks.

NORMALITY

The opening of a screenplay needs to do two things at once. It needs to draw the audience into a world that they recognize, and at the same time to create a sense of dramatic tension so that they continue to watch.

The way to do this is to begin with an active dramatic scene in which a character (the main character or another) has a goal that we can immediately recognize. However far travelled your script will be, begin with something the audience can hold on to. Don't dive in with a complicated problem. Start with a simple issue. It could be finding money for the parking meter; or getting the kids up to go to school; or yearning to buy that expensive guitar.

If the setting is exotic – a jungle war-zone or an alien planet – it is even more important to ensure that we can relate to his goal: the need to find shelter, running out of water, wanting to take a rest.

And the protagonist should be facing an obstacle, even if it's as small as trying to cross a busy road or having to placate an angry child.

Introduce us to the normality of your central character's life. This will of course vary enormously from character to character: he could be fighting terrorists or starting a new school. Most importantly, you should show how your protagonist's normal life isn't working. Something is wrong – and that problem will relate directly to his inner flaw:

- In *All about My Mother*, we're in a hospital. A patient flat-lines and Manuela, one of the staff, phones to offer his organs for transplant. We cut to her domestic life. She has a loving relationship with her only son. However, something's not right. It's to do with something related to her past, and in particular her son's father, whom she refuses to name. All is not as good as it seems.

- *The Terminator* opens in Los Angeles – in the future. A high-tech fight is taking place but a title card soon tells us that the real battle is in the present – tonight. We flash back to now. A garbage-truck driver is having difficulty getting his truck to work. A flash of lightning, and he flees in fear. A violent man appears and goes looking for a woman called Sarah Connor. Soon, we meet Sarah herself, happy-go-lucky, late for work and unaware …

Normality could in theory continue for ever, unchanged. Manuela could continue to avoid answering questions about her son's father. Sarah Connor could continue to be late for work and be bullied by customers for the rest of her life. But if the story is to start, this state of affairs mustn't last.

 Key idea

Normality is flawed, but could go on for ever.

Write

Develop the key events that will begin your story: a scene showing your protagonist's normality and its drawbacks. Include a sense of the dominant mood of your story, to draw us in, and a small dramatic moment to involve us from the start. Don't try to tell us everything that's going on. Allow us to wonder and guess for a while.

QUESTIONS AND ANSWERS

The temptation with the first act is to fill it full of information. At this point, the audience doesn't want information; it wants emotion, suspense, someone to care about. Many writers make the mistake of giving all the answers straight away. Questions are more important than answers.

A story starts by posing a question (we're in a harbour at night – why are we here?) – and then, before you answer the question, pose new ones (a man is lying as if shot – what's happened? who is he? is he dying?) – and, before you answer *those* questions, pose a new one ... and so on.

Keep overlapping questions as the story unfolds.

Key idea

Questions are more important than answers.

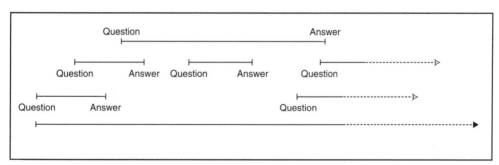

Figure 7.1 Story timeline

A TASTE OF HONEY

One small, easily forgotten, scene is crucial to your story at this point. The script won't work if the audience doesn't fully appreciate what's at stake for the character – what he stands to lose. So, as soon as possible in the first act, you should give us a glimpse of what happiness looks like for him ... just before you snatch it away. A taste of honey.

This might be a scene where we see how good protagonist's life now is, for all its flaws. Such as where we see Sarah Connor enjoying life, riding her bike in the sunshine, or chilling out with her flatmate.

Alternatively, it could be a scene which shows us what success might feel like in the future. You could show the two lovers meeting for the first time and finding an instant rapport. Or the detective protagonist solving (or thinking he's solved) a case.

In *All about My Mother*, Manuela finds a new connection with her son and promises to tell him the truth about his father. They watch her favourite play and share an insight into her past. But, before she can share more, that new connection is brutally smashed. Esteban is run over by a car and killed.

The taste of honey, while brief, powers the whole of the rest of your story. It's what your protagonist is fighting to get back.

Snapshot exercise

Write a scene with a glimpse of happiness. Show us what success might look like for your protagonist – before you snatch it away.

STORY

Story differs from normality. A story begins when the character has a problem that refuses to be ignored but must be urgently solved. His life cannot go on like this for ever. The job of the writer is to destroy the balance of his normal, flawed life.

A story begins with a shock that rattles the bars of the central character's cage. This incident, often called the 'inciting incident', knocks his world out of shape. Things are changing and he has to deal with them.

The inciting incident will normally pose the main story question that must be answered by the end of the film or series. (If not, then the question will be posed by the First Act turning point, see Figure 7.2 and below.)

Key idea

We shift into story when there is a new situation that cannot go on for ever, and must be resolved, one way or another.

You must place this within the first ten minutes (ten pages in professional layout). Any later and the audience will begin to feel impatient:

- In *The Terminator*, the inciting incident is the moment when Sarah Connor first hears that someone is killing people called Sarah Connor and that she could be in real danger.
- In *All About My Mother*, it's the shock of Manuela seeing her son die.

A CUNNING PLAN

As a result of the new situation, the protagonist generally does what any sane person would do: he tries to return life to how it was. No matter that life was not that wonderful, there's comfort in familiarity. So almost every lead character will try hard to

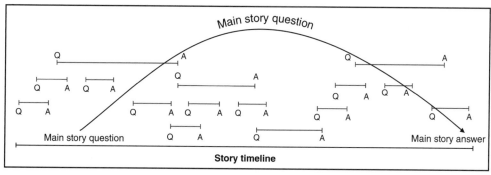

Figure 7.2 The main story question (Q = question; A = answer)

pretend that nothing much has changed, and develop a cunning plan for putting things right again:

- Sarah Connor does the natural thing and tries to contact the police for help.
- Manuela tries to go back to her normal life and agrees to Esteban's heart being used in a transplant.

As we have already seen, stories are made of a succession of decisions. The same decisions that reveal the inner life of the characters form the spine of the outer story and give it the energy it needs to drive forwards.

This first plan will probably follow the path of least resistance. A mistake many writers make is to have their characters do more than seems necessary. Most people just want an easy life.

 Key idea

Villains are keen. Heroes are reluctant.

At this point, and for the next 15 to 20 pages, it may seem as if normality has returned. The protagonist tries to enact his cunning plan. He deals with the conflicts that arise, and attempts to return to the status quo. However, you cannot allow this to happen.

The job of the writer is to push the lead character into greater and greater difficulties, because only the greatest difficulties will force him to reveal his true nature. The inner story and the outer story interact and interfere with each other. Increased levels of conflict, throughout the story, peel off the layers one by one until he sees himself for what he really is (see Figure 7.3).

 Key idea

The job of the writer is to push the lead character into greater and greater difficulties.

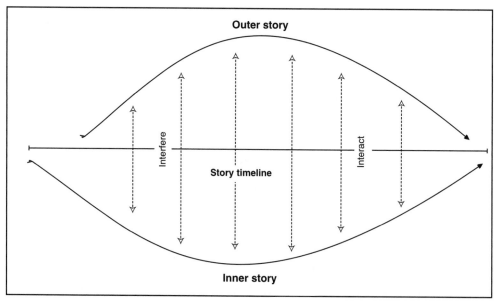

Figure 7.3 Inner and outer stories

Write

Develop an inciting incident. Make it rattle your protagonist's cage. How does he first decide to deal with it?

FIRST ACT TURNING POINT

This comes to a head at the climax of the act. Disaster strikes and the original plan fails. It was too simplistic and it failed to grapple with the reality. Now, reality strikes back and throws everything into chaos. The lead character needs a better plan. This plan will be the one that carries him through the rest of the story.

Every act builds to a turning point with:

- a surprise, *leading to*
- an emotional climax *and*
- a new challenge *forcing*
- a new decision.

At the end of any act, except the final one, the protagonist faces a new challenge that will form the basis of the following act. At the end of each act, something crucial has changed, though not irreversibly.

- Sarah Connor, expecting help from the police in escaping Kyle, is attacked instead by the Terminator.
- Manuela realizes that she can't get her son back.

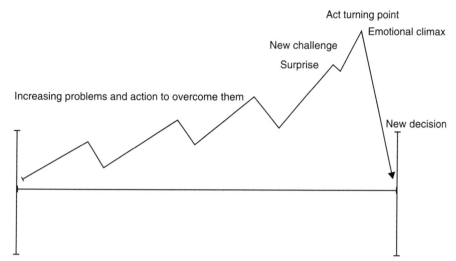

Figure 7.4 The structure of an act

SURPRISE, DISASTER AND CHALLENGE

The surprise is often missed by beginner writers. They either leave it out of the script or they don't communicate it to the central character. The new disaster twists the story in a new direction, one that the audience isn't expecting. If the climax is predictable or logical, then there is no clear distinction between the acts.

The protagonist also *must* know about the surprise in order to be forced to face up to the new challenge. It doesn't work if another character knows what's occurred and the lead character doesn't.

Of course, disaster can mean subtly different things, depending on your story and genre. In a love story, the 'disaster' may be the moment when the lead character falls in love and realizes that his entire world is about to be turned upside down. In a noir, it may be the point at which the protagonist lands the job that will let him kill the husband of the *femme fatale*. In a biopic, it may be the scene in which the would-be singer first finds his true voice and sees the way ahead – a path that could lead to success but also to personal turmoil.

John Sayles, writer-director

'In terms of audience rhythm and patience, I subscribe to certain broad rules. By the end of the first half hour they'd better know what the game is and who the players are. The proposition of the movie, the backbone question that will be decided, must be stated. New characters can be brought in after this point, new sub-propositions raised, but all the basic stuff should be established.' ('Thinking in Pictures')

Key idea

The surprise brings disaster and challenge in its wake.

In *All about My Mother*, the climax of the first act comes when Manuela decides, against all advice, to trace the recipient of her son's heart. She finds the man but, to her own surprise, is unable to face him. This inner obstacle is underlined by the outer obstacle of her colleague's criticism of her for going against all the rules. Her original plan for reconnecting with her son, and with her maternal feelings, is in ruins. She decides to go back to Barcelona, the city where her son was conceived.

Sarah Connor's plan to seek help from the police is thrown into confusion when the Terminator attacks. To her surprise, Kyle, the man who she'd noticed following her, and who she'd taken for the murderer, now comes to her rescue. She has to decide whether she can trust him or whether he is indeed trying to kill her. With bullets flying and little time to think, she's forced to trust him, at least for the time being.

Workshop

Sketch out and share some initial ideas for your Act One turning point, with a climax, surprise and new challenge. Aim to make it a disaster that destroys your central character's initial plan. Force him to rethink. You may well already have the core ideas on your character grid; if not, you'll need to invent a new climax and insert it at one of the character steps.

You should now have an opening scene, inciting incident and Act One turning point, and probably fragments of some of the scenes between.

Discuss whether they are powerful enough. Are they challenging the central character, or merely giving information? Do they draw the audience in strongly, or is there something you could add or improve? Brainstorm the possibilities.

Where to next?

The challenge at the end of Act One forces the lead character to make a new decision. The old plan doesn't work, after all. He needs a new plan. And that plan will underpin the rest of the story.

8

Act Two – the project

The beginning is over. Normality seems a long time ago for your central character. After the climactic reversal of the end of Act One, he has to make the essential decision that will fuel the rest of the story. He must either settle on a new goal or decide on an entirely new way to go about achieving his old goal. Then he must go about putting this new plan into action.

Writing the second act can feel very intimidating at first. It will occupy at least half your screenplay. This means around an hour of a classic 100 to 120-minute movie – an expanse of 60 pages that you have somehow to fill without losing the plot.

The key to understanding the second act is what I call 'The Act Two Project'. This will bring the second act to life and give it shape and forward momentum. Without it, your story will wallow without a rudder.

The story decision and the to-do list

An audience watches a story in the future tense – that is to say, what occupies them is not what happened in the past, but what might happen in the future. An involving story makes them *hope* for good things and *fear* bad. However, they can do this only if they know what might occur. A poor script leaves them uninvolved, without being able to engage actively in the hopes and fears of the protagonist. (This often happens if the lead character is passive – that is, only reacts to events as they happen to him.) In a good script, he takes control of his story and develops his own new plan. A good script will ensure that the audience understands his plan, so that they can engage with it, and anticipate every obstacle and diversion along the way.

The first step is to have your character make a clear story decision – a commitment to solving his problem himself. This will be his Act Two Project.

 Key idea

The protagonist must take his story into his own hands.

The second step is to make a list. In essence, you create a 'to-do list' for your lead character. This list may or may not be shared with the audience up front. However, it drives the story forwards and allows you to break down the second act into manageable sequences.

Five to nine steps should be sufficient at this stage. The twists and turns that arise during the story will be more than enough to add complication and surprise.

 Key idea

The to-do list allows you to divide the second act into manageable parts.

In *All about My Mother*, Manuela has resolved to find Esteban's father and resolve their outstanding issues, as a way of coming to terms with her son's death.

Her to-do list might read something like this:
- Return to Barcelona.
- Go to the father's old haunts.
- Make contact with old friends.
- Find Esteban's father (the transvestite Lola).
- Tell him about his son.

In reality, her inner story (her insecurities and need to relearn how to be a mother) get in the way, so the to-do list becomes more complicated:
- Return to Barcelona.
- Go to the father's old haunts.

- Make contact with old friends.
- Help another transsexual prostitute sort out her life.
- Put off seeing the father (the transvestite Lola).
- Get a job caring for the actress her son admired just before he died.
- Care for Rosa, a young nun made pregnant by Lola.

Sarah Connor similarly needs a to-do list to help her fight the Terminator. Again, only the first steps may be apparent to her (and us) at the start of the act:

- Run away from the Terminator.
- Find out more about Kyle to see whether she can trust him.
- Look for a place to hide.
- Go to the police for help.
- If this fails (which it does), help Kyle fight the Terminator.
- Learn about the Terminator – why it's there and what its weaknesses might be.
- Plan to destroy the factory that is inventing the robots in the present, so that the future Terminator never gets built.

Snapshot exercise

Watch or read the script of your favourite film or TV programme and decide what the protagonist's Act Two project might look like. Write down his to-do list in bullet points. Mark where events force the list to change, as the act unfolds.

Making things worse

Having established your protagonist's to-do list, now do your best to disrupt it. Writers' agent Julian Friedmann says that writers are generally too nice to their characters. This is not the time to play the nice guy. Your job is to think of the worst things that could happen to him and then make them worse still.

Julian Friedmann, agent

'Make things go from bad to worse for your central character ... then to worse, to worse, to worse ...'

Manufacturers test their materials to destruction because it's the only way to be sure how strong they are. The only way to know how strong your central character is is to make things as hard for him as you can possibly make them. And then see how he reacts.

In the Belgian crime series *Salamander*, police inspector Paul Gerardi is pitted against two rival sets of conspirators. In the earliest episodes, he is outmanoeuvred, given no support, then suspended from his job, but still he fights on. His best leads are killed. His best friend betrays him. He is chased and shot at. When you think things can't get worse, his wife and daughter are blown up in a car bomb intended for him.

You can always make things worse …

Write

Check that your lead character has a clear Act Two project. Ensure that he makes a decision to act and doesn't remain passive and reactive. Break the project down into a to-do list of five to nine parts.

Now brainstorm all the things that could go horribly wrong. Don't stint. When you think that you've thought of the worst possible, go further.

Key idea

As fast as your character grows, make the obstacles grow faster.

Shaping Act Two

Once you're clear on your protagonist's Act Two project, and you have an active protagonist and a strong antagonist, you can start to shape the second act. (If you prefer, you can explore the possibilities with more freedom and come back to this section when you edit your first draft.)

Classically, Act Two divides into four roughly equal parts, which run approximately 15 pages each in a 90-to 120-minute feature, fewer for a shorter piece. These show how the arcs of the outer and the inner story interact and interfere with each other:

1 **Denial** The first sequence, coming immediately after the drama of the Act One climax, allows for a period of retraction. Here the protagonist, having made the decision that leads him into the main story, does what most humans will do: he goes into denial. He may have decided to go after the new goal, but he will do it in the easiest way possible, ideally without actually changing on the inside.

2 **Commitment** The period ends with the realization that this is not good enough – he must move on. Often, the point is marked in a symbolic scene. For example, having set out to drive to Newcastle, but with no intention of dealing with his flaw of lack of courage, this may be the moment where he faces down a very small spider in the service station loo. The next 15 or so pages are devoted to an energetic pursuit of his goal, and the first steps towards making a serious inner change.

This part ends at the **midpoint,** where we gain a glimpse of possible success, a moment of celebration and triumph, however premature it may be. For many writers, the midpoint is as important a turning point as the act turning points. It certainly helps to have the story turn significantly here. The stakes become higher. The story shifts.

3 **Respite and interlude** Following all the action of the last section, the third quarter of the act often brings a slower pace. This is a chance for you to show other sides of the protagonist's character; it's a time for romantic interludes, or other subplots, before reality bites back. Any triumph at this stage is actually too early. He may have changed, but not nearly enough to overcome the obstacles that are growing by the minute …

4 **Disaster** In the final section of the second act, things go from worse to worse. Everything is going wrong. As fast as the protagonist grows internally, it's not fast enough. This section ends with the Act Two climax, when all seems lost. (See Figure 8.1.)

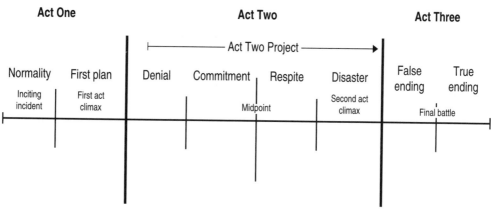

Figure 8.1 Three-act structure

In *Tootsie*, the first part of the act begins with Michael auditioning for a part disguised as Dorothy. It ends symbolically after he has lost his temper and is asked, by the producer, whether he was acting. For the first time in the script, Michael shows his diplomatic side and says, 'Whichever will get me the job.'

The second quarter follows his first days in the job and ends at the midpoint with the arrival of an unexpectedly large delivery of fan mail. He's a hit. In the third quarter, we develop the romantic subplot with Julie, his co-star, and in the fourth quarter everything falls apart. Julie thinks Dorothy has been making lesbian advances, Julie's father proposes marriage, and the studio extends the contract – he's stuck.

Escaping the impossible

Ideally, you should end up with your protagonist in an impossible position. There's no way he can escape now. But, of course, he must. Somehow you must get him into Act Three. He needs a new turning point – a surprise and a new challenge. But what can they be?

This is typically a difficult sticking-point for writers. You think of every possible avenue, but none of them works. They are either unbelievable or uninteresting.

The problem is made worse by the fact that this is also a low point in your protagonist's inner story. He thought he was improving, but his flaw has not yet been overcome. If he knew how to solve his inner story, he could solve his outer story. But he's not strong enough yet.

And because he doesn't know, you – the writer – don't know how to progress. How to move on?

Here's the answer: work backwards.

 ## Key idea

If you don't know how to get into the final act – jump to the end and work backwards.

Jump to the end that you know you want. You may not yet know the details, but you know the rough aim. You have a feeling for the final situation, if not how to get to it.

Visualize the ending. Now ask yourself: 'Why?' What happened just before, that made it happen? When you have that, ask yourself: 'Why that?' What happened just before that? And what happened before that? Keep working backwards until you are almost back to the end of the Act Two.

Let's say we're developing *Juno*. By the end of the second act, Juno is stuck. Pregnant, while still at school, through a single act with her friend Paulie, she has decided to give the baby up for adoption. But everything has gone wrong. Paulie has turned against her, because of her attitude. Vanessa and Mark, the ideal couple she chose for the baby, are splitting up. She's stuck, and she's coming to term – a nine-month ticking clock. How does she escape? We have the emotional climax. Now we need the surprise.

Let's jump to the end. We have a sense that the film ends with Juno and Paulie together, though we don't yet know how.

At the end they will sit in the sunshine, like normal teenagers, singing and playing guitar. Why?

- ... because Vanessa is at home with the baby. Why?
- ... because Juno chose to give the baby to Vanessa, after all. So what happened before?
- ... Paulie raced to the hospital to be with Juno. Why?
- ... because he noticed that she wasn't at the track, watching him run. Why?
- ... because she'd gone into labour. So what happened before?
- ... she made up with Paulie. How?
- ...she told him she loved him. Why?

- … because she left the Tic Tacs he loves in his mailbox. Why?
- … because she realized that she loved him, and he loved her. Why?

Joining the dots

We're almost there. We just need to connect the last dots. To find a way to get from Juno in despair to Juno realizing she really loves Paulie.

This is the easy bit. Because, surprisingly, the one place you can do something stupidly simple is here, at the end of Act Two. Here is the one, and possibly only, place in the story that you can get away with cliché, coincidence, luck, to make the story move on, anything from a raid by pirates to a ruined videotape. And that applies to the greats, all the way back to Shakespeare and before.

- It's pirates that allow Hamlet to escape from the ship taking him to England and return to Elsinore for the final confrontation with the man who murdered his father.
- It's a ruined tape that allows Michael Dorsey to declare his real identity on live TV in *Tootsie*.
- It's a foolish phone call to her mother that gives away Sarah Connor's hiding place to the Terminator and sets up the final battle.
- And, in *Juno*, it's a surprise conversation with her stepfather that makes Juno realize what she's been avoiding all through the film.

The dots have been joined. We have our surprise and Juno knows what her new challenge is: to get back with Paulie.

Focus point

If you're stuck – jump to the end and work backwards. Find a simple turning point that joins up the dots between the end of Act Two and the start of Act Three.

Joe Eszterhas, *The Devil's Guide to Hollywood*

'Slug it out with your second act. The second act is the most difficult to write because the first and third acts have built-in, sure-fire dramatic potential. But in the second, you have to move your story and your characters along as speedily as possible. The director of Jagged Edge *(Richard Marquand) and I kept taking the film out to preview audiences and getting dismal responses. But when we cut eight minutes from the film's second act, audiences erupted at the end of the movie with applause.'*

Workshop

Take a pad of blank Post-its and a large board or wall (you can also use 3×5 cards and pins or a card-style outlining feature in a computer program, such as Scrivener or Final Draft).

On each Post-it or card, write an element of the main storyline and any subplots. Be as detailed as you wish, depending on how you like to work. Some writers like to plan the details of each step on a card. Others prefer to scribble down ideas as they come: a single word, a character step, a scene, a goal, a turning point ...

Begin to arrange them in an order that feels right to you. Outline the rough shape of your first and second acts. Combine elements that you feel should be together. Look for logical connections. For example, a 'character' Post-it might usefully be stuck to the scene he's introduced in, together with a Post-it showing his goal and another showing his primary flaw. A sequence of scenes can be stuck together, and if necessary moved as a group. Subplots can be integrated so that they flow and intercut naturally with the main storyline.

Make things as bad as possible for your protagonist. Make sure that the last section has a strong surprise, climax and a new challenge.

Share and discuss the key moments. Ask whether you've made things tough enough for your protagonist. Share ways in which you could make things even worse.

(This board with its notes and story breakdown will be a useful tool to keep near you as you continue to develop the treatment and script.)

Where to next?

At a low ebb, facing a fresh crisis, the protagonist must make one more crucial decision. All is still to be won, or lost. We are entering the third and final act.

9

Act Three – the final battle

In the final act, protagonist and antagonist will come face to face. At the end of the previous act, the lead character was once more facing disaster until another turning point, as at the end of Act One, changed the story in a crucial way.

Now, however, he himself has changed. He makes a decision that sets up the final battle. Whatever the genre – from romantic comedy to sci-fi action thriller – the story climaxes with a confrontation that will finally resolve the main issue, for good or ill.

William Wyler, director and screenwriter

*'A lot of people come to me with great openings. I don't want a great opening.
I want a great ending, because with most stories you can't find a good ending.'*

The battle

Once again, depending on the size of the climax at the end of Act Two, you may have earned yourself a short respite. This gives you (and the audience) a chance to breathe and reflect on other matters. You may return to a subplot here, say goodbye to a good friend, remember a loved-one, or merely prepare the hero's armour for the fight.

Soon, however, you are fully engaged in the battle. It may be a literal battle or a metaphorical one. Either way, the goals should be clear by now. Act Three is not the place to introduce complex explanations or new dramatic ideas. We're heading down the home straight. And the stakes are the highest – a matter of life and death … or more important than that.

Tom Hooper, director

'There are three big endings: revenge, tragedy and forgiveness.'

Snapshot exercise

Take another look at your favourites – what do they use as a final battle? Do they ring the changes to find fresh and unusual ways of staging the big confrontation? If so, how?

Often, this act includes the obligatory climactic scene. In every story, there is one scene that cannot be dodged. Invariably, it's a long-delayed confrontation between protagonist and antagonist. Most frequently, the scene takes place during the final battle itself, although on occasion it may take place earlier in the act, or in the previous act. It will develop key themes and may involve moments of confession and an awareness that the two characters are more similar to each other than they thought.

In the movie *Heat*, the obligatory scene is the meeting in a restaurant between homicide detective Vincent Hanna and Neil McCauley, the violent thief he has been tracking. In this scene, they both lay out their goals and personal creeds, and make it clear that each would each kill the other if he got in the way.

Write

Decide on your own final battle. What will best suit the style and genre of your story? Should it be physical or verbal, spectacular or comic? How can you best challenge your central character to prove how much he has grown?

Joss Whedon, writer-director, *Firefly*

'People love a happy ending. So every episode, I will explain once again that I don't like people. And then Mal will shoot someone. Someone we like. And their puppy.'

The false ending

Halfway through Act Three, things come to a head. It looks as though we've reached the ending. The lead character has won or lost. But this is a false ending.

Perhaps the hero is wounded, apparently mortally, with a sword cut to the heart. Or the heroine has won the boxing match and turns her back on her opponent (*Million Dollar Baby*). Or the husband and wife have finally agreed to divorce. But it's not over yet.

With the false ending, it might *look* as though everything has been resolved – but it hasn't. The reason lies, once more, in the inner story. The protagonist has almost achieved his inner change, but not quite. He has yet to prove that he has changed – by enduring one last twist. Or, alternatively, he must take what he has learned and show that he can apply it to the rest his life. His work is not yet done.

Key idea

The false ending is not a true ending because the central character has not yet grown enough:

- In the final act of *The Terminator*, Sarah and Kyle do battle with the robot. It steals an articulated lorry and tries to run them down, but they blow up the truck, and the Terminator appears to be destroyed in the fireball that ensues. Sarah and Kyle embrace with relief. However, this cannot be the true ending because this is Sarah's story. She is supposed to be learning to stand on her own feet. So far, she has only succeeded with Kyle's help. She's not yet done it alone.

- At the start of *Tootsie*, actor Michael Dorsey found he was unemployable, largely because of his difficult attitude. He set out to prove that he could do the work, posing as actress Dorothy Michaels and landing a plum job on a hospital soap. By the end of Act Two he's achieved his goal, but is now stuck in his new persona. The woman he loves, Julie, thinks he's a lesbian, and her

father has proposed marriage. He is desperate to escape. Then he learns that the show is going to be broadcast live. We know (because it has been planted earlier) that he has a tendency to go off-script, and now, as Dorothy, he does so with a vengeance – in an extravagant improvised speech that ends with him whipping off his wig and revealing himself to the world as a man. He has extricated himself with wit and elegance. But there are still too many loose ends for the story to finish here.

Satyajit Ray, director

'Last, but not least – in fact, this is most important – you need a happy ending. However, if you can create tragic situations and jerk a few tears before the happy ending, it will work much better.'

Snapshot exercise

List the false endings in your favourite screen stories.

Write

Develop your own false ending. What is it that your character hasn't yet learned, or has to prove that she's learned?

The true ending

The final section of the story brings the plot to a close, both in terms of the outer and inner story. If your protagonist has changed enough, he achieves his happy ending. If he fails to grow enough or changes too late, then the story ends in tragedy. Partial change may leave you with a mixed ending – happiness and sadness together.

In this last sequence, the false ending may be reversed – victory may turn into defeat, or vice versa. Or victory may have been achieved in theory, but must now be confirmed and consolidated. The protagonist must return to his normal life and show us that he has really changed. His new-found virtues must be shown to be permanent.

As with other acts, Act Three needs an emotional and dramatic climax, a final surprise, a challenge and one last action.

The story ends because this final action makes return impossible. It's over. The lead character cannot ever go back and travel this road again.

- To their horror, Sarah and Kyle realize that the Terminator is still fully functioning and deadly. Kyle is killed and now Sarah must do battle on her own, proving that she can indeed fight for herself. She lures the robot into the jaws of a heavy-duty machine, where she crushes him to death, piece by piece. In a coda, we see her driving to some far-off place, pregnant with Kyle's child and dictating her story so that her son can grow up to be a hero himself. She is alone and self-reliant. Her transformation is complete.

- In the true ending of *Tootsie*, Michael Dorsey must go back and sort out the mess of his private life, applying what he has learned. He returns the ring to Julie's father, and manages to remain friends. Now he must reconcile with Julie, who is still angry. His manner is entirely different from the Michael we saw at the start of the film, and it wins her over. He was, as he says, 'a better man as a woman than he ever was as a man'. She agrees, tentatively, to see him again. As long as he doesn't wear her dresses.

Problems with endings

If you're unable to work out an ending, it's probably because you haven't pushed the inner story far enough. The protagonist can solve his outer problem only if he's fully dealt with his flaw. This is the true theme of your script. Go back and look again at how he was at the start. What did he need to change? Has he changed enough at the end? For Sarah Connor to fully stand up for herself, she had to do it alone. Kyle had to die. How much further do you need to push your protagonist to prove he's learned his lesson?

If your ending is a tragic one, you need to show that your protagonist has gone as far as he can. He cannot grow any further. Is there a moment where he sees this? When perhaps he glimpses the possibility of change, but ultimately draws back? Or when he makes the change, but it's too late?

In *Chinatown*, private eye Jake Gittes has been hurt too often before. His suave cool covers a fear of trust and intimacy that only finally breaks down near the end. In the false ending, he takes the risk of trusting Evelyn Mulwray and we glimpse the possibility of salvation. But he has not changed enough. It takes very little for him to suspect her motives and, although he quickly realizes his mistake, it's too late. His suspicions have set off a chain of events that lead to her death. He tried to deal with his flaw but, tragically, not soon enough.

 Key idea

Ending, inner story and theme all work together – if you have a problem with one, look at the other two.

Write

- Sketch out your lead character's final battle. Describe the key elements – decision, final confrontation, false ending, true ending. Does it appropriately reflect the emotions of the genre (comic, dark, action-led, etc.)?
- Plan out a scene from the false ending. How can you show what your protagonist still needs to achieve – internally and in the outer world? What obstacles and actions can help you put this on the screen?
- What is the final climax, challenge or surprise? Is it irreversible?
- Who makes the final decision? What is it, and what does it say about life after the story ends?

Workshop

Go back to your planning board and add Act Three. Look at the balance of all three acts, now, and rearrange them as feels right, aiming to keep the lengths of the acts proportionate.

Discuss the shape you now have, and listen to feedback. Does it work? Are the ideas fresh, unusual and dramatically sound? Remember: a recipe only works well with the best ingredients.

Where to next?

As the overall story begins to take shape, with the main elements of the structure in place, it might be tempting to plunge straight into writing the script. However, this urge is best resisted for a little while longer.

First, we need to stand back and see our plans in perspective. In the next chapter, we're going to draft the story out in a shorter, more manageable form. We're going to write the treatment.

10

The treatment – fanning the flames

With the structure and characters beginning to form, it's time to write the first treatment. As we'll see, a treatment is an outline or synopsis of the overall story, beginning, middle and end. By allowing you to stand back and see the whole in just a few pages, it helps you plan ahead, see the story's strengths and potential weaknesses, and adjust any major issues at an early stage. This will be much more difficult to do once you have a hundred or more pages to play with.

There are three times to write a treatment. The first is the planning treatment, written before you sit down to write the script itself. The second will be written between drafts. This redrafting treatment helps you regain perspective. There are always unexpected issues that arise when you write a draft and the redrafting treatment is the best way to take stock of these and rearrange the story before you plunge back into the next.

The third time is when you write a selling treatment. This will often be demanded by producers and agents, before they agree to read your script. This can be very frustrating, as you may well feel that a short treatment can't do justice to a 99-page screenplay. It is certainly true that much that is good about a script can never be put in a treatment – there has to be room for a certain magic, for the evolution of small but significant details, for tone. However, there are also important elements that can be detected in a synopsis that, if absent from the script, will sabotage it. Moreover, producers and agents will argue that their time is precious and, if you can't convince them in two or so pages, that's your problem, not theirs.

Most of this chapter talks about the treatment you'll need to write for a single self-contained story – or for a given episode within a series. If you're writing a TV series, you'll also need a longer series proposal. I'll describe that at the end.

 Key idea

You need clear, well-written treatments to plan, redraft and sell your script.

The good news is that the same techniques apply to each type of treatment – indeed, the better the treatment reads as a selling document, the better it will serve you as a planning or redrafting document. The challenge of communicating with total clarity will force you to think harder and more dispassionately about your plans – and save yourself days, if not months, of wasted effort when it comes to writing the draft. And vice versa – writing the most effective planning treatment will help you immeasurably when you come to selling the finished script. A well-planned script has an unmistakeable tightness and sureness of purpose that stands out.

The bad news is that treatments are rarely easy to write. They demand a high level of skill, perspective and thought.

Treatment, outline or synopsis?

Before we move on, let's look at some definitions. No matter what some gurus may try to teach you, in the industry the words 'treatment', 'outline' and 'synopsis' mean exactly the same thing.

In particular, there are no accepted definitions that define them as having different lengths. If you are asked to supply a treatment (or outline, or synopsis), your first question should be 'How long?' You may be surprised at the answer. A producer you think wants a ten-page treatment may ask for a single page. And a financier you expect to ask for a half-page may demand five.

You must deliver whatever length they ask for – and not a word more. Producers (and competition judges) look with jaundiced eye on a treatment that comes in a page longer than what they requested. (And using 6-point font, no paragraphing and quarter-inch margins is not the solution either.) From here on, I will (as everyone else does) use the terms 'treatment', 'synopsis' and 'outline' more or less interchangeably.

David Newman and Robert Benton, screenwriters, *Bonnie and Clyde*

'After nine years in this business we can state with some authority that nobody knows exactly what a treatment is. Some producers want one, some don't. Some mean an outline of the plot, maybe ten or fifteen pages. Some mean a sort of "presentation" of the idea, two or three pages. And some mean what we took it to mean; our "treatment" was, in effect, a full shooting script minus the dialogue, seventy pages long, including cuts, dissolves, key camera set-ups, even music cues.'

What everyone does agree on is that a treatment must:

- **be written in the third person.** This is not the place for the first-person-narrative 'I'. The exception is a POV treatment – a treatment that tells the story from the point of view of an individual character. But this is normally just for your own use (see below).

- **be in the present tense.** If your background is in writing novels or short stories, you may feel more comfortable in the past tense, but treatments, like scripts, are always written in the present. The one exception was Graham Greene, whose treatments for *The Third Man* and *The Tenth Man* (which was unproduced) read as excellent past-tense stories in their own right. But he was Graham Greene.

- **contain the beginning, middle *and* the end.** Not to include the ending shows you to be an amateur. Without the ending, it's a blurb – what you might see on the back of a DVD. The ending gives meaning to the whole and shows that you do actually have a satisfying way to finish the story. If the ending contains a major twist, you still have to tell it.

- **be roughly in proportion to the script.** You will probably have much you want to say at the start but, however long the treatment, the length of each section should approximate to how the story plays out. This is not easy to achieve but, if you're struggling to get the opening to length, it probably means that you're trying to say too much.

- **be readable.** It should flow easily and be clearly laid out. Use any standard font, with generous margins and short paragraphs. (It doesn't have to be laid out as strictly as a script.) Don't ever be tempted to try to sex it up with multiple fonts or colours. And there certainly shouldn't be any pictures. Your job is words.

- **generally not contain dialogue.** There is no need for dialogue in a treatment. It holds up the story, and while you may have scintillating lines that you want to show off, they rarely look so good out of context (however, see the information on the master scene treatment, below).

- **contain your contact details at the end – if you're sending it out.** You'd be surprised how often treatments get detached from their covering letter/email.
- **most of all, be brief and to the point.** A treatment has only two possible jobs to perform: it must help you write the script and it must entice someone to read the script when it's finished. To do this, it summarizes the story in a short form, leaving out as much as possible. Anything, and that means *anything*, that gets in the way of these two jobs is redundant.

Film industry treatments

There are a number of different kinds of treatment used in the industry – from one-sheets and POV treatments to step outlines and master scene treatments. As a professional, you need to know, and be able to write, them all, if needed:

STANDARD TREATMENT

This is a summary of the story. It may be of any length, from one paragraph to ten pages or more, conforming to the rules above.

ONE-SHEET

This can have two meanings. Some people use 'one-sheet' simply to mean a treatment that runs for a single page. However, a one-sheet can also be a one-page document that summarizes the project, rather like an executive summary, with a logline (a one- or two-sentence summary), one-paragraph treatment, and brief information about the project and yourself.

POV TREATMENT

This is a very powerful development tool – a treatment written from the point of view of a single character. This would normally be written for your own eyes only and is the only time that it's acceptable to write a treatment in the first person.

As with the first-person CVs you wrote earlier (Chapter 5), this is a good method for developing both character and plot, and is a very useful step towards writing the full treatment.

In the POV treatment, you can write only what this person does and sees, from when the character first enters the story to when she leaves. The advantage is that by stepping into a character's shoes, even those of a very minor character, you gain a three-dimensional view that invariably brings you new ideas and insights. It's useful to do this for every single character in your story, no matter how small.

For an amusing, tragicomic riff on this, see Tom Stoppard's play (and film) *Rosencrantz and Guildenstern Are Dead*, which follows the on- and off-stage lives of two minor characters in *Hamlet*.

Write

Take any of your characters and write the story from their point of view. Stick to the rules: you can write only what they see and do.

What and who do they first encounter? Where have they come from? What action do they take? What do they feel about it? What happens next?

STEP OUTLINE OR BEAT SHEET

A step outline is a longer treatment that breaks down the story into key steps or story beats. Each beat will be an individual scene or sequence of scenes, given a short paragraph to itself, often numbered.

Another very useful part of the planning process, it makes the overall structure very clear before you start writing the script itself.

SCENE-BY-SCENE

Similar to a beat sheet, a scene-by-scene tends to be used a great deal in television, breaking down the story into individual scenes and locations, so that the production team can check that the story or episode can be shot to budget.

MASTER SCENE TREATMENT

The longest kind of treatment, a master scene treatment can run to 50 pages or more, and it looks very similar to a full-length script. Indeed, it may well be formatted like one. The purpose of the master scene treatment is to see the story played out in something approaching the full length of the screenplay, with all its twists and turns and character development.

However, unlike a script, you can jump over the finer details. You can also combine scenes and generalize, for example saying, 'They argue and then make up,' or 'He runs every morning for five weeks' – scenes that would need to be fleshed out properly in a script.

While you can include dialogue if it helps, the joy of a master scene treatment is that you are able to write the bulk of the script without needing to get into dialogue or action details until you're ready to, and so it can be a very useful stage between outline and first draft script.

SERIES PROPOSAL

As with a series premise, a series proposal needs to show that the series has the potential to run over many episodes. It will normally include a one-sheet executive summary, character biographies, an outline of the world the series is set in, the CV of the writer and treatments for sample episodes (see later in this chapter).

Key idea

The many different kinds of treatment are there to help you develop your ideas in the way that feels most suitable to you as the writer – changing perspective from a grand view, to a character's point of view, to almost full length, as you feel appropriate.

How to start writing your treatment

As with writing the script, there are three ways of approaching the job of getting the treatment on to the page:

1 You can start with the premise and build up, gradually getting longer.

2 You can write a long treatment in one go, and cut it down, gradually getting shorter.

3 You can mix the two, bouncing from short to long and back again.

Asghar Farhadi, screenwriter and director

'I tend to jot down moments, lines, interactions that don't really make any sense. I try and explain these scattered notes to my close friends, and they become more and more logical. I see screenwriting as a bit like a math equation which I have to solve.'

Which you choose depends on how you like to work. Each has its advantages and disadvantages.

1 Starting with the premise has the advantage of clarity, but you may find it difficult to let your style flow.

2 Starting long and then cutting down allows your style to flow more easily but it can be harder to gain perspective on what to cut.

3 A mix could give you the advantages of both, allowing you to step back and step in at will.

Key idea

Try the three different approaches in turn to see which you feel most comfortable with.

The following takes you through from short to long (with a few detours). To use the other methods, work backwards through the steps, or mix and match as feels right. The method is less important than the final result.

The one-paragraph treatment

A one-paragraph treatment is useful to allow yourself to see the essentials of your story. You will also need it for any executive summary, proposal or one-sheet (see above).

For the shortest treatment, we're going to start with the outer story – in six sentences, two sentences per act:

- The premise you've developed should give you the basis of **your first and second sentence**: your protagonist, her life and the big challenge that kicks off the story (Act One turning point).
- **Sentences three and four** outline her Act Two project (*so she sets out to... or and along the way she has to ...*) leading to the Act Two challenge (*only to discover/realize that ...*).
- **Sentence five and six** bring us the final battle (*So she has to ... and finally ...*)

If you find you have to spend more than a sentence to set up your character's world, be ruthless. This is about the bare bones of the story, nothing more.

Juno – *in one paragraph*

Sixteen-year-old Juno discovers that she's pregnant. She decides initially on an abortion, but at the clinic realizes that she can't go through with it. Instead, she settles on having the baby and giving it up for adoption, and finds a couple – Vanessa and Mark – who she gets on with well. But she discovers, as she approaches term, that they are splitting up. She goes into labour, and has the baby. Now she has to choose between giving the baby away and life as a single mother, but she gives the baby to Vanessa.

Notice that you have to be very focused here. You'll see no mention of the romantic subplot (with Paulie, the father of the child), or indeed any other subplots, and almost no other characters. We're after the very essence of the outer story.

This gives us the fundamental story pulse, without distractions, and tells us whether you have a workable through-line. The through-line drives the outer story, and without it any screen story will founder.

Key idea

The outer-story short treatment highlights the story's through-line and shows whether there's enough momentum to hold an audience.

If you're any good as a writer, this bare-bones discipline will be enormously frustrating. There will be a thousand ideas, lines of witty and dramatic dialogue, exciting visuals and gripping moments of action that you know will add power to your story. Write them down in your notes and keep them out of the short treatment. They don't belong here.

Write

Write down your six-sentence outline of the outer story. It's OK to go to a little longer at this stage, but aim as close to six as possible. The discipline will reveal where you know your story structure and where you are still unclear.

The half-page to one-page treatment

However, on its own the outer story feels rather mechanical. It doesn't give us the character arc or theme. This comes from the inner story, and that's what we have to include next.

For each sentence of the outer story, add a sentence on the character's personal journey. Link the dramatic through-line that you already have to her primary flaw and her struggle to change. This gives us the underlying meaning of the action and stops it feeling so mechanical.

Juno's major flaw, at the start of the story, is that she has grown up too quickly and left some important part of herself behind. In a sense, she's very similar to Michael Dorsey at the start of *Tootsie* in that her masculine side dominates her feminine side. With her child's father, Paulie, she takes the dominant role. She's the one who decided to have sex. She has the (stereotypically) masculine, offhand attitude towards their 'one-armchair' stand. The film even shows her sitting in the armchair, with a pipe in her mouth. Her young pregnancy is a symbol that she's living her life the wrong way round (a view she herself echoes in the script).

Her character journey, in this coming-of-age story, is to rediscover what it is to be a young female today and find a way to start again and do it the right way round.

Juno – a fuller treatment

Strong-willed and precocious 16-year-old Juno discovers that she's pregnant after a one-night stand that she initiated. More or less bulldozing the father, the rather wimpish Paulie, she decides initially on an abortion. But at the clinic she is put off by the staff's rather offhand approach and she can't go through with it.

Instead, she settles on having the baby and giving it up for adoption; and she finds a couple – Vanessa and Mark – who she gets on with well. Dismissive of Paulie, who clearly loves her, she tells him that they were never a couple. Indeed, she seems to get on better with Mark, spending time together, chilling to punk rock and horror movies.

However, as she approaches term, she discovers that Mark and Vanessa are splitting up. At the same time, she angrily confronts Paulie for asking another girl to the prom. But he tells her that she's the one who broke up with him.

Realizing her true feelings, she tells Paulie that she loves him, and they make up.

She goes into labour and has the baby without telling Paulie, who's needed in a school track meet. However, he guesses what's happening and joins her in hospital. Now she has to choose between giving the baby away and life as a single mother, and she gives the baby to Vanessa.

As the story ends, Juno's an ordinary teenager again – dating Paulie and resolved to do things in the right order this time.

Again, we have only the very barest bones of story, but now we know why the story is being told – we can see the theme and the character's journey. Now we can appreciate how the audience will engage with the story, and where their empathy will lie.

If you're asked for a half-page or one-page treatment, this is the best way to produce it.

Write

Copy your one-paragraph treatment and add the inner story, in roughly alternate sentences. You don't have to be slavish. Allow yourself a little flexibility in the way you mix phrases and sentences, but continue to be disciplined. You are still giving the barest essentials.

Bring out the core character journey, starting with the flaw. If you are still not clear about the flaw and the journey, that's fine. It's a process that takes time. Keep digging – and remember that the flaw and the journey can often be best discovered by seeing how your character has changed at the end. If necessary, look at how she finishes up, and work backwards.

Write your first draft one-page treatment now.

Polishing one-page and longer treatments

When sending out a treatment, put the title, centred, on a cover page, together with your name as writer and your contact details – it's amazing how many people forget that. Covering letters and emails get lost.

On the next page, you should again put the title and your name. Next, specify the genre. This is to avoid any misunderstandings. A comedy treatment can look dangerously like a tragedy if you haven't been forewarned, and vice versa.

Many writers like to put their one-line premise at the top of a treatment. This is an excellent way to start off the document as it ensures that the reader knows exactly what she's getting and will approach the treatment in the right frame of mind.

Leave a space, perhaps with a line across the page, and then divide the remainder of the treatment roughly in proportion to the story – that is, a quarter for the first act, half for the second and a quarter for the third.

As you grow your treatment, you can use the three-act structure you've drafted out in previous chapters. Be determined to include only the most essential information, and avoid subplots as far as possible. You still don't have room.

Continue to alternate between the outer and the inner story to help the reader. Treatments are often hard to read, and a reader's patience can wear very thin. A constant flow of action (outer story) will leave the reader with mental indigestion. A treatment that gives only the character's inner journey (inner story) will leave the reader hungry for specifics – wanting to know how this inner journey will be shown on screen. You need to keep a good balance between the two.

Snapshot exercise

Find a story outline, for example on a website such as Wikipedia or IMDb. Does it flow well? Do you feel that there is a good balance between outer and inner stories?

Print it out and go through it, marking outer and inner story elements with different-coloured pens.

Could you improve the treatment? If so, how? Are there techniques you can learn from this writer's approach to the treatment? If so, what are they?

RHYTHM AND FLOW

Variety of rhythm and a good flowing style are vital at all levels, to smooth the storytelling path.

Look once more at the treatment for *Juno*. It uses a variety of sentence rhythms and ensures that the sentences flow naturally from one to the next, using four main techniques.

1 Generalizations – in a script you must be specific, but a good treatment also includes generalizations to ease the flow – *strong-minded, gets on well with ...*

2 Sequencing – compressing a number of scenes together to avoid clogging up the story – *spending time together, chilling to punk rock and horror movies, goes into labour and has the baby ...*

3 Link words and phrases – *but, instead, initially, indeed, however, at the same time ...*

4 Varying the word order, avoiding starting every sentence with the subject – *More or less ignoring the father ... Finally admitting to herself ...*

Beware of treatments that become a stodgy list of actions: *And then ... and then ... and then*. The best linking words of all are *but* and *however* ... because they imply surprise and conflict. But using them all the time would become monotonous, too. So build up a good vocabulary of links and study how other writers use them. Such as:

- moreover
- meanwhile
- in the last resort
- while
- not knowing that
- to her surprise

- against all expectations
- in desperation
- hopefully
- on the other hand
- in the other room
- on the other side of the planet
- five centuries later …

GENRE, TONE AND STYLE

Remember your genre and ensure that the tone and style of your treatment reflect the feeling you're aiming for. If the film is going to be a sparkling comedy, then lighten the style and show some wit. If it's a dark horror, choose words and images that will chill us to the bone. Look at your vocabulary and sentence structures. A thriller will need to be written in short, tough sentences, whereas a historical drama would benefit from a more literary tone.

Read the great writers to see how they achieve their effects, especially short-story writers from Chekhov to Poe to du Maurier to Carver. Short stories are an excellent way to tune up your treatment writing.

Be careful, though. Short stories are allowed to be oblique and use suggestion in ways that would feel irritating in a treatment. A story may hint, where as a treatment has to come out and say what it means. Nevertheless, the best short stories can still teach us a great deal, not least through their command of tone and their ability to create atmosphere with very few words.

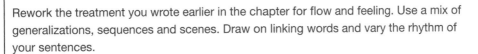

Edit

Rework the treatment you wrote earlier in the chapter for flow and feeling. Use a mix of generalizations, sequences and scenes. Draw on linking words and vary the rhythm of your sentences.

Most importantly, ensure that the style you adopt reflects the emotions of the story. Set the tone through your choice of words and images.

Writing a treatment for a series

As with the premise, if your series or serial follows a single overarching narrative, write one treatment for the entire story. Create this in the same way as a single film or drama, but showing the episode breaks. This would apply to any series with a dominant storyline, such as *The Fall*, *The Killing* or *Homeland*.

However, if you're creating a series without a dominant storyline, such as *The West Wing*, *House* or *Fawlty Towers*, you should write a series proposal as part of your planning process. This will also be essential later, when you come to market the project.

A series proposal presents the key aspects of the series with clarity, sketching in the elements that will attract an audience and give life to a variety of different stories.

A series proposal should contain the following items:

- **A one-sheet, giving an overview of the characters, their world and likely stories.** At the top, put the title, the genre and your series premise or logline. Then summarize the key points of the series, the dynamics and tensions, and the main selling points. Finish the page with brief suggestions or loglines for sample episodes.

- **Fuller details of the story world and the tensions within it (one page).** Bring that world to life, specify what the main elements are, where the power lies and what the main issues are going to be.

- **The main recurring characters** – a page on the central character, if there is one, and half a page each on the others, showing their strengths and flaws and points of contact, based on your character constellation. Show how they'll strike sparks off one another.

- **Detailed treatments of two sample episodes** to show the variety of possible storylines. The first might run to a page and a half, while the second might be a little shorter.

- **Shorter synopses of a further two or three,** a paragraph each, and individual loglines for episodes to follow. These ideas should be varied enough to show that the series can generate a variety of stories and won't be the same idea repeated each week.

Creating a detailed series proposal at this early stage will give you confidence that your idea has at least the potential to succeed. (Later you'll use the same format to market to the industry, to be sent with a sample episode script.)

Some writers like to use the same proposal format to market single-story or mini-series ideas, in which case the longer treatment, of course, will give the whole story, from beginning to end.

Workshop

Workshop your one-page treatment. Note the strengths and weaknesses. Are there areas that come to life on the page? These might include scenes that you hadn't even thought were that important before. Are there areas that dip or become vague? Where does your attention sharpen and where does it drop away?

Discuss the mix of inner and outer story. Is the balance right? Does the style flow? Does the story work? Do we believe in the character? Do we care?

Where to next?

You have a first draft treatment, possibly a number of draft treatments of different lengths. But this is only the start. Does it form a solid, reliable foundation for the screenplay you're going to write?

11

Troubleshooting treatments

Good treatments aren't written, they're rewritten. You will rewrite your treatments as much as your scripts, probably more. Get good, reliable feedback and listen to what the readers say.

Problems with treatments are almost always symptomatic of problems with your core ideas: perhaps certain aspects haven't yet been fully thought through, or an idea needs strengthening. A treatment can't solve every problem; ultimately only writing the script itself will fully reveal what you are trying to do. But it's worth spending time dealing with issues now, before you invest time and effort writing scenes that will have to be changed or abandoned later.

Go back and read GOATS (in Chapter 3). First, are you clear about who your lead character is, what her goal is, what's stopping her and what action she sets out to take? Protagonists often become passive and reactive at this stage – letting events push them around. Make sure that your central character takes charge of the story, develops a clear plan of action and sets out to try to make things happen herself.

Some characters obviously have a smaller capacity for action than others. A 90-year-old woman or a nine-year-old boy are unlikely to sprint after criminals or leap over walls to catch a spy. But this is no excuse to allow them to remain passive. They can be instrumental in taking the crucial action that pushes the story forwards – pointing the way, insisting that others take notice, not allowing less motivated characters to give up.

Also, check that you've told us what the stakes are, and why they are important. Why should we care that the boy gets the girl? Why might it be so dreadful if the heroine fails to win her Nobel Prize?

 Edit

Do a GOATS check on your draft treatment – goal, obstacle, action, tactics, stakes. Are they all there? Do you need to strengthen one or more? Which? How could they be improved? Redraft the treatment with these improvements in mind and see whether it works better.

Typical problems with treatments

THE TREATMENT FAILS TO COME TO LIFE

Sometimes you can think too much and lose the spirit of the story. Often this comes from the pressure to squeeze the story into a few lines. When this happens, we can find ourselves including all the boring parts and leaving out the fun.

To counter this, forget about length for a moment, and write the story freely, at any length and in any format you like. Let the words flow without trying to edit. This is the speed-writing we talked about in Chapter 2. Whether you write one page or 50, your aim is purely to get the words down and edit them later.

If the act of writing itself makes you self-conscious, record yourself as you tell the story out loud – to yourself or a friend.

The result will be overlong and messy, but by allowing yourself the freedom to write or speak without restrictions, you'll find your storytelling voice more easily. Then you can start to edit it down.

You can repeat the process as often as you like, alternating between free writing, or speaking, and editing, until you have a version you're satisfied does the job.

Raymond Chandler

'A good story cannot be devised; it has to be distilled.'

Write

Speed-write your treatment. Just get the words on the page, without trying to get it right or sticking to a given length. If it helps to get you started, begin 'Once upon a time …' For this version, there are no rules – you can write in the past tense, if it helps, or in the first person. Ramble as much as you like.

All you have to do is write the story, beginning, middle and end. Agree with yourself that you will do no editing or corrections as you go.

When you've finished, put it aside for a time, if you can, and then come back and read it through, again without stopping.

Mark the best parts, and begin to tidy it up.

THE TREATMENT FEELS PLOTTY AND CLOGGED

Are you falling into the trap of *and then … and then …* ? Too many specific scene descriptions will become constipated and difficult to follow without lightening them.

When reading a scene in a treatment, we automatically ask ourselves, 'So what? What is the underlying meaning?' A good treatment will constantly answer such questions, stepping back and putting the action into context.

To do this, ensure that you are shifting easily from specific scene descriptions to sequence writing to generalizations and back again. Give us the meaning as well as the action.

THE TREATMENT FEELS VAGUE

This is the exact opposite of the previous problem: a treatment that focuses too much on the generalities – on the genre or the inner story. Such a treatment will lack substance. You need to give us the specifics that prove your case. Like a lawyer addressing a jury, you need to bring us hard evidence.

Faced with generalizations, a reader will ask 'For instance? Give me an example of that?'

If you assert that tension grows, you must deliver at least one tense moment involving the central character, and the action she takes. If you say that the protagonist grows more confident, you need to find an action she takes which will demonstrate her growing self-esteem.

Check your treatments carefully to make sure that you have substantiated all your claims and that we have the evidence we need to judge that the story does what you say.

Edit

Go through your treatment. With each specific scene description, ask 'So what?' And with each generalization, ask 'For instance?' Does the treatment immediately answer these questions?

If you find unanswered questions, fill in the gaps.

THE STORY WORKS, BUT ISN'T EXCITING ME

It's all too easy to focus so much on making the outer story work that you forget that it's the inner story that draws us in. As we saw when you developed the premise, this is where a good writer engages personally, however fictional the material.

Go back to the inner story and the central character's struggle with her flaws. Ensure that you know what it is, and show her flaws from the start.

Make it personal. You shouldn't ignore the audience, but you can worry so much about writing for them that you lose what makes your story special.

Chris Rice, Development Executive, Independent TV, Los Angeles

'Where I can see someone trying to figure out how to tick all the boxes, it puts me off.'

Snapshot exercise

Step back and look honestly at yourself. How do the issues you care about relate to those of the protagonist? What is it that you're trying to explore ? Is there anything you're shying away from, perhaps because it's too close to home? Can you look deeper into what makes your protagonist tick?

THE TREATMENT IS OUT OF PROPORTION/TOO LONG

Most, if not all, first-draft treatments spend too long setting up the story. I see many two-page treatments that spend one-and-a-half pages describing the situation, leaving only half a page for the story and resolution. This gives you no room to do justice to the second and third acts, which form the most dynamic parts of your script.

The only solution for this – or any other parts of the treatment that are over-length – is to be tough with yourself and cut, cut, cut:

- First, cut all negatives. It's a waste of space to tell us what *isn't*, as opposed to what *is*.

- Next, take out all but the most essential facts and descriptions. Then look at those that remain. How many of those do you really need for us to understand the essential plot? Keep cutting. You'll be surprised how little setting up a story requires.
- If you still need to reduce the length, cut most of the 'colour' – extra moments of wit, tension, horror and so on that are intended to give the right tone for the genre. A single well-chosen adjective or verb can often be as effective as a whole sentence.
- Finally, look at what you have left and find ways to say it more succinctly. If you are using two adjectives to describe a character, use one. Instead of a long phrase, find a better verb. Trawl a thesaurus for crisper ways of expressing your ideas.

However, be careful not to cut all the inner story and leave only the outer action. The balance must still be right.

Snapshot exercise

If you're having difficulties with length or proportion, search film and TV websites, such as IMDb and Wikipedia, for a treatment you like that's roughly the right length. Examine the structure of the treatment and how much information is given to the reader and in what order.

Now use that synopsis as a template to tell your story: for each phrase, substitute your own, using the same rhythm and sentence structure, but your voice. When you've finished, you should have a treatment that's almost exactly the same length, but in your own words.

How much of this new treatment could you use? Are there phrases that could help you? Paragraphs? The whole of it?

MY STORY IS NOT STRAIGHTFORWARD …

Simple linear stories are more easily written as treatments than those with more complex structures. Multiple storylines, complex flashbacks, fractured narrative or even multiple protagonists make writing the treatment even more of a challenge than normal.

The trick is to step back and see the whole. Your job in writing a treatment is not to mirror everything that happens in the script, but to give an overview, so that the reader understands the key ideas and the important dynamics as the story unfolds.

If you have multiple protagonists or storylines, you need to find the nutshell. This is the element that unites them – their common theme or aim.

In Paul Haggis's *Crash*, there are eight intersecting storylines with different protagonists, who also appear in one another's stories. But the theme that unites them is – in a nutshell – race. Every story is in some way related to how the people of Los Angeles cope with the racial tensions that divide the city. The nutshell encompasses your whole story and will almost always be connected with the survival of the group around whom the stories revolve.

In writing a short treatment of *Crash*, you wouldn't attempt to detail every single plot-line. You'd outline the theme of racial tension. For Act One, you'd briefly introduce this theme (which is the common flaw that runs through all the characters) and an overview of the storylines, focusing on two or three as examples. For Act Two, you'd show the key developments, alternating between overview and examples as before. And in the third act you'd show how they are resolved.

Simple flashbacks are best treated when they occur in the script – in other words, if a story begins at the end, such as in *Sunset Boulevard*, begin as the script does. Start with the body floating in the swimming pool, and jump back to tell the story that led up to it.

More complex flashbacks, as in The *Usual Suspects*, would be better treated in the same way as intersecting storylines. In The *Usual Suspects*, we have two storylines: the interrogation of Verbal Kint and the story he tells. Alternate between the two but simplify the number of jumps, depending on the treatment length.

A severely fractured narrative, such as *21 Grams*, where the timeline cuts almost at random, still has a three-act shape, despite its apparent randomness. A treatment would focus on this, introducing the characters at the beginning, the development of the story in the middle, and what we learn at the end.

Readers understand that treatments are not scripts, so you can stand back, as the writer, and say things like *As we jump from past to present, we learn ...* In this way, you can simplify a complex shape and give the overall idea of the film, leaving the details for the script itself.

(For more on fractured time and multiple storylines, see Chapters 19 and 20.)

THE PREMISE SEEMED GREAT, BUT SOMEHOW THE FIRE HAS DISAPPEARED

A good premise catches fire at some point. It's then, when the spark ignites for you and for the people you pitch to, that you know you have a workable idea. One of the dangers, when developing the idea, is that the process of making a story work can take you away from the very thing that excited you in the first place.

Let's say you had a great pitch for a romance involving two people living on opposite sides of the United States. In developing it, you get involved with the comedy of the woman's relationship with her boring boyfriend, and the man's insistence on remembering his dead wife. The man's child becomes an increasingly interesting character. The man and woman meet frequently, but their relationship keeps hitting dead ends. As does the treatment.

The problem is that you've lost the very thing that made the idea catch fire – the two people divided by a continent.

In *Sleepless in Seattle*, writers Nora Ephron, David S. Ward and Jeff Arch had to take great care to keep the story focused on the distance between Annie and Sam (both literally and metaphorically). They had to ensure that we never get distracted by other issues or lose focus on the core idea that drives the script.

If you've lost the original fire, return to your initial premise. Remind yourself what excited you about it, and put that spark back into the story.

Snapshot exercise

Go back to your premise. Remind yourself what the spark was and what excited you. If your treatment has changed, does the change have more spark or less? If the new ideas are better than the first, then revise your premise.

If not, how can you get the spark back? Where is the expanded story missing the point? Where did it go astray? Step back, return to a point where it was working and rebuild from there.

THE TREATMENT FEELS FLAT AND FULL OF TALK

One of the largest traps of treatment writing lies in describing the dialogue. Inevitably, you will be dealing with scenes in which people talk. However, nothing is more off-putting than long stretches of *he says … she describes … he explains …* This creates the impression of static, wordy scenes.

If your treatment is filled with such talky language, ask yourself first whether this is right for your genre. If not, can you replace the talking with more visual, cinematic scenes?

Where possible, the verbs you use should be dynamic and visual. Look for cinematic action – such as *she sprints … they set the fuse … he grasps hold …*

If, however, dialogue is what is needed for your story, then you must focus on what the character is trying to achieve through the talk. Draw on verbs that bring out the drama of the scene, such as *he argues, she persuades, they confront, she cajoles …*

Stronger verbs excite the imagination and give specificity, depth and a higher level of believability. (For an excellent and exhaustive list of useful verbs, see Judith Weston's book *The Film Director's Intuition*.)

 ## Write

Create a list of strong action verbs building on those given above, and keep it handy, so that you can be vivid and varied in your choices.

Workshop

Reread your treatment once more. Try it on friends, writing colleagues and workshop members.

Does it have drive and energy? Does it give the reader a flow of action and at the same time the meanings behind the action? Does it suffer from any of the troubleshooting issues above?

Listen to feedback, and rework again.

Where to next?

As the treatment grows longer and more detailed, so we need to look at the building blocks of the story – the scenes.

12

Scenes and sequences – the building blocks of a story

While characters form the basis of your story and the structure gives it an overall shape and forward drive, it's the individual scenes that provide the narrative power, moment to moment.

Time, place and change

In *Story*, Robert McKee defines a scene as a unit of storytelling that takes place in a single time and location, at the end of which some aspect of the story changes.

A scene runs continuously from beginning to end. If you jump in time, either forwards or backwards, even by a few minutes, then you have effectively created a new scene. In the same way, a scene occurs in a single location. A shift of location leads to a new scene.

The change that takes place could be small or large. It could be as simple as the protagonist being hungry at the start, and having stolen a sandwich by the end; or as complex as his needing money at the start, and agreeing to sleep with a potential client at the end.

In the first scene of *His Girl Friday*, Hildy arranges with her fiancé for him to wait for her while she says goodbye to her ex-husband and ex-boss, newspaper editor Walter Burns. By the end of the scene, she has left to go and speak to him. A small change.

In the sixth scene, Walter persuades Hildy to write one last interview, to help a murderer who's been unfairly condemned to hang. A large change.

McKee defines a sequence as a collection of scenes, at the end of which something significant has changed. The first six scenes of *His Girl Friday* combine to make the first sequence – at the end of which Hildy has agreed to write the interview and delay her departure for Albany and the quiet life of a housewife.

Your aim should be to develop scenes that will string together to make powerful sequences, each pushing the story forwards within the overall structure of each act, to tell your story.

 ## Key idea

A scene is a continuous unit of storytelling in which something changes. A sequence is a series of scenes in which something significant changes.

 ## Snapshot exercise

Look at the scenes you already have in mind. Does something change at the end of each one? If not, can you find an element that could change?

Choose at least one of the scenes, preferably one that's hot, a scene you're looking forward to, and sketch out in treatment form how it might go.

Can you already see sequences forming? Does something significant change at the end of each sequence?

> ## Greg Marcks, screenwriter
>
> *'Think of story as the plan and screenplay as the execution. A screenplay is a story told in scenes, each scene necessary to tell the story. When planning a screenplay, I try to write the story in prose first, without dialogue, with each scene represented by either a sentence or a paragraph. Then I read and revise, omitting what is unnecessary.'*

Dramatic scenes

The scene is the fundamental power unit of a story, and as such the majority of your scenes will need to be show dramatic movement. Dramatic, once again, means GOATS – Goal, Obstacle, Action, Tactics, Stakes. A scene that's missing one of these five elements becomes what Hitchcock called a 'no-scene scene' – that is to say, a scene without narrative thrust.

> ## Key idea
>
>
>
> Even a small scene needs Goal, Obstacle, Action, Tactics, Stakes – all five.

THE SCENE'S GOAL

A scene needs to have a protagonist. The protagonist of a scene will usually be the protagonist of the main storyline, but not always.

As with the overall story, the protagonist of a scene must have an outer-story goal – a goal that we can see on camera – small or large. His goal could be to destroy a robot or merely to cross the road, and we may well already know his goal before the scene starts.

> ## Key idea
>
>
>
> The protagonist of a scene will often be the protagonist of the main story, but not always.

THE SCENE'S OBSTACLES

There needs to be at least one obstacle – anything from a nuclear bomb to a ringing phone. Be aware of the value of small obstacles. There is only room for a few large obstacles in a story – too many major obstacles throw the story off track. But medium and small obstacles – from a car that won't start for a few seconds to a picky shop assistant – can bring a scene to life in surprising ways.

In *The Seven Samurai* there are only three major obstacles to the samurai's goal of defending the village: the bandits, the suspicion of the villagers and (in the final battle) the weather. Adding more in a given scene (say, an earthquake, a war, government troops, a corrupt politician) might be tempting, but would overload the film.

Instead, individual scenes focus on smaller obstacles: working out how best to build the defences, training the villagers to fight, and so on.

 ## Key idea

To develop strong scenes, create a large number of small obstacles.

THE SCENE'S ACTIONS

Now the protagonist needs to take action – visibly and/or in dialogue. His actions, as we saw earlier, will also reveal his character and inner thoughts.

In an early scene in *The Seven Samurai*, Kambei, an experienced samurai warrior, is called on to save a young boy who's being held hostage. The obstacle is significant: if he attacks openly, the child will be killed. As we watch, he shaves off his distinctive samurai top-knot, puts aside his long sword, disguises himself as a priest and asks for two rice-balls. We learn from his actions that he is clever, humble enough to remove the emblems of his trade, if needed, and adept (in seconds, he's snatched the boy and killed the kidnapper).

 ## David Mamet, playwright

'Every scene should be able to answer three questions: "Who wants what from whom?" "What happens if they don't get it?" "Why now?"'

THE SCENE'S TACTICS

The protagonist also needs to have a number of possible tactics to follow. A typical weakness, found in many scenes, comes when the protagonist has only a narrow range of predictable choices. This tends to lead to flat, predictable writing. Instead, don't think of a scene in terms of its ending, but in terms of its possibilities.

For example, say you decide to write a scene where the protagonist ends up killing his blackmailer. If you write the scene with the end in mind, you risk narrowing the possibilities.

In real life, we enter a situation with many possibilities in front of us. Depending on his character, the protagonist would have a number of choices. He might try to confront the blackmailer, trap him, argue with him, beg for mercy. The scene begins with him exploring these possibilities. Unfortunately, things don't pan out that way …

In the kidnapper scene from *The Seven Samurai*, we sense that Kambei has many possible tactics to choose from. He could storm in and risk the child dying. He could enlist help. He could give up. Not knowing which he's planning to choose keeps the scene alive for us.

Key idea

In a richly textured scene, the protagonist can choose between many possible tactics. Not knowing which he'll choose keeps the scene alive for us.

THE SCENE'S STAKES

There has to be something at stake – small or large.

Ask yourself: is it clear why the action of the scene is important to the characters? Is it clear why we, the audience, should care?

Sometimes the above elements (Goal, Obstacle, Action, Tactics, Stakes) will be set up within the scene. More often, they will be set up beforehand. And very often you will use a scene to set up elements for the scenes that follow.

Developing the scene – an example

You need to write a simple scene showing Esther crossing the road. Her goal is clear, but this could easily be a no-scene scene. So you throw in an obstacle (a red light) and already the scene becomes stronger. Higher stakes? She's late for a crucial meeting (a fact we learned in the previous scene).

Now challenge her tactics. Normally, Esther would wait for green, but for once she takes a risk and runs across, dodging the traffic. In the process, she drops some important papers, which are now out of order, setting up a problem for the next scene.

In this way, you keep the narrative flow pushing forward and add extra story value on a number of levels.

Write

Take a character – from your current story or not – and give him or her a goal. Try out three different obstacles, and for each obstacle try out three different ways to overcome it. You now have nine possible scenes. Which combination of obstacle and action works best? What do they reveal about the character? Where might they lead next?

Using action and dilemma in scenes

In the example above, Esther begins with a clear goal – crossing the road. This presents her with conflict – the traffic – and a dilemma – should she wait or run? The action she decides on leads to a further problem, and a new goal.

This succession of goal – conflict – dilemma – decision – new goal runs through almost every dramatic scene, large or small. (We'll look at the few exceptions in Chapter 22.)

Key idea

A strong scene normally centres on a dilemma.

A dilemma presents the protagonist of the scene with two or more difficult choices, neither of them desirable. Neither waiting nor running across the road is a choice she would normally make, but she has to decide, and now.

The issues and dilemmas may be massive or apparently trivial, but they energize the story. The character may have to choose between two kinds of latte or between which of two people he really loves. In both cases, they draw the audience in and reveal the kind of person he really is.

Write

Going back to your nine possible scenes in the previous exercise, insert a dilemma into each. Now your protagonist must make a difficult choice, with no time to delay. Force him to make it, right or wrong, and see what problem now arises.

Creating a sequence – the obstacle chain

Another major mistake most screenwriters make at first is to let their characters solve their problems too quickly, too predictably and too repetitively. They understand that stories are about conflict, so they dive straight into a big conflict with large obstacles, resolve it and are then forced to create a new one. Before they know it, they have a script crammed with big scenes, no breathing room and massively in need of cutting.

The solution is to realize that not every scene needs to be big, nor should the problem be resolved too soon. Obstacles, especially small ones, are your best friends once again. They keep the narrative moving in the right direction.

What you need is an obstacle chain. An obstacle chain uses a continuous flow of small, new obstacles to create involving sequences that draw an audience along, whatever the genre.

Key idea

A chain of obstacles is vital to holding the audience's attention as you develop your story.

To create an obstacle chain, break the action down into smaller steps. Begin with the protagonist's goal in the scene and imagine what the first obstacle might be. Next, ask what he might do (given his character) to overcome that obstacle. If possible, force him into a dilemma, which makes him choose new tactics – and take actions he wouldn't normally take. Then, when he has managed (or failed) to overcome the small obstacle, present him with a new obstacle, which he now has to find a new way to overcome. Continue this way until you relent and allow him to reach the end of the chain – only, of course, to start a new chain …

When creating an obstacle chain, it's important not to repeat yourself. Each new obstacle and action should be different; otherwise the audience will rapidly become bored. Also, be truthful and avoid cliché. We've all seen chase sequences, for example, which repeat the same essential trick time and time again.

Building a chain – an example

You're planning a story in which a young woman, Naomi, thinks her mother is having an affair with her boyfriend. At a certain point Naomi learns that they're meeting in a nearby motel, so she sets out to uncover the truth.

You develop a scene in which Naomi goes to the motel, sees the couple, confronts them and storms out, threatening never to see either of them again. This is a good scene, but not necessarily the best option to take. It gives us a small amount of character insight, but is rather linear and predictable. An alternative might be to place more obstacles in Naomi's way, to force her to take more action and reveal more about herself and the theme of the story.

In this second version, Naomi arrives at the motel to confront the couple (goal/tactics), but (obstacle) she doesn't know where to find them and there's no one on the desk to ask. She sneaks a look at the register (dilemma/action), but before she can see very much she is interrupted by the returning receptionist (obstacle). She lies (dilemma/action) and says her fiancé made a booking and she wants to surprise him, but the receptionist says nobody has booked in that day at all (obstacle).

So Naomi goes into the bar/restaurant to look around (tactics). The couple are not to be seen (obstacle), so she starts to flirt with the barman (dilemma/action), hoping to ask whether he's seen anyone who looks like them. However, the barman is suddenly called away by the manager (obstacle). Suspicious, Naomi decides that the staff know more than they're saying, so she …

And so on. After a few more beats, she finally discovers the couple and confronts them. Can you see how that could be a much more interesting way to develop the sequence? We are drawn more strongly into Naomi's quest and we learn more about her. We see her overcoming dilemmas – she takes chances, lies, flirts and so on – and she grows as a character.

Write

Write more links to the obstacle chain above. Keep it fresh and interesting. Find a succession of small new obstacles and actions that Naomi can take.

Occasionally, cut her some slack and allow her a small success or two, or she'll never get to the end!

Workshop: chain of obstacles

Decide on a new character, give him or her a clear, concrete goal, a location and an end point. One of the workshop members begins the sequence by introducing the first (small) obstacle and what action your protagonist takes to overcome it. The next member picks up the story immediately with the next obstacle, and the next action … and so on, round the group.

Each writer takes turns to invent the next obstacle and an action to overcome it. Each obstacle and action should be different from the previous ones, to avoid repetition, but otherwise try to accept whatever each says and move on with what they give you. Notice however, that large obstacles or actions might derail the story or change the genre.

See how many times you can go round the group before you finally reach the end point that you agreed on.

Some writers may find this exercise easier than others. It's worth persevering – you're exercising a vital muscle. If you can become fluent at the chain of obstacles, you'll have mastered one of the most important skills in screenwriting.

Where to next?

So far, your characters have been more or less mute. It's finally time to get them talking. In the next chapter, we start to create dialogue.

13

Hearing voices – creating dialogue

Good screen dialogue is very different from any other kind. It is different from stage dialogue, very different from dialogue in novels and short stories and, although it seems very natural, it is still markedly different from everyday speech. It has its own rules and demands, and varies from film to film, even from character to character.

Well-written dialogue can't salvage a badly constructed story or weak characters. However, flat dialogue can sabotage an otherwise good script, while good dialogue gives a screenplay a special sizzle.

Samuel Goldwyn, to Billy Wilder and I.A.L. Diamond

'You have all the scenes. Just go home and word it in.'

When to write dialogue

Experienced writers will often leave dialogue writing until surprisingly late in the process. They are aware that dialogue is greatly influenced by the structure, theme, genre and characters of a script and that it's a mistake to rush into writing dialogue scenes before these elements are firmly in place. Once written, those draft scenes can be very clingy – sticking in the writer's memory long after their usefulness has gone.

However, it can be just as great a mistake to spend too long on notes and outlines, so that when the dialogue is finally written it is mechanical, stale and empty.

The solution is to develop the dialogue in three stages:

1 Jottings – for example speed-writing, fragments, character monologues
2 Research – listening to how real people speak, and researching language and style
3 Writing from left-field – this can be your first draft written at speed, with the sound of the characters in the writer's head as much as possible but without self-criticism.

1 Jottings

Write some dialogue sketches from the start – in the form of notes, experimental scenes, fragments and monologues. These can be very important early stages in the development process, and they keep the project fresh and alive while the drier decisions of structure and narrative are being sorted out.

These scraps can be invaluable in setting the tone and style. You begin to see and hear how scenes might work and how characters interact. However, by not writing the script itself, you remain free to shift, drop and adjust your ideas as the outline develops, without feeling tied in to existing material.

Focus point

While planning the script, keep writing scraps and sketches to explore the characters' voices.

SPEED-WRITING

We talked earlier about writing as fast and unthinkingly as possible, to leap away from the analytical editing brain and allow the creative brain to play. I recommended beginning every day's work with ten minutes speed-writing – without plan, subject, rules or revision.

If you are doing this, continue to build up your of speed-writing practice each day, but now begin to look back as well.

Snapshot exercise

Return to your speed-writing notebooks and begin to reread them. They will probably be a mess, which is fine. Don't try to edit them, but look for nuggets of gold – a turn of phrase here, an insight there. Mark anything you find with a coloured pen or highlighter.

Look, in particular, for a sound that might form the basis for a character's voice. Copy useful passages into a notebook or file for future use.

CHARACTER RIFFS

This exercise, a variation of the one we used in Chapter 5, is a very powerful method for developing a character's individual sound. Pick a photograph and write freely in the character of one of the subjects in the picture. This time, however, have her talk specifically about the story.

Example: Gemma

I'm feeling stressed today. My husband has like smashed our only car and I have to catch a taxi to work. It's not the first time he's done this, is it? You know, it's I think he's jealous that I love my work. You can see the car in the background of the picture, the one with the crumpled fender … etc.

Write

Speed-write a character riff for your lead character for the first time we see her. Write for at least as long as it takes to begin to hear her in your head.

CHARACTER STEP MONOLOGUES

It follows that, as you develop your characters, you'll become better at hearing their voices and the better you hear their voices, the more strongly you'll be able to develop their characters. The two go hand in hand and reinforce the development process.

Key idea

Developing your characters goes hand in hand with developing their voices.

Write

Create a character riff for each emotionally important point in the story. Put her in different situations and hear how her voice changes (or not).

How does she respond to pressure? To indifference, praise, love or fear?

Example: Gemma

It's a Sunday morning, and I totally wake to find that my husband isn't in bed. At first, it doesn't bother me. He's way too obsessed with his running, and he'd run round the city twice a day rather than go and find himself a proper job. But his trainers are like still in the corner of the bedroom. So, I pull myself out of bed and then I notice the broken window and that's when I start to seriously freak out…

Edit

Collect up the character riffs for your protagonist and read them though. Mark the sections where you feel her voice is starting to come through.

Collect them and build on them by writing new character riffs, where you strengthen that voice. Listen for the different voices she uses, in different contexts.

William Faulkner, novelist

'I listen to the voices, and when I put down what the voices say, it's right. Sometimes I don't like what they say, but I don't change it.'

DIALOGUE SCRAPS

Scraps of dialogue can jump into your head at any time. But those golden turns of phrase will vanish rapidly if not immediately written down.

Keep a notebook and pen close to your hand when you work, and in your pocket whenever you are away from your desk. Or keep a 'fragments' file, open and ready at all times, on your computer or phone. Some apps can usefully be set to synchronize between different devices so that you can access all your fragments at any time.

Focus point

Always be ready to write down fragments, turns of phrase, scraps of dialogue when they come to you – wherever you are.

Write

This is a speed-writing exercise with modifications. The same rules apply as always: no rereading while you write, no editing, revising or crossing out; just keep the hand moving as you go.

This time, however, you're going to have two or more characters talk to each other, allowing them to 'speak' straight on to the page without editing or over-prescribing. This allows you to discover their tone and style without the pressure of having to deliver a professional 'scene' in a script.

For this exercise, there is no requirement to create dramatic interest, only to explore sounds, rhythms and interactions.

2 Research

To improve your dialogue writing:

- listen to how people talk
- read voraciously, especially scripts in your genre.

LISTENING

Listening to how people really talk will sharpen your ear for voice, subtext and language. Hear how people express themselves, manipulate one another, let slip what they really think and feel, make friends, console, share their love. Keep a notebook with you at all times, and jot down any interesting conversations you overhear and unusual or revealing turns of phrase. (Just don't be too obvious about it …)

Listen to how people speak on the radio and on TV. Listen for when they're putting on a voice they feel is appropriate, and when they are speaking naturally. Listen for when they're concealing and when they reveal their true selves.

Key idea

Listen to how people really use language when they speak.

Keep a note of any useful lines, interchanges, slang or anything new that catches your attention. Language is changing all the time.

If your story takes place in a particular place or time, you may need to put in some serious legwork. If necessary, go and talk to the experts.

David Newman and Robert Benton, screenwriters, *Bonnie and Clyde*

'[We went to East Texas] to listen to the language patterns, the speech cadences, the colloquialisms, so as to insure absolute accuracy. It wasn't enough that each character should sound like Texas, but that each spoke with a voice distinct from the others.'

READING

Good writers are good readers. Reading will help you develop your feeling for what dialogue works on the page and what doesn't.

Keep reading as many scripts as you can in your genre. Look at how they handle dialogue. Which passages work and which don't? Examine why. Keep clips and notes of the passages that work best.

Key idea

Read widely to see how other writers have created dialogue on the page.

Read newspaper and magazine articles, interviews, discussions of changes in language. Listen out for new words that you could use (though don't be afraid to invent your own slang if you wish – many writers do).

If your story is set in the past, you'll probably want to read material from that period, though you shouldn't copy it slavishly.

LISTENING TO YOUR OWN DIALOGUE

Good dialogue writers hear their characters speak as they write. Some can do this automatically; however, for many it's a skill that can be learned.

To train your dialogue ear, speak your dialogue aloud. You can do this as you write, either at the keyboard or pacing around the room. (This is not so easy if you write in a library or coffee shop.) Another powerful method is to read your dialogue back to yourself afterwards. You'll very quickly learn to hear where a voice sounds right and where it doesn't, where the dialogue picks up and where it falls flat.

Listen carefully for your characters' voices. Sometimes a single word or phrase provides a key to a character. Suddenly, the character comes alive for you. Note that phrase down in your character files and use it as a reference point.

John Steinbeck, novelist

'If you are using dialogue, say it aloud as you write it. Only then will it have the sound of speech.'

Snapshot exercise

Take a scene between any two characters, where they each have important goals to achieve, and enact their dialogue aloud. If you have the space, do it for real, moving and sitting as they do. Write down their dialogue (speaking aloud again if you wish) and then read the scene back to yourself, aloud. Record it and listen to the recording.

Each time, listen for the moments where the voices come to life. Even if it's only one sentence, or even one phrase, what do you hear? Can you build on it?

SCREENPLAY DIALOGUE VS REAL LIFE, NOVELS AND PLAYS

While screen dialogue draws on real speech, and literary and stage dialogue, it is nevertheless distinctly different.

In real life, people ramble, interrupt themselves, lose the point, speak vaguely and often incoherently, and yet somehow we make sense of (most of) what they say. On screen, you haven't the time, and the audience hasn't the patience.

In a novel, we are happy to read long, beautifully crafted speeches, using literary language that sounds unrealistic and flat in the mouths of actors.

Watching a play on stage, we delight in lengthy, static dialogue scenes that would kill a movie or TV show stone dead.

Screen dialogue:

- **needs to sound realistic,** even though it is a tidied-up impression of the rhythms of natural speech. It needs to give us the music and the flavour. Being realistic also means being credible: in other words, we believe that the character would credibly say what he says in the given situation.
- **is oblique,** mimicking the way people rarely say what they mean, leaving the meaning 'between' the lines – in the 'subtext'.
- **is motivated** – in other words, as we discussed earlier, screen dialogue is a form of action. Characters speak when they want to have an effect on someone: to impress them, to persuade them, to convince them.

Key idea

Screen dialogue is a form of action.

Snapshot exercise

Take a scene where you are clear about the character's goals and obstacles, and visualize the situation. Who would be the first to speak? What would they realistically say?

In real life, we rarely come straight out with what we want, so ask yourself how you'd work up to the issue, if it were you. How would you introduce the subject? Now ask the same question about the character. Does he blurt it straight out, or is he more canny, working round to it? Does he try to manoeuvre the other person and get them on his side?

Now, how does the other person react? How would you react? Do they answer straight out, play for time or simply ignore what's been said?

Continue through the scene – don't worry about the quality of the writing; focus on the lines being realistic, oblique and motivated.

3 Writing from left-field

None of this means that you can't have scenes where the characters talk about trivialities. In fact, it's crucial that you allow your characters to have left-field moments, such as how they can't stand burnt toast. Those moments are often the strongest of all, because we learn about the characters from what they're not saying.

One of the best-loved scenes from Quentin Tarantino's *Pulp Fiction* is a riff on two gangsters arguing over the kind of hamburgers they sell in France. One of the clips most shown from *When Harry Met Sally* leads to Sally demonstrating how to fake an orgasm. Don't be afraid to follow your imagination, wherever it goes. You can always edit it later.

Write

Take any two characters (from your story or freshly invented). Now set them to arguing about something totally trivial – opening a window, who won the FA Cup in 1961, who last had the Muse CD.

Let the dialogue go anywhere, and watch how their foibles, attitudes and flaws grow as much through what is not said as what is.

(As before, don't try to write *well*. Just do the exercise, have fun with it, and if you find there's something you want to use, you can always tidy it up later.)

Here is some dialogue from *Annie Hall* in which writers Woody Allen and Marshall Brickman take a simple idea and run with it:

FADE IN:

INT. DOCTOR'S OFFICE - DAY

Alvy as young boy sits on a sofa with his mother in an old-fashioned, cluttered doctor's office. The doctor stands near the sofa, holding a cigarette and listening.

> MOTHER
> He's been depressed. All off a sudden, he can't do anything.

> DOCTOR
> Why are you depressed, Alvy?

> MOTHER
> (Nudging Alvy)
> Tell Dr. Flicker.
> (Young Alvy sits, his head down)
> It's something he read.

> DOCTOR
> Something he read, huh?

> ALVY
> The universe is expanding.

> DOCTOR
> The universe is expanding?

> ALVY
> Well, the universe is everything, and if it's expanding, someday it will break apart and that would be the end of everything!

Disgusted, his mother looks at him.

                    MOTHER
         What is that your business?
                   (she turns back to the doctor)
         He stopped doing his homework.

                    ALVY
         What's the point?

                    MOTHER
         What has the universe got to do with it?
         You're here in Brooklyn! Brooklyn is not
         expanding!

                    DOCTOR
         It won't be expanding for billions of years
         yet, Alvy. And we've gotta try to enjoy
         ourselves while we're here. Uh?

He laughs.

Figure 13.1 From *Annie Hall*, screenplay by Woody Allen and Marshall Brickman

Snapshot exercise

Reread the scene above and discuss the ways in which Allen makes the dialogue realistic, giving the music of New-York-Jewish speech, yet not entirely real. Look at how he gives each a character a different style of speaking that reflects their attitudes and their emotional state.

Bring out the subtext. For each line of dialogue, write about what is being revealed. What do we understand that is not being said?

Actors and directors analyse character motivations line by line. Take each line and find what the character is trying to achieve by saying it. What effect is he or she trying to have on the others? Are there places where the same line is intended to have different effects on the two people listening? Are there any lines that aren't?

Workshop

Speed-write any scene from your story. Don't try to make it good, just aim for lines that are realistic, oblique and have motivation.

Have fun with it, and let it go where it wants to go.

Have the other participants read the parts and description, while you listen. What works? What could be improved in the next draft? What have you learned that you didn't know before?

Where to next?

With the dialogue under way, we're in a good position to move towards the first-draft script. However, before we can begin that, we need to look at the non-dialogue parts of the script – the descriptions.

14

Writing the descriptions – adding pictures and sounds

The descriptions in your script go to the very heart of what makes it television or cinema. These visuals and sounds, your choices of setting, props, décor, movement and sound atmospheres are important storytelling tools. They will also profoundly affect the mood and emotional impact of your script, and ultimately of the finished production.

And yet they are not the finished production and must be sketched in the most delicate and subtly suggestive strokes, where a short sentence must do the work that in a novel could take long paragraphs. As a writer, you must see and hear the action as clearly as a director, but what you write is as condensed and inventive as a Japanese haiku, creating striking images in our minds but using the fewest possible words.

All descriptions must be dramatically relevant at the time

The fundamental rule is that every line of description should further the dramatic thrust of the script at the time that it is needed.

Key idea

All description should further the drama.

DRAMATICALLY RELEVANT ...

Any descriptive detail must help progress the goal, the obstacle, the action, the tactics or the stakes. If it doesn't move the story forwards, it shouldn't be there.

In a novel, you need details to help the reader visualize the scene – the colour of the walls, the bird that sings overhead, the white rose that lies on the coffin, the shine on the shoes of the mourners ... However, in a script, all such description merely slows the story down.

If it isn't relevant to the story, you're wasting your time, and the reader's.

As you read more and more screenplays, good and bad, you'll grow to appreciate how much work readers must put into following the action, and how overloaded they can become if there is too much irrelevant detail. Overloaded readers rapidly become impatient and irritated readers, and irritated readers rarely turn into buyers.

Keep the descriptions focused and to the point. If you have lovely ideas for how to stage the story and create poetic shots, keep a separate file of notes. The production team may well find them valuable – but only after you've sold the script.

The corollary also works: if you have a visual idea that's particularly important to you, then build it into the story. If it's dramatically relevant that we see a white rose on the coffin, the art department has a solid reason to ensure that it's there in the shot.

Key idea

If you want a detail included in shot, make it part of the story.

... AT THE TIME

In a play, it is conventional to list the details of the set, the characters on stage and sometimes even the props, at the start of a scene. This is precisely what you do not do in a script.

If there is a bed on the left, two chairs and a table in the middle of the room, with carnations in a vase, you don't need to tell us in advance – wait until they are used.

Of course, if the scene opens with something strange, unusual or atmospheric that would immediately attract the characters' or the audience's attention, then it is dramatically relevant to mention it:

```
INT. CID OFFICE — DAY

A large box covered in Christmas wrapping paper sits
on DC Gerard's desk.
```

But you don't need to tell us precisely how many people are in the office, that the phones are ringing (or not) or what else is on the desk ... Less is more.

Reading screenplays for descriptions

As you did with dialogue, you should buy or download a large number of screenplays, good and bad, and examine how they handle description. You will find a wide variation. Some well-known screenplays over-describe – however, they are often either written by the director or have the finance already in place. Screenplays from the 1950s or earlier often include camera shots, as do post-production scripts or transcriptions from the finished movie.

Modern scripts are generally less descriptive, yet you still have a degree of choice as to how much to write. Some use language, sparingly, to bring out the drama or poetry of the story while always remaining dramatically relevant at the time. On the other hand, others gain from leaving almost everything to the imagination.

Figure 14.1 gives the opening of *The Green Mile* by Frank Darabont. It's at the detailed end of the spectrum – this has probably the most description you could get away with in a screenplay. And yet every word is dramatically relevant at the point in the script where it appears.

EXT. FIELD - DAY(SLOW MOTION)

… where cattails sway in the sepia-toned heat. A small scrap of fabric is snagged in the nettles, fluttering languidly …

COLOR BLEEDS SLOWLY IN as mosquitoes swarm and dragonflies skitter, showing the fabric scrap to be pale yellow …

Suddenly, a MAN WITH A SHOTGUN comes crashing through the cattails, wiping through frame and exiting…

… then ANOTHER MAN … and ANOTHER … armed with rifles, plowing through the brush, exiting frame …

… and now comes KLAUS DETTERICK, a farmer one step above shirt-tail poor, a double-barrel shotgun in the crook of his arm. He pauses, horrified, seeing the scrap of cloth. He pulls it loose, turns back, screaming something in anguish…

… and still more men come crashing into view, flooding by us with dreamlike, slow-motion grace. ONE MAN is leading a team of DOGS, trying to untangle the leads. DEPUTY ROB McGEE is shouting for everybody to stay together…

… and under it all, we hear a sibilant, frightening whisper:

> WHISPERING VOICE (V.O.)
> You love your sister? You make any
> noise, know what happens?

And off that horrible voice, we

CUT TO:

INT. GEORGIA PINES NURSING HOME—MORNING(PRESENT DAY)

A CLOCK RADIO spews the morning weather report, abruptly pulling us into the present with a prediction of rain. PAUL EDGECOMB, late 70's/early 80's, wakes to another day …

Figure 14.1 From *The Green Mile*, screenplay by Frank Darabont

Note that Darabont breaks the description down into short paragraphs, giving a strong sense of movement, almost as if we were seeing the film, shot by shot. Each paragraph is a new development, setting up questions in the reader's mind. Not a word could easily be cut.

At the other end of the spectrum, scripts such as Nora Ephron's *When Harry Met Sally* serve as good examples of how to build a witty scene with minimal description. In the following extract we are in Sally's car. In the scene shown in Figure 14.2, she is driving them both from Chicago to New York.

```
EXT. CHICAGO STREET - DAY

Harry takes out a bunch of grapes, starts to eat
them.

                    SALLY.
          I have this all figured out. It's
          an 18 hour trip, which breaks down
          to 6 shifts of 3 hours each. Or,
          alternatively, we could break it
          down by mileage. There's a map
          on the visor, I've marked it to
          show the locations where we change
          shifts. You can do three hours?

                    HARRY
               (offering her one)
          Grape?

                    SALLY
          No. I don't like to eat between
          meals.

Harry spits a grape seed out the window, which
doesn't happen to be down.

                    HARRY
          I'll roll down the window.

After a lengthy silence.
```

                              HARRY

          I hope this isn't going to be one
          of those trips with a lot of long,
          awkward silences.

                              SALLY.

      Me too.

    A long awkward silence.

                              HARRY

          Why don't you tell me the story of
          your life.

Figure 14.2 From *When Harry Met Sally*, screenplay by Nora Ephron, Rob Reiner and Andrew Scheinman

Ephron uses the brief descriptions to develop a dry, laconic style that suits the movie. The gag with the closed window is carried off in just six words. The echoing of 'long awkward silence' in just four. We are told nothing about what Harry or Sally look like. Their emotions, tone and almost all of their actions are implied. And yet the reader gets the comedy and forms a clear picture of the scene, between the lines. Such economy and control show a screenwriter on top of her craft.

Richard Holmes, Head of Production, Creative England

'*I like to see evidence in the language, especially the description, that the person has read other scripts. You feel you're in the hands of someone who knows what they're doing and will deliver.*'

Write

Take a passage of description from a favourite novel, short story or play and rewrite the scene as if it were in a screenplay. Does the description appear in a place that feels right for the narrative of a screen story? How much description can you cut and how much do you need to retain for the script to work? Is there anything that the writer has left to the reader's imagination, but which you need to add for a screenplay?

Once you've written a first draft, go through it again. Is every detail really *dramatically relevant at the time?*

No mind-reading or editorializing

Novels and short stories are allowed both to make grand generalized statements and go inside the heads of their characters. As we saw, treatments also need to do both from time to time. However, in the screenplay itself you are not allowed to do either. Everything must be capable of being either seen or heard by the audience.

This means that you must be very careful not to write anything that the audience could not easily understand from the shot, the action or the soundtrack. You can't tell us what someone's thinking (mind-reading) or comment on the action (editorializing).

For example, you can write:

`Raj stares at the photo and tears come to his eyes.`

– it can be filmed by the camera – but not:

`As Raj stares at the photo he remembers the smell of his father's aftershave and how he used to wish that he didn't work so late every night.`

… This is mind-reading.

You can write:

`The sun beats down on their heads.`

– which we could see on screen – but not:

`The desert is a cruel and murderous place.`

… which is an editorial comment by the writer. Beware of such tendencies. The problem is that you might think you've communicated this idea to the audience when you haven't. If that idea was important to the story, you've unwittingly left a hole in the script.

 ## Key idea

Only write descriptions that could be filmed or recorded on sound.

You *can* include descriptions that could plausibly be acted (*Hannah grows angry*) but not ideas that could only be understood with dialogue or different, more specific visuals.

Best of all, show, don't tell. Rather than telling us that Hannah's angry, give her an action that shows it (*Hannah thumps the table*).

Focus point

Find ways to show what can't normally be filmed, through action.

Props and other images can be very useful here, especially if you took the time to give them significance earlier in the story. For example, if you've established that Victor never goes anywhere without his phone, finding the phone covered with blood in an empty house will immediately convey meaning.

Similarly, in many Westerns, the cruelty of the desert is revealed when the protagonists come across the skeletons of families who have died there, all their possessions scattered on the sands. Of course, such images rapidly became cliché. It's your job to find images that are fresh and different.

Be observant. Watch people, their gestures, actions, style and the way they use their possessions. Keep notes of useful images, locations or props that could be of use in future scenes. Build a vocabulary of useful visuals to draw on in dramatizing your scripts.

Stanley Kubrick

'Observation is a dying art.'

Snapshot exercise

Find examples in your treatment where you have described what someone is thinking, and where you have made generalized statements.

How might you use action and description to show, not tell? Try to find ways that use as little dialogue as possible, preferably none. Be inventive.

Key idea

Find images that are fresh and haven't been overused. Keep a notebook of actions, gestures and other ideas for visual storytelling in future scenes.

Writing for emotional effect

Work at developing a style that's appropriate to your story. Learn from short stories and novels, as well as produced screenplays. While, as we've seen, certain literary effects aren't open to you, you do have a range of styles you can draw on.

As with a treatment, your descriptions should evoke emotion, especially the primary emotions of the genre you're writing in. Writing a horror film, make us shiver. A thriller needs to have us on the edge of our seats. See how thriller screenwriters use short, punchy sentences to raise the tension, while romantic and historical scripts tend to be written in a more flowing, gentle style.

And everyone appreciates a little humour and wit, in any script.

Write

Write a short scene in which a man goes into a post office to look for a friend he's supposed to be meeting, but who hasn't turned up. Now rewrite it in three different ways:

- Rewrite it the first time as if it's a scene in a **horror script**. Find language, imagery and incidents that evoke a sense of horror, without changing the essential structure of the scene.
- Now rewrite it as a **social drama**. What language and so on will bring out our sympathy, place him in society and evoke the power struggles he faces?
- Thirdly, rewrite the scene as **comedy**. Bring out the humour in the situation. If you're working in a different genre (sports, science fiction, war, etc.), then you might like to rewrite it for that, too.

Now show it to a friend or colleague, and see whether they can spot which genre is which.

Contrast your locations

For most films, you should seek to vary your settings and avoid repeating the same location time and time again, especially in consecutive scenes.

However, television and low-budget films demand fewer settings because every set and every move to a different location cost money. You'll make a low-budget producer very happy if you can set most of your story in one place – a warehouse (*Reservoir Dogs*), a coffin (*Buried*) or an office (*The Office*). However, this places great responsibility on you, as the writer, to ensure that the story still works. If your story is restricted to a small geographical area, maybe even a single house, then there is a danger of the audience feeling trapped.

The trick is to break the location into mini-locations, as can be seen in Jean Renoir's classic *La Règle du jeu* (*The Rules of the Game*). Set largely in a French château, each room is given an individual character of its own. The château's elegant drawing room, for example, is where the characters generally meet for entertainment, the dining room is a place of refuge, and the armoury, where the guns are stored for hunting, is where many of the fights take place.

Even a lengthy sequence (or a whole story) that takes place in a single room can benefit if you give a different 'location' feel to different parts of the room. Except for the opening and the closing shots, *Twelve Angry Men* takes place entirely in a jury room, but the script breaks the room into different areas and also makes use of the claustrophobia, the heat of the day and the changing light to add emotion to the story. *They Shoot Horses, Don't They?* is located almost entirely in a sleazy dance hall, where couples compete to be the last standing. Again, much is made of the claustrophobia, plus the passage of time, the different parts of the room – the stage, the dance floor, the audience – and the rare escape to the changing rooms or the outdoors.

Snapshot exercise

Take a single location for a longer scene and divide it into smaller parts, say, for example, a hotel reception area. Choose at least three different parts of the location and give each one a distinctive role and feeling.

Sound effects and music

While concentrating on the visuals, remember also that you have at your disposal a wide range of possible sounds – atmospheres, sound effects and music.

Key idea

Don't forget the power of sound.

SOUND ATMOSPHERES

A sound atmosphere is the background sound of a location or situation: the singing of birds on a summer's day, the drilling of a team mending a road, the roar of a football crowd. Your choice of location will often automatically bring its own natural sounds.

You don't need specifically to describe the sound of a place, unless it's particularly remarkable for some reason, but you do need to be aware of how a location's natural sounds will affect the story. Have a second look at your settings and ask yourself what they will sound like. Have you set scene after scene in places that will sound identical, or that have no distinctive sound at all – such as an office?

Key idea

You don't need to specify sound atmospheres, but bear them in mind when you choose your settings.

Is the sound atmosphere (or lack of it) going to help your scenes or drag them down? Think of the alternatives – the sound potentials of (say) a breaker's yard, a flamingo park, a sewer (*The Third Man*), a jazz parade, a clock repair shop, the whispering gallery in St Paul's, an empty swimming baths, a pigeon loft …

Remember, too, that the atmosphere can add variety to the way the characters speak – for example shouting over the noise of a rock band, or whispering backstage during a play.

SOUND EFFECTS

A sound effect, sometimes known as a 'spot effect', is a specific sound, such as a gunshot or a screech of brakes.

Sound effects can highlight a story point, a new development, or a decision made or deferred. It might be the scraping sound made by a table in a room that was supposed to be empty; the smash of a glass being dropped; or the sound of a text message arriving.

Sometimes, simply the choice of verb can evoke a sound, bringing that moment to life-as in 'he SCRATCHES his name', 'she HAMMERS on the door', 'the engine SHUDDERS to a halt'.

MUSIC

Music can be useful, if made part of the drama, but there are pitfalls. Tempting as it is to include swathes of musical references, these can rebound against you. If the music is well known and recent, it will probably be in copyright and expensive to use. Or it may distract the reader. If it's not well known, then it may just annoy the reader, who will be left feeling ignorant.

Never add generic music directions, such as 'SUSPENSE MUSIC PLAYS', as this should be left to the director and composer. Create suspense through your story and choice of language.

If the music is played by – or to – characters in the story, then describe it (briefly) in terms that make it clear to the reader what it sounds like and why it is dramatically relevant at the time – for example:

```
He hears a piano in a nearby house playing a Chopin
nocturne - sad and reflective - and stops, staring
thoughtfully into the darkness.
```

 Write

Write a scene in which you tell the story as much as possible through sounds. Perhaps the lights have gone out, or the important action is taking place off-screen. Choose a location, atmospheres and effects that tell the audience precisely what's happening without showing it in visuals or dialogue.

Workshop

You're almost ready to write the first draft. Develop the treatment and scenes into a longer treatment, showing the main beats, characters and locations. Include fragments of dialogue if you wish. Keep it flowing, so that you can feel the emotional energy and see the overall shape with some of the new details that are beginning to emerge.

Don't limit the length – make it as short or as long as feels right. Don't worry if many scenes are very sketchy at the moment – you want to leave some things to discover when you write the draft screenplay itself.

Discuss this in workshop. Is the spark of the premise still there? Can you follow the general dramatic thrust? Is there variety? Are there some fresh ideas? Do you bring your own personal angle to the story? Is it heading in the right direction?

Where to next?

You can only plan so much. After a while, you have to jump in and write. The time has come to write the first-draft screenplay.

15

Learning to fly – writing the first draft

At some stage, it becomes time to write the first draft of the script. Depending on the approach you prefer, you may well have a detailed plan, or no plan at all; a clear understanding of your characters, or a generalized sense of their voice; a pile of fragmentary scenes and sequences that you've been experimenting with, or a blank screen. What you almost certainly *won't* feel is ready.

The next step is for you to write the first draft of your screenplay, or sample episode. We'll look at what a first draft needs to have, how to schedule the writing and how to get the words on to the page.

When to write the first draft

Learning to tell when the time is right to dive into a first draft takes experience, and to some extent no writer ever really knows. But beware of the desire to go and hide in the planning and researching process. It is better to write a draft that is only partially planned than never to write it at all.

For this chapter, you will be working almost entirely in 'first gear' and 'third gear' – that is, visualizing and creating, without judging or editing. Those come later. (See Chapter 2.)

The three golden rules of writing the first draft

The rules for writing a first draft are simple and few. A first draft must have:

1 **a beginning**
2 **something in the middle**
3 **an end.**

That's all. If it has all those three, it's a perfect first draft.

It doesn't have to be any particular length or format (although it may be helpful to use the correct format from the start; see Appendix 2). It doesn't have to be clever, or witty, or impressive, or well structured, or correct, or incorrect, or any of those things we worry about.

Most of all, it doesn't have to be good.

It just has to be written. This is the creative gear that you've been practising when speed-writing. Making it good comes later, when you edit. But you can't edit what you haven't yet written. The sole job of a first draft is to provide you with material that you can edit for the second (and following) drafts – nothing more and nothing less. This is *your* first draft, and nobody else needs see it. It's a sketch for the finished article, a rehearsal, full of mistakes, half ideas, thoughts, moments of passing inspiration, glimpses of glorious things, awful clichés, meanderings and false starts.

> ## Stephen King, in *On Writing: A Memoir of the Craft*
>
> *'Write the first draft with the door closed, and the second with the door open.'*

The first draft is there to show you what *shouldn't* be in the script, not what should. Yes, there will be moments of inspiration, but most of it will resemble the wrong side of a carpet – all the threads and none of the picture.

Focus point (again)

Don't get it right, get it written.

Write your first draft in the shortest time possible. There are two good reasons for this. First, it gives you less time to worry. Writing a first draft is rather like running through a haunted forest – critical and doubting voices will hiss at you from all sides, but if you stop or look back, you'll be turned to stone. As you run, you'll see dozens of such writers, frozen to the spot, unable to escape. However, if you plunge on, without a sideways glance, I promise that you'll get to the end.

Stephen King says he writes 'just fast enough so that his fears don't catch up with him'. The playwright Alan Ayckbourn takes 11 months to plan each of his plays and then writes the plays themselves in just two weeks.

The second reason is to stop you making the first-draft process too important. If you take longer, you'll only be tempted to write well, and that will kill your draft stone dead.

Ernest Hemingway, author and journalist

'There is nothing to writing. All you do is sit down at a typewriter and bleed.'

1 A beginning

The best way to start is to start. Don't worry too much whether you've found the perfect starting place; you almost certainly haven't. Indeed, you almost certainly will never find it until you start writing. Most often, you'll find your start buried in later pages, but you'll only find it if you get going in the first place.

Plan a nice moody opening, appropriate to the genre – tense, funny, thought-provoking – and scenes that show the protagonist's inner problems. Then plunge straight into the middle of something. It doesn't matter what. Go straight into the world of the story, with its stresses and problems. Put someone in a difficult situation – physically or emotionally – and take it from there.

Have fun, enjoy diving in, and start writing.

Explore the normality of your protagonist's world, and his flaws. As this is the opening, you may find that these pages go more slowly than any other part, while you find your voice. This section should aim to cover the first ten pages to the inciting incident, a good climax to finish your first chunk of work, the first major disaster to hit your central character and his first decision to deal with it.

There are no rules, aside from the three above: beginning, something in the middle and end. It's just for you, so, if it helps, write it on your iPhone, in longhand on yellow legal pads or in green ink on the back of a lobster shell. As long as you write.

Having said that, your edited screenplay will need to end up in standard industry format, so you may as well start now. Some software will automatically set this up for you, but, if you have any doubts, see Appendix 2 at the end of this book.

Write

No matter where you are, write an opening. Start with a mood and put someone in difficulty. Take it from there. If you have your treatment planned out, leave yourself some freedom to improvise. Discover what it's really like to be in the middle of each scene. Be open to any and all ideas that come to you, as long as they don't take you into a different story. Don't try to be economical or write well – just get the words on the page. Throw stones at your protagonist and watch him respond.

2 Something in the middle

Once started, the most important thing to do with a first draft is to keep writing. Don't edit, revise or even reread.

Divide the rest of your script into steps – each, say, approximately 15 pages long. If you're writing a feature-length script that fits into the structure we've been outlining, allocate two steps each for the first and third acts and four steps for the second. Aim to end each section with a juicy climax and a decision. This gives you something to look forward to.

Some writers like to warm up a new session by reading back over the last few pages. That's OK as long as you are not seduced into trying to correct or improve what you see. It's better, if you can, to avoid rereading for the simple reason that, if you see faults, you may be distracted or, worse, become self-critical. Conversely, if you see good writing, you may feel inhibited, under pressure to reach that standard again.

Many writers like to leave each writing session with something undone – a half-finished scene or even a half-finished sentence that they can come back to for an easy start the next day. Others prefer to finish cleanly, but have a clear idea of the next scene. Try different ways, to see which works best for you.

Most writers write in story order, but some hate doing that, and prefer to jump around the script, working on whichever scene feels hot and appealing. It really doesn't matter which you do, as long as you write.

The mind plays all kinds of games when first-draft writing, and the most important thing to be aware of is that you cannot write and edit at the same time. The editing and the creating brain do not function together. When you're being creative, you may feel that a scene is brilliant – only to look at it the next day and realize that it is overblown or flat. On the other hand, the speech that you were convinced is completely awful turns out on inspection to be exactly right.

 Key idea

Remember: you cannot judge while you are writing, and you cannot write while you are judging. Separate the two.

If the idea of writing dialogue intimidates you at first, then write all the scenes with description and action but few, or no, specific lines of speech. This is technically called a master scene treatment, and is a very useful stepping stone (see Chapter 10).

Then, when you've got to the end, start a second draft and add the dialogue. Again, use speed-writing. Give yourself the freedom to let your characters flower and sort out the problems later. Don't agonize about the quality. Get the words on the page and polish them later. Inspiration turns up when you sit down and work for it.

 Focus point

In case you missed it the first and second time:

Don't get it right, get it written.

A routine helps because writing starts to become bedded in as a habit, like brushing your teeth or getting dressed. Find the time of day that works for you. Maybe you tend to write your best when you first wake in the morning, or late at night. (Many writers like to write when they feel a little sleepy, to help bypass the internal editor.) Better to settle on a regular regime than wait for perfection, even if it's half an hour before you go to work, or a page a day in your lunch break.

Brené Brown, author

'Even if you plot, sometimes you won't know what is coming until the words appear on the page. Something happens when you commit to writing regularly, and you write through the frustration, annoyance and self-criticism.'

As you write each day, you'll have to make some quick decisions. Be prepared to think on your feet, change ideas and jump over problems, leaving them to be solved later. That's all fine. Focus on your lead character, and ensure that he is active and comes to life. Other matters can be sorted out in the edit.

3 An end

… And then, at some point you come to an end. Stop. Write, FADE TO BLACK.

It doesn't matter if it's page 10 or page 1,000, you've finished a draft screenplay. It has a beginning, something in the middle and an end.

Most importantly, you will have learned things about your story from writing the draft – and finishing it – that you will never learn any other way. There is a magic about finishing a draft. The very fact of coming to the end will yield unexpected insights. You will understand your story in ways that you can't while it remains as an idea in your head. Some scenes and characters will have turned out less exciting than you thought they would, while others will have flowered in surprising ways.

A beginning, a middle and an end, that's all it needs. If you've done this, whatever else you've done, you've written a perfect first draft.

Chuck Close, artist

'Inspiration is for amateurs – the rest of us just show up and get to work.'

As you're working with the study door closed, there's no workshop exercise this chapter.

Where to next?

Sometimes speed-writing a draft is easier said than done. Problems can and do arise. In the next chapter, we look at some of the issues that might come up in the middle of a first draft, and how to deal with them.

16

Troubleshooting the first draft

Most of the problems with first drafts come from one or other of the four gears. Some writers call their problems 'writer's block'. Others insist that writer's block doesn't exist; it's merely a catch-all phrase for a number of possible problems.

I can't think of any ideas (1)

Assuming that you've worked out your premise and planned the story, what you mean, presumably, is that don't know how to translate a scene or story step from your treatment into an actual script.

Are you visualizing? Close your eyes and let images come to you, as if you had a screen in your mind. Don't judge them, watch them. Imagine the stage of the story you've reached and see the characters in action. Set up their conflicts. Whatever you see and hear, write it down. Remember, it doesn't have to be good. Don't get it right, get it written.

Focus point

Run the start of the scene in your mind. Write down what you see. Now, visualize what happens next …

Get excited about details. The creative mind loves details. Be vivid, tactile, emotional. Use all five senses – see, hear, feel, smell, taste … Once you begin to trust the details, the ideas will flow.

Make it as true as you can. Say you have a moment between two minor characters: a police sergeant talking to a nurse. It's too easy to think in flat stereotypes. Have you ever actually met a sergeant or a nurse? Can you draw on your memories to see and hear them as real people? If not, can you draw on memories of other people you've known, from other areas of your life? I was once stuck creating the character of an elderly Portuguese farmer for my Portuguese epic. Casting around, I lit on my grandmother, as having the right spunky energy and sharp humour, though she'd probably never stepped on to a farm in her life.

Try reversing the stereotypes. Make the sergeant a woman, and the nurse a man. Give them goals and obstacles. Imagine that the sergeant is desperately hungry and the nurse has had too much to drink. Try anything that will give the pictures in your mind fresh life.

I can't think of any ideas (2)

Look around you. An experienced writer learns to use everything and anything that comes to mind. Watch out for useful triggers for imagination. They can come from anywhere and everywhere:

• places

• people

• sounds from outside

• interruptions

• passing thoughts

- odd memories
- research notes
- objects
- problems
- lines of dialogue said previously by the characters
- lines of dialogue not said by the characters
- misunderstandings and misreadings
- typos and mistakes
- random and surreal connections
- rhymes.

Maybe you hear a car reversing outside your window and decide that the police sergeant is going to have a short rant about being unable to park near her house, and that reveals another side to her. This now sparks a sarcastic reply from the nurse, leading you into their real issues by a roundabout, but more interesting, route.

 Key idea

Utilize everything and anything around you.

If you utilize whatever comes to keep the flow, you'll find you discover all kinds of random unexpected patterns and possibilities – including character psychology, theme, hidden ideas, subtext and status.

Most of all, make it fun.

My writing is flat/overblown/boring/stupid/ no good

Stop trying to judge. I can guarantee that your writing will look completely different once you've gone all the way through. It may be better; it may be worse! But whatever judgements you make now will be misleading and stop you writing the draft. Speed-writing is right brain, from your unconscious mind, flowing, uncritical, accepting, prepared to be wrong, happy to be bad. Keep moving; don't stop, look back or try to be good. A first draft will ramble, go off on tangents, include longueurs and passages that are unclear, but resist the temptation to edit – just keep ploughing on.

 Erica Jong, novelist

'I went for years not finishing anything. Because, of course, when you finish something you can be judged.'

Keep going to the end: commit to finishing every draft that you start, however bad it may be. Then edit. The good news is that the more insistent your inner critic, the more you can trust yourself to edit thoroughly later. Remember, you never need to show your first draft to anyone. Indeed, you never need to show any draft to anyone else until you've made it the best you can.

If it helps to calm your inner critic, make an agreement with yourself that you'll never allow any draft to be seen by anyone else until you're fully happy with it. And then get back to putting the words on the page.

Ray Davies, musician

'Being in control by being out of control. When you let the writing control you, it springs into life. You can do anything. If you try to control the writing, nothing lives.'

I've lost faith in the idea

In the middle of the jungle it's possible to lose your way. Go back to your premise and remind yourself what excited you in the first place. If you had faith in your idea once, you'll find it again. Relight the spark.

One powerful trick is to find a talisman – an object (or a poem, line of dialogue or piece of music) that reminds you of the theme. Keep this by your computer as you work.

Researching my Portuguese adaptation, which was based on the lives of port wine farmers in the early twentieth century, I picked up a piece of the flinty rock that the farmers had to smash every year to turn their arid land into earth that could grow grapes. I brought it home and placed it by my monitor. It summed up, for me, the hard struggle they faced, and reminded me, every morning, why I wanted to write the script.

I've lost faith in myself. I'm sure I can't write this

Join the club. All writers have doubts. That's fine.

And by the way, if you're at all sensitive to your characters, you'll pick up their feelings as you write and be fooled into thinking they're your own. How's your central character feeling at the moment? If you feel depressed, angry, lost, stuck and unable to move on, it could well be your protagonist who is feeling those emotions in the story.

Accept the feelings and use them. Have one of the characters voice the very doubts that you are having yourself. Let the protagonist announce (if only to himself): 'This isn't working. I can't do this. I'm no use ...' – and keep writing.

I don't feel very inspired

You often won't. Amateurs write when they feel inspired. Professionals write because they have to. The job of writing is simply turning up, day after day.

If you aren't inspired, find something to help you get into the scene you've reached. Visualize. Use what's around you. Create conflict in the scene. Invent a new obstacle for your protagonist – an external problem or an inner challenge, something in her mind that she has to overcome. Or just write rubbish, knowing that you can fix it later. (And it may not turn out to be such rubbish after all.)

And keep rolling on.

I've planned out this scene and I can't get into it

You know too much. You may be focusing too much on the ending of the scene, rather than the dramatic ebb and flow. Slavishly following the treatment can make writing very linear and plot-bound. You can know your story too well.

Writing is a process of exploration and discovery. You need to step away for a moment. Try writing against the content. Trick yourself into forgetting what you've planned by writing the opposite. If Sanjay is intent on murdering Ben, write a scene in which they talk about apples … football … the weather … anything but what the story is about.

Willy Russell, playwright and screenwriter

'Part of the process of writing a play for me is to discover what I don't yet know I know.'

Key idea

If the scene isn't coming to life, try writing against it.

I've had a much better idea for a script

I guarantee that you will be struck by great new ideas at least once during the draft. When you allow your creative mind time to grow, it rewards you with yet more creativity. But, however brilliant the new idea seems, don't on any account abandon your current draft to write a new one. Sometimes these siren songs are merely ways of avoiding the work in front of you. If you stop and start a new script, the same thing will happen next time, and the next … and you'll end up with a dozen started scripts and none finished.

When that great, sparkly new idea comes to you, stop. Take five minutes to jot it down and put it aside in a special folder for new ideas. Then go back to the current script. Afterwards, like waking from a dream, you may well find that the idea wasn't so exciting after all. Or you may discover that you do indeed have a strong premise for when you're ready to write the next one.

My plot and/or characters are taking the story in a totally new direction

This also happens, and this time there's no hard-and-fast rule. On the one hand, the grass can often seem greener on the other side of the fence, and a new plot twist can often seem fresh and attractive purely because you've been thinking about the old one for so long. On the other, sticking too slavishly to your plans can make a script stiff and rigid. Characters grow and may start making decisions you'd never planned on.

If the changes are small and improve the story without requiring a total rethink, allow them. They may require revisions earlier in the script (perhaps you've discovered that your protagonist is actually married, not single). Don't go back now, or you'll be tempted to start editing. Make a note to deal with any issues in the next draft.

If, however, they demand a complete change to the remainder of the script, take a few minutes to think through the implications. Will the premise still work? Will the premise be better? Is there some other reason why it will sabotage the story or will it strengthen it? There's no single answer. New directions can be a sign that the story is alive and growing, or that you've lost the plot.

There are three possible situations:

1 **The change will spoil the story.**

2 **The change is good for the story.**

3 **You don't know.**

If you decide that the new ideas aren't worth pursuing after all, then nothing's been lost. Indeed, you may have gained new insights into what does work. Mind you, if you've already veered off in a wrong direction, you'll need to retrace your steps. Save a safety copy of the draft as it is, remove the offending scenes and continue down the path that you'd originally planned.

If, however, you decide you like the new ideas, then keep going.

And if you don't know, that probably means there's no wrong answer. Do either. You can always fix it in the next draft.

In the long run, you're the boss. It's often said by writers that the characters 'took over'. It's a useful myth, but characters can't actually take over. They're fictions. You're in charge – and, once you've decided on your plan, have no qualms in insisting that your characters do what they're told.

Whichever way you go, keep the thinking to a minimum and get back to first-draft writing as quickly as you can.

I can't bring myself to write the next scene(s)

There are three main reasons why writers freeze up. One is that you find the scene you planned in your treatment boring. The second is fear of failure. The third is that you find it raises difficult emotions.

If it really bores you, then you have to leave it out. If you find it boring, so will the audience, and the one sin you can't afford to commit is to be boring. Jump to the next scene and write that. You'll probably find you never needed the one that bored you in the first place.

If the scene is really essential, then you must find something to interest you in it. Bring in a new character or theme. Raise the stakes. Clarify the goal. Make the obstacles more exciting. Find a personal angle on the character's inner challenge and put your own feelings into the scene. Or leave it to one side. Write a scene that gets you going, and leave that one till later.

 Raymond Chandler, novelist and screenwriter

'When in doubt, have a man come through the door with a gun in his hand.'

If you are hesitating because you are afraid you'll fail, then here's the news: you quite possibly will. Most writers write bad scenes in their first drafts. And the sky doesn't fall in. In fact, nothing awful happens at all, apart from some bruised feelings. Because they're writing with the door closed.

The question is not whether you'll fail to write a good scene now, but whether you'll fail to make it better when you edit. And you can't possibly make it better if you haven't written it in the first place.

So write it.

The third reason you may freeze before writing a scene is that it raises difficult personal emotions. Perhaps it draws on painful memories or embarrassing fears.

In this case, you absolutely must write the scene. Never avoid a scene for emotional reasons, or the heart of the script will fade and die. Face your feelings and give them to the characters. It's only words on a page, and remember, nobody will ever see it until you are ready to show it to them. If they're that difficult, then go and get therapy. But write the scene!

Focus point

Never avoid a scene for emotional reasons.

Once you've written your way through it, you'll find that your writing becomes more powerful, honest and convincing. When you look back at it (not now, but when you come to rewrite), you'll probably find that it looks completely different from how it felt at the time. Most importantly, you'll be able to judge whether it's right (or wrong) for the script. But for now, go through the fire and get the words on the page.

Where to next?

Once you've finished the first draft, congratulate yourself and celebrate. Getting through a first draft is a major, emotionally draining, journey for all writers. Buy your favourite food, sit and do nothing, hold a party, whatever works for you.
You never have to write a first draft of that script again.

Print it out, make a safety copy on a flash drive and keep it somewhere very safe. Wait for as long as you can bear.

Then, when you are ready, get it out again. You're ready to make it good.

17

Revising structure – the first edit

The best way to edit your script is in stages, starting with the big picture. If you try to rewrite the whole draft in one go, one line at a time, you'll lose sight of the context and waste an enormous amount of time. There is no point in spending an hour revising the first line of description when the whole scene needs to be cut. You'll waste time polishing lines of dialogue, if later you decide to change, or delete, the character who's speaking them.

Your aim, therefore, should be to work from large to small, overview to detail. First, you should analyse and adjust the aim and structure of the whole screenplay. On a second run, you should revise the characters, and then, in succeeding edits, the individual scenes, the dialogue and the descriptions, finishing with a general tidying up and check for presentation. By giving yourself permission to concentrate on one thing at a time, you will be able to focus efficiently and avoid tinkering.

Focus point

Plan to edit the script in successive runs – working in order from overview to the smallest detail of action and description.

First reading

After allowing as much time to pass as you can, bring the script out and find yourself a quiet place where you won't be disturbed. Lock the door, turn off your phone and email, and read the entire script through in one sitting. First impressions are crucial. This is the closest you'll ever come to seeing the script fresh, as others do. Take in the whole shape of it in one go, the dips and climaxes, the energy and the momentum, or lack of it.

You can read on the computer screen, but I recommend reading a printed copy, to give yourself a new perspective. Read it either in your head or out loud.

Key idea

Read the script first time without interruption – this is the closest you'll ever get to seeing it with someone else's eyes.

Keep a pen in your hand and scribble marks and notes as you go – not too detailed because you want to keep the flow of reading. But mark anything that seems relevant – passages that flag or are particularly strong; characters that blossom or that are contradictory; sparkling lines and shifts in tone. If you have a new idea, jot it down as fast as you can and go back to reading.

Keep going until you get to the end. Then – however good or bad you think it is – congratulate yourself. You have written something that you can now make better.

Most writers find their first reading a mixed experience. At worst, you'll wonder how on earth you could have written scenes as bad as some in the script. How did you allow the story and characters to get so lost? How did the dialogue and action become so flat/ unbelievable/overwrought/undercooked?

But there will also be reasons to be hopeful – if only that it will never be that bad again!

Now the real work starts.

Snapshot exercise

Put the script aside, and ask yourself what it's all about. Where is it most alive? Now turn back to the premise you made when you first planned your script. Does the script reflect it, or has it shifted? If so, is that shift one you want to keep, or should you think about revising the script so that it more accurately reflects the original idea?

What's it all about?

It's very easy to lose sight of the original spark in the process of getting the words down. Suppose the heart of your premise is a twist on a 'boy meets girl' story, set in outer space. Whenever you mentioned the space element, people's eyes lit up. That was the spark. But somehow, in the writing, the setting has been pushed into the background. The characters could be anywhere. Perhaps, in future drafts, you should bring the location into the foreground – ensuring that everything from plot twists to subsidiary characters builds on the specific stresses and strains that arise from living in space.

By contrast, you may have discovered a new and richer seam of story as you wrote the first draft. Space has become less important and new settings work better. Maybe you've discovered that the original flaw – inhibition – masked the real flaw – jealousy. In such cases, go back to the premise and rewrite it.

A third possibility is that on reading the script you realize that there is a major flaw in the premise that needs to be attended to. Perhaps the goals aren't strong enough, the obstacles not consistent enough, the inner story or stakes not clearly enough defined. If necessary, work though Chapter 3 again until you are confident that you have a premise that works, based on the new information you've gained from writing the story from beginning to end. Make it as strong as you can now, and the next stages of revising will go so much more smoothly.

You might like to write your premise (changed or not) on a Post-it note and stick it close to your monitor as you revise.

Write

Without referring to the script or treatment, write an outline of the story from memory – the overarching goal, the shape of the inner and outer stories, the main plot and subplots, the key characters and scenes.

Now look back at the treatment and script. What did you forget or miss out? Do you really need them?

We often automatically improve stories when we recall them. It's possible that your memory of the structure will be a good guide to where the script should now be heading and that the parts you didn't remember might well be those which can safely be cut.

Checking for tone

Getting the tone right will be one of the most important tasks of the rewrite, but it will take time. To begin with, you may see it only in glimpses – a scene here, a line of dialogue there. There may be only one or two places in the entire first draft that feel right, but you'll know when you read them.

Joe Eszterhas, screenwriter

'Tone is everything. The tone of your script is even more important than the structure of it. It is the key to your script's success. If your tone is off, the movie will not work.'

Mark these moments most emphatically, so you can build on them in the next draft. Look back over them. What do they have in common? Find a particularly strong section and pin it up next to your computer, to remind yourself what you are aiming for.

Starting to revise

For the moment, don't try rewriting the script itself. Step back and take the long view. The best way to develop your second draft is to write a new treatment. If you wrote a treatment earlier, you can revise this, or you may find it easier to start again with a blank sheet.

If you didn't write a treatment earlier, but dived in without a plan, you must write one now.

A fresh treatment allows you to take an overview and see the shape. It is much easier to rearrange the elements of your story as a treatment than dive into the confusion of your 90- to 500-page first-draft script.

Key idea

Start your second-draft script as a treatment.

Go back to the basics. Look back over the chapters on structure and remind yourself of the essentials, especially GOATS: Goal, Obstacle, Action, Tactics, Stakes. Look at where your script holds to these, and where it deviates from them.

Look at the overall length of the script and the relative lengths of each act. Look carefully at the actions of the central character, and her growth, or otherwise.

There are certain flaws you will almost certainly find you need to deal with. They occur in 99.9 per cent of first-draft scripts.

YOUR SCRIPT IS FULL OF CLICHÉS AND THINGS THAT DON'T WORK

Yes, it's a first draft. That's what they're like. The question isn't whether they're in the script now, but whether they'll be in the script when you've finished editing.

To avoid that, let me introduce you to my cliché buster.

The problem with most scripts is that their writers hold on to their bad ideas for too long. This applies to all kinds of ideas – of structure, character, lines of dialogue, moments of action – and all kinds of writers. Inexperienced writers hold on to a bad idea because they're afraid they may not find a better one. Experienced writers also hold on to bad ideas, but they generally do it because the idea worked in the past so therefore ought to work again. This is often not the case.

Both kinds of writer go into denial – saying things like 'It's not really important' or 'The director will fix it.' But it's a lie. You don't want bad ideas in your script, however trivial they may seem. And what if the director doesn't fix it? There'll be enough mistakes that you don't spot – it's your responsibility to fix those you find.

 ## Focus point

If you spot a problem, it's your responsibility to fix it, and yours alone.

The cliché buster works because most bad ideas come in one of two forms:

1 **They work, but they're familiar and clichéd, or simply boring.**
2 **They're exciting and different… but they don't work.**

To use the cliché buster, take a page of your notebook and divide it into two columns. The first column you label 'Boring but works' and the second 'Exciting but doesn't work'.

Now, when you have a problem, of whatever kind, you brainstorm all the possible answers. Each possible solution will either work but be boring, or be fresh and different but not work. Write it in the appropriate column. Keep going, filling up the page, going on to further pages if necessary.

At some point, I guarantee it, you'll find a solution that both *works and is exciting*. When you find it, write it across both columns, give a loud cheer and use it. You've used the cliché buster.

Boring but works	Exciting but doesn't work
boring workable idea	exciting unworkable idea
boring workable idea	exciting unworkable idea
etc…	etc…
Solution – works and is exciting!	

Let's say you were writing *Gravity* and were stuck trying to find the cause for the astronauts to be marooned in space. You'd had a first idea – a power failure. It works, but it's rather dull and a cliché. You turn on the cliché buster. You have a thousand thoughts. You think of more workable clichés – a fuel leak, a computer glitch, a human error. Other ideas are wonderful, but just don't work for your story – an alien attack, or one of the astronauts is a terrorist or has a nervous breakdown …

After a time, it hits you: a cloud of space debris. It's not a cliché but it works. In fact, it's exciting – a very real contemporary threat. Fanfare. You move on.

Boring but works	Exciting but doesn't work
a fuel leak a computer glitch a human error …	an alien attack one of the astronauts is a terrorist a nervous breakdown …
a cloud of space debris!!!	

You can use the cliché buster for all kinds of script issues, from the overall concept, to character details, right down to a single line of dialogue or description. The solution will usually arrive in a few minutes or even faster. Just occasionally, it will take longer – maybe much longer. Stay with it, even if the problem seems trivial. The longer it takes to find the answer, the more important it is that you find it, and the more it will transform your script.

I once, for example, spent days trying to work out what a relatively minor character did as a job. I was growing annoyed with myself, but no answer to this apparently trivial problem satisfied me. Finally, after what felt like weeks, the answer came out of the blue. That answer entirely transformed the story, and became the basis of my most successful script.

Edward Burns, writer-director

'It's an enormous wall that's built between you and your dreams. And if every day, you just chip away … It may take ten years, but eventually you just might see some light.'

YOUR SCRIPT IS TOO LONG

Length is not important for a first draft, but it must be addressed for the second. If you've laid out the script professionally, using the industry format and Courier 12-point font, then your script should run at roughly one page per screen minute. This is approximate and varies according to genre and style.

Dialogue runs faster than description. So a page of action could take much longer than one minute on screen. At the extreme, the wedding scene in the first act of *The Deer Hunter* (written by Deric Washburn and Michael Cimino) famously took up no more than a few lines of script and ran for 51 minutes in the final movie). Conversely, a very dialogue-heavy script may run faster than a page a minute. This is common in TV scripts, especially soaps, which tend to have more dialogue than cinema films. A soap script could typically come in at 60 pages for a TV half-hour.

However, in most scripts, with an average balance of dialogue and action, this will balance out.

If writing for cinema, you should normally aim at delivering 90 to 110 pages. UK producers prefer scripts just under 100 pages long, whereas US producers are a little more flexible with early drafts. TV dramas vary between feature length (90–120 minutes), TV hour (48–54 minutes) or half-hour (24–27 minutes) – with the page lengths pro rata (subject to the point about soaps above).

Too long and you're probably overwriting, or have too many plot strands or major characters.

The other possibility is that your story is simply too complicated. Ask yourself whether it would work better as a series. But be honest – length doesn't necessarily mean depth. For your script to work as a series, you'll need more than just a long story, you'll need a story that sustains over time. Rather than overstaying your welcome, it's always better to leave the audience wanting more.

 ## Edit

Look first at the structure. Is there a plot strand that could be lifted out and leave the main storyline unchanged? Are you giving us information we don't really need? Are there distracting diversions, however entertaining they may be? If so, they should go. They're not helping your story and are simply taking up valuable space. If cutting them would remove something you'd miss, find a way to put that something in somewhere else.

Be determined in your cutting – you'll be amazed by how much better the story runs.

YOUR SCRIPT IS TOO SHORT

Too short and you probably haven't fully developed the characters, or your scenes are too dry and need fleshing out.

However, it could be that your story actually works better as a shorter drama, and that you should be aiming for a different time slot, after all.

 ## Write

Give yourself time on the page to enjoy each scene and bring out the emotions and the action that they deserve. If your story is very linear, you may need to add a subplot or two, and possibly develop minor characters or add new ones to give us different perspectives and a variety of pace.

 ## Paul Thomas Anderson, director and screenwriter

'Screenwriting is like ironing. You move forward a little bit and go back and smooth things out.'

THE FIRST ACT IS TOO LONG

Every first draft takes too long to get to the point. We all believe the audience needs to know stuff before the story starts, and mostly we're wrong. Even if you've worked hard to try to avoid this in the treatment, you'll still find scenes that are there to 'set up' what happens later. Cut them. You'll surprised how little the audience needs to become involved in a story. We don't have to know your hero's full backstory – the fact that he was abandoned when he was one year old, went to army college, flunked out and got a girl pregnant. Not yet. All we need to know is that there's an interesting, flawed guy in jeopardy. The vital points can be slid in later, once the story is up and running.

Karl Kraus, playwright

'A writer is someone who can make a riddle out of an answer.'

Cutting all that information allows you to intrigue, tease and draw the audience in. You can leave hints and suggestions of a darker past, without going into boring detail.

Key idea

Intrigue us, don't bore us.

Another reason for a slow Act One is that the plot points aren't where you think they are. You may well feel you have an inciting incident on page 10 and a turning point on page 27, as all the books advise – but do you? Very often, in first drafts, it turns out that the climax on page 27 would work much better as the inciting incident and moved up to page 10. And the most effective Act One turning point can regularly be found lurking around page 60 or even page 90!

Key idea

Almost every early draft takes too long to start.

The dangers of a late Act One turning point can be seen in the 1987 thriller *No Way Out*. US Navy officer Tom Farrell meets Susan Atwell and they begin a deeply felt affair. However, unknown to him, she is involved with his boss at the Pentagon, Secretary of Defense David Brice. The first act is clearly building towards a confrontation, which doesn't come for 45 minutes, during which plot details are 'set up' for later in the film – making that section of the movie feel at least 15 minutes too long.

Luckily, when the climax to the act finally comes, there's a big enough shock twist to compensate for the delay and the audience is recaptured. But, maybe because of the flawed Act One, the film has never quite achieved the classic status it could have.

Edit

Remove all surplus setting-up scenes. Create questions, not answers.

Now, ask yourself where your strongest turning points are in the script. Where does the protagonist have to deal with the really big challenges? At what point do things go completely wrong and he has to make the big decision to sort them out?

Seek out your real inciting incident and Act One turning point, and move them up to where they belong. Cut anything that gets in the way. To do this will probably mean deleting even more 'setting-up' scenes. Great.

THE PROTAGONIST DOESN'T KNOW SHE'S IN TROUBLE AT THE END OF ACT ONE

The protagonist must know he's got a problem before the start of the second act. It's no good if we know but he doesn't.

The Terminator would not work if Sarah Connor didn't know at the end of the first act that the Terminator was trying to kill her and that she has to run. She may not know what it is or why it's there or how to deal with it yet, but she knows she's in deep trouble.

Key idea

If your central character doesn't know he has a serious problem, it's not your first-act turning point.

Harry and Sally know that they face a massive personal challenge if they are to stay friends and not sleep together. The murderer in Louis Malle's *Ascenseur pour l'échafaud* (*Lift to the Scaffold*) knows that he's trapped in a lift and will be arrested if he doesn't escape. Ron Woodroof, in *Dallas Buyers Club,* knows he could die of AIDS and that to get the medical drugs he needs will mean breaking the law.

So, if your protagonist doesn't yet know he's in serious trouble at the end of Act One, your turning point is to be found later – when he does.

Edit

Locate the point where your central character knows he's in deep trouble, and cut, move, amend anything that is needed to ensure that we get to it on page 25–27, or before. Be professional. Anything less is selling yourself and your audience short.

THE PROTAGONIST IS TOO PASSIVE AND REACTIVE

Something about the process of writing a first draft brings all the other characters into sharper focus than the protagonist. We feel closest to the central character, and as a result we see the story through his eyes – but also give him less to do. In almost every first draft I've seen, the protagonist is passive – failing to take action when needed – and fails to push his story forwards.

One crucial job of the second, and any following, draft is to give the story back to the central character. He must make his own decisions and take control. It must be he who drives the story and takes action wherever possible.

Search through the script for all instances where other characters take over, minor instances and major. Where his boss unlocks a door, have *him* unlock it instead. If the protagonist's husband decides they should save their son, make it *her* decision.

In *Gravity*, Dr Ryan Stone is not an experienced astronaut; she's a medical engineer on her first mission. But when she's marooned in space, she doesn't remain passive but fights constantly to find ways to return to Earth. In *12 Years a Slave*, Solomon Northup has next to no rights or powers, and yet he is constantly active despite the dangers and constantly facing moral dilemmas. His decisions are sometimes negative – keeping his head down, refusing a fellow slave when she wants to die – but often positive – fighting his first owner, writing for help.

 Edit

Go through the script again, marking each point where the protagonist could action, each instance where he stands back instead of taking the story into his own hands.

THE PROTAGONIST'S GOAL IS CLEAR BUT THE STORY STILL FEELS UNFOCUSED AND WEAK

Have you focused the forces against him? Do you have a strong enough antagonist? Do you have a clear antagonist at all?

Your protagonist can only be as strong as the forces that face him. His obstacles must be large to draw out his full potential. This may mean a 'bad guy' antagonist. Or it may be a romantic antagonist – in many romance stories the lovers are their own antagonists, each forcing the other to change. In some stories, such as some war movies, the enemy is invisible for much of the time – in such cases, you need to seek out closer antagonists to focus the narrative, such as oppressive senior officers and untrustworthy or difficult fellow soldiers.

Be careful to ensure that your antagonist runs the distance. The 1960s thriller *Bullitt* is mostly famous for a climactic car chase through the hills of San Francisco. This takes place at the midpoint of the movie. However, the chase ends with the death of the film's most dangerous hitman. Unable to replace his threat with one that is as great, or greater, the movie loses energy and the second half fails to live up to the promise of the first.

More careful attention to the antagonists could have ensured either that the most threatening character survived to the end, or that he was followed by one who was even more vicious, so as to raise the stakes.

In the series *House*, it's important that Gregory House is faced with credible, strong opponents to focus the stories. In most of the series, the hospital administrator, Lisa Cuddy, is the primary antagonist, with individual episodes bringing House into conflict with different members of his team, patients and their families.

However, too many antagonists could weaken a story. Keep the conflict focused. In *What's Eating Gilbert Grape*, almost everyone in Gilbert's circle is to some extent his antagonist, stopping him growing up. To avoid confusing the audience with so many antagonists, the main storyline focuses on the difficulties caused by his brother Arnie. He creates Gilbert's most pressing problems throughout.

 Key idea

Build up the antagonist and focus the conflict.

 Snapshot exercise

Make sure that you are clear where the main challenges to your protagonist are coming from. If necessary, create a new character, build up an existing antagonist or combine more than one to ensure that the conflict is focused and not diffused.

THE ENDING IS TOO SHORT

This may feel counter-intuitive, especially if your first draft runs to 300 or so pages, but while first drafts generally spend too much time at the start, they tend also to run out of energy at the end and finish before they've done the story full justice. In the last chapter, you were asked to race through the third act, to give it energy, jumping plot holes and leaving questions unanswered. Now is the time to revisit it.

If you've discovered your Act One turning point hiding three-quarters of the way through the script, then you may already have realized that you need to do more work on the second and third acts. Even if the Act One revisions are not quite so drastic, you will almost certainly find, on closer inspection, that your central character has not quite completed her journey.

 Key idea

Most early drafts need more development of the end.

Problems with endings usually mean that the writer hasn't fully worked through the inner story. In the movie *What Lies Beneath*, Claire, the wife of a renowned scientist, begins to suspect that her husband may be involved in a murder. As the tension grows, she finds herself being haunted by a woman who might have been the victim. However, the writers fail to develop a coherent inner story for her. Matters come to a head but, without the inner journey to help them, the writers can't work out how to end the story. The film ends in a series of melodramatic, but repetitive, twists. The failure to create a satisfying last act spoils what is up until then a very watchable thriller.

It would have been tempting to end *Tootsie* at the point where Michael Dorsey has revealed his true gender live on TV to an audience of millions. But his story is not finished. He has learned to connect his masculine and feminine sides, to temper his aggression, but now he has to prove that he can do the same in his ordinary life. He has to patch things up with the father of the woman he loves, and then face the woman herself, whom he has lied to all this time. Only once he has done all this, and not relapsed into his old self, will the story be over.

Key idea

Ending, inner story and theme – if you have a problem with one, look at the other two.

Write

Look at the ending and ask yourself what the protagonist has still to learn. Have you fully tested her out? If she's supposed to be growing more caring, have you really proved it? Does she need a final challenge to deal with any last doubts? Does she have to take what she's learned back to her world and show that she has really changed?

Being cruel to be kind

If you find you are cutting out scenes and plot points that you love, that probably means that you should be! If you are in love with a scene that's causing problems, that's often a sign that it's tilting the script out of balance and needs to be examined or ditched – if only because, if you didn't love it, you'd have cut it already!

You've started editing, and editing is part nurture, part murder. You must be caring and ruthless. The famous instruction is 'Kill your darlings', variously attributed to many writers but most probably coined by the poet and critic Arthur Quiller-Couch. It's often misunderstood. He didn't mean you must cut every moment you love. A good script needs some odd moments and surprises. Resist the temptation to polish away all the interest.

If in doubt, go back to the cliché buster. If it works and is interesting, then keep it. If you still can't decide between something that works and something that is interesting, choose the interesting. The world likes writers whose ideas work, but there are far too few writers whose ideas are interesting.

 Joe Eszterhas, screenwriter, *The Devil's Guide to Hollywood*

'Don't "nice" your script up.'

However, this is not an excuse to be lazy. 'Kill your darlings' means don't be precious. Cut anything in your script that gets in the way of telling the story. And, most tellingly, it's probably the very character/scene/line of dialogue that you love that is holding everything up.

If you have a problem cutting out your favourite parts, the solution is simple. Cut them, and keep them in a separate clips file. When you reread the script, I guarantee that in almost every event you'll forget they were ever there. If you do miss them, you can always put them back.

And if you don't, you have a store of great ideas for use in some future script.

 Key idea

Editing is part nurture, part murder. Be caring and ruthless.

 Edit

Go back to your board of Post-its or cards, and cut, add and rearrange until you've found a shape that works better. Keep going until the structure feels solid. Trust your gut instincts.

Next, redraft your treatment to match the decisions you've made and workshop it (see below).

 Edit/write

Keep a safety copy of your first draft script and rework your screenplay to match the new treatment.

Writing the second draft will involve shifting gears many times from editing to creating, as you go from cutting and moving scenes to creating new ones. This can be tricky. Remember, as before, that when you're creating a new scene you're back in first draft speed-writing mode.

Don't try to edit at the same time as creating. Don't try to make it good. Don't worry, for the time being, about the quality of the writing. All that matters for this run is the structure. The rest will come later.

Discuss the changes and your reasons for them. Listen to feedback and make any further changes you feel will help.

Where to next?

Now that you've begun work on the big picture, it's time to focus in on some of the other story strands in your script – the subplots.

18

Revising subplots – adding texture to the story

With the main planks of the structure in place, it's time to look at the smaller timbers. Without any subplots, a story can feel very restricted. Subplots add variety and give you the opportunity to show the audience different sides of your main characters which the main plot cannot, by its nature, reveal.

To avoid feeling too one-paced or claustrophobic, a movie or single drama should have at least one subplot, and can have up to five, although the fourth and fifth plot-lines will need to be very simple to avoid overbalancing the whole. More than five subplots will be too complicated for a one-off, and the average is two or three.

For example, in John Ford's classic Western *The Searchers* (screenplay by Frank S. Nugent), Ethan Edwards and Martin Pawley spend years on the trail of Debbie, Ethan's niece and Martin's adoptive sister, who has been abducted by a Comanche war party. The main story focuses on the long search and shows Ethan's fierce determination and Martin's growing self-confidence.

Meanwhile, the first subplot develops their personal relationship, coloured by the fact that Ethan shows elements of racism, and Martin has some American-Indian blood. Initially antagonistic, this subplot allows Nugent to show a softening of Ethan's attitude that could not have been shown in the main plot.

A second subplot follows the growing but complicated romantic relationship between Martin and a girl from a neighbouring ranch, again allowing the script to draw out otherwise hidden sides to his character, while keeping the script moving forwards.

How to develop and edit subplots

The same techniques apply when creating and editing subplots as with the main plot: GOATS – Goal, Obstacle, Action, Tactics, Stakes.

Decide who the lead character of the subplot is – usually it will be the same protagonist as in the main story, though not always. What is his goal, what's stopping him, what actions does he take, what new tactics is he forced to adopt, what's at stake?

Larger subplots may have a detailed three-act structure with turning points, although smaller subplots will be simpler, with perhaps only two turning points, or one. A very short subplot may contain as little as a brief beginning with a single turning point leading to the final battle.

> ## Key idea
>
> Subplots have similar structures to a main storyline, but generally simplified.

Often the turning points of different plot-lines will be close together, to avoid multiple climaxes – indeed, one event may be a turning point in two or more plot-lines. For example, when Rosa goes into labour in *All about My Mother*, this is a turning point in the main story, and also in Rosa's own subplot.

A subplot may be resolved at the end or sometimes be left hanging – although you should avoid leaving your story with too many loose ends. The resolution may indeed come through the resolution of one of the other plot-lines, For example, an important character may die, bringing to an end two subplots that concern him.

However, subplots cannot live alone, separate from the main plot. They need to feed into the main plot and influence it in some way. If you can lift a subplot out completely and have no effect on the main story, then it probably should (and very likely will) be cut.

The Rosa subplot directly affects the main story, as it brings Manuela's procrastination to a halt, and forces her finally to meet the father of her son.

 Key idea

A subplot must directly influence the main storyline.

Relationship-line subplots

Many subplots develop the relationships in a story. A subplot like this will be called a 'relationship line'. One or more relationship-line subplots are very useful, especially in a more action-oriented film, to contrast with the action line of the main plot.

In *Seven*, the main story follows two detectives as they try to stop a serial killer. One relationship-line subplot develops between them. Mills is new and angry and Somerset is tired and about to retire. They have very different views of policing (a potentially clichéd 'buddy movie' subplot, but one which is written with delicacy and freshness here). Meanwhile, a second relationship-line subplot develops between Mills and his wife, revealing tensions within their marriage. Both relationship lines come together when she shares news of her pregnancy with Somerset. The subplots directly complicate the plot when, in the climax, the killer goads Mills with the fact that Somerset knew and he didn't. Although each subplot is given a very simple structure and very little screen time, you couldn't remove either of them without profoundly changing the resolution of the main plot.

Action-line subplots

If your main story is itself a relationship story, you may need an action-line subplot for contrast and to give the story a stronger spine.

The screwball comedy *His Girl Friday* tells the story of Hildy, ex-ace reporter and ex-wife of editor Walter Burns, and his fight to get her back. To do this, he hires her for the day to help reprieve a condemned man. This action-line subplot complicates Hildy's increasingly desperate attempts to leave and take up the new (quiet) life as a housewife that she's been hoping for. By the end, she wins the reprieve and realizes that she could never be a housewife. Walter wins back his ex-wife (though for how long is a question that the film leaves open at the end).

Action stories also often need action subplots to develop important side issues to the main plot. A bank heist, for example, may spark an action-line subplot involving a separate job that threatens to sabotage the main robbery.

Snapshot exercise

Is your main story an action-line story or a relationship-line story? Are there any subplots that are already present, perhaps in embryo, or which could be coaxed into life? What could they bring by way of new perspectives on the main characters or the story?

For each subplot line, define the main character (of the subplot), his goal and main obstacles. What actions will be demanded of him? Will he be challenged to change his tactics and grow, and how? What is at stake?

Finally, does each subplot directly affect the main plot? If not, look for ways to ensure that it does.

Focus point

Create subplots to explore hidden sides of your character and add contrast to the main plot.

Series subplots

Developing strong and revealing subplots is particularly important for a TV series. However, there is a limit to how many plot-lines the audience will be able to keep in their minds. To avoid confusion, many subplots should be kept short, possibly lasting only an episode or two.

Each of the main characters in *The West Wing* has at least one relationship line – C.J. Cregg, for example, has a running subplot that concerns her ageing father and another that concerns her abortive love-life.

Meanwhile, the main plot spins off into different action lines as the story evolves. However, not all are running at the same time. Each episode will focus on one to two main issues and around two to three subplots, some of which may never reappear again.

Dennis Potter's series *The Singing Detective* centres on a novelist, Marlow, who is in hospital with a life-threatening skin disease. The first action-line subplot follows the plot of a spy thriller that he is writing/hallucinating as he undergoes treatment. Relationship-line subplots develop out of his acerbic feelings towards his fellow patients and the staff, his more lustful feelings towards the attractive Nurse Mills, and his memories of a key event in his childhood. Potter keeps these relevant by making it clear that they all (including the thriller) not only reflect his inner journey but will have a direct effect on his struggle to be cured.

Subplot – pattern and repetition

Subplots have an additional role in giving you space to develop other aspects of your themes, widening perspectives and providing balance. To do this, you can deliberately create patterns and reversals, repeating motifs and reflecting similar situations with different outcomes.

For example, if your main story concerns a father–son relationship, there will be limits to how much a single story can explore alone. Including a subplot which involves another father and son can allow you to develop new angles and possibilities.

Techniques include the following:

- **Reflections** – developing a parallel to your main story in which different situations reflect the same themes. For example, a detective is tracking a murderer while his wife is trying to find out whether he's cheating on her.
- **Reversals** – showing how similar situations can go in totally different directions. For example, the protagonist is a slum kid gone wrong, while in the subplot we follow her best friend who went right.
- **Widening perspective** – one or more subplots that show many different angles on a problem, such as different forms of addiction.
- **Pattern** – repeating motifs help point out meanings and parallels, such as in Shakespeare's *King Lear* where the plot and subplots repeat images of blindness, madness, parent–child relationships, fear of betrayal and so on.
- **Balance** – creating subplots with contrasting tone or pace helps give variety to the overall story. A main plot that is very full of action could be balanced by a subplot that is more contemplative and interior, such as a romantic relationship. Conversely, a more intellectual main plot might be usefully balanced against a subplot which is energetic and visually active.

In Truffaut's autobiographical movie *Les Quatre Cent Coups* (*The Four Hundred Blows*), we follow the story of Antoine's increasingly fraught attempts to grow up in the backstreets of Paris without being crushed by authority.

Relationship lines complicate his personal search as he discovers that his mother is a street-walker, tries to find a way of living with his stepfather and stays overnight with the family of his best friend. Each of these lines explores different attitudes towards family and different kinds of adult behaviour. Each ends up making his life worse. None, though, gives him the solution to his problems, which he must work out for himself.

The West Wing often balances subplots with a different tone, while using other subplots to explore different angles of the same issue. In one storyline that runs over two episodes – 'Gaza' and 'Memorial Day' – a congressional delegation to Gaza is blown up by a roadside bomb, four people are killed and Josh's PA, Donna, severely injured. The main plot concerns finding out who's behind the killings and how to retaliate.

One major subplot contrasts this high-tension storyline with flashbacks of Donna talking to Palestinians and Israelis – a more thoughtful strand that explores the corrupting emotions of revenge from a different angle. A second, romantic subplot follows Josh as he flies to see Donna in hospital and grows to realize what he feels for her. A smaller subplot develops the question of honesty vs duty when a new NSC aide, Kate, speaks out of turn about the dangers of retaliation.

Write

Examine one of your subplots and how it relates to the main storyline. Brainstorm possible repetitions, patterns, reversals and motifs that you can bring out more strongly.

Set the tone and pace so that it contrasts with the main story and with the other plot-lines, to give variety.

Do this with each subplot in turn.

Subplot structures

Subplots can be run alongside the main plot, overlapping with it throughout the story; they can also cut across the main plot, taking the story in a new direction (a crossplot); or they can virtually stand alone.

OVERLAPPING

In most cases, a subplot will arise naturally out of the story and intercut with it, adding complication. It may start before the main story or after. It should ideally end before the main story. If it can only be ended after the main story, ensure that you end it quickly or you'll risk leaving the audience with a feeling of anticlimax, as the outcome of the main story will almost always be more compelling to them than any of the subplots.

CROSSPLOT

In some films and series, a crossplot can take over for a long period of time, before we return to the main plot. This can be dangerous. If the audience is more invested in the main story than the crossplot, they will feel cheated, or simply bored, by this new storyline. Alternatively, the crossplot could turn out to be more interesting and take energy from the main story. However, if the crossplot is equally strong and has a clear and direct effect on the protagonist's main goal, this structure can be very effective.

Examples include *Witness*, where the entire second act effectively suspends the main story while the lead character recovers from his wounds, hidden in an Amish village, before

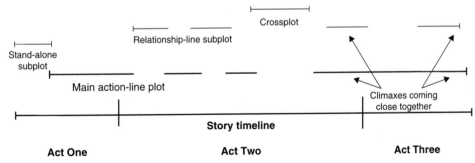

Figure 18.1 Typical subplots

the principal storyline resumes in Act Three. (For a detailed analysis of the subplots in *Witness* and in *Tootsie*, see Linda Seger's classic *Making a Good Script Great*.)

STAND-ALONE

One of the most useful functions of a subplot is to fix an otherwise flat opening. Some stories are forced to build slowly. We need to know the situation and characters before anything makes sense. However, you can't afford to write ten or more undramatic pages while we wait for you to explain the intricacies of life in ancient Mesopotamia or why two detectives are staking out a gangster's girlfriend. This is where an opening stand-alone comes in.

Starting the film with an energetic subplot gives you a stronger opening and buys you time to develop other ideas, introduce characters and build up the information we need before the main story can begin. This subplot could continue to run through the main story (overlapping) but such a subplot may not be logical or desirable. Creating a stand-alone subplot solves the problem. A small, self-contained story can draw the audience in and lead into the events that follow.

 Key idea

A stand-alone subplot can solve problems such as a necessarily slow opening.

The danger with stand-alones is that they do exactly that. Like any subplot, they need to be linked strongly in to the main story.

In *Stakeout*, Chris, a detective, falls in love with the ex-girlfriend of a brutal escaped convict, whose home he's staking out. The story needs time to develop their relationship before the murderer appears. But this would yield a very slow start. So Jim Kouf's script opens with an energetic chase sequence. This introduces the lead character, but now in high-level action. As a result of the mistakes Chris makes during the chase, he is carpeted by his boss and given this stake-out as a punishment – ensuring that the stand-alone sequence is bound tightly into the main plot and doesn't float free.

Workshop

Outline at least two possible subplots in the workshop and listen to feedback. Do the subplots fit with the overall story? Do they feel part of the whole? Does each affect the main storyline or does it risk floating free? Discuss any other action or relationship lines that might add balance and new dimensions to the story.

Where to next?

As we've seen, almost all cinema and TV screenplays work best in three linear acts, progressing forwards in time. However, in attempting to fit the template, you may genuinely find that you are doing your story a disfavour.

You may find that something essential isn't working. You may find that the order feels wrong, or that you're distorting the meaning, forcing it into a shape that feels untruthful. In such cases, you may have a story that needs a different structure. In the next two chapters, we look at situations when you may need to jump in time, fragment the story or write in other structures than the standard three acts.

19

Playing with time – flashbacks and non-linear stories

Most screen stories run seamlessly forwards, without large jumps in time. However, there may be occasions when you need to break this rule. Changing the timeline can be very useful in dealing with a number of storytelling problems. However, playing with time, through flashbacks and fractured or multiple timelines, should be relevant to the story, not imposed upon it as a gimmick, and also introduced with care, so as not to lose the audience.

> ## Linda Aronson, in *The 21st-century Screenplay*
>
> *'Flashback is one of the most exciting storytelling techniques available to screenwriters.'*

Using time jumps to help your story

We saw earlier that a slow opening can be countered by creating a more dynamic subplot that can start the story. Another powerful method would be to open with a flashback from a more dramatic scene later in the script. More radical changes to the storytelling order (the timeline) can be used to balance screenplays that change pace awkwardly or even shift genre – say, from action to drama.

There are essentially seven ways you can change the timeline of your story. However, each also has its particular uses and meaning:

1 **Flashback from the Act Three climax**
2 **Redemptive flashback**
3 **Incremental flashback**
4 **Exposition flashback**
5 **Ironic flashback**
6 **Parallel timelines**
7 **Fractured timeline.**

(For much of the material in the first half of this chapter I am indebted to Linda Aronson and her excellent breakdown of flashbacks and fractured narrative in *The 21st-century Screenplay*.)

> ## Key idea
>
>
>
> Each type of flashback has its own meaning.

1 FLASHBACK FROM THE ACT THREE CLIMAX

If the ending is tragic (such as the death of the hero), consider starting your story at the end with a flashback from the end. By telling the audience how it ends in advance, you prepare them for the bad news. Linda Aronson calls this kind of flashback 'detective story of the human heart'. The central question of the story now becomes not 'What's going to happen?' so much as 'Why?'

In *Sunset Boulevard*, the film begins with a body floating in a swimming pool. We flash back to find out who he was, and why he's there. At the end of the film, we find ourselves back where we started, but with a deeper understanding. However, the story doesn't always end there – once we have returned, there will normally be one more twist that deepens or subverts the meaning one final time.

2 REDEMPTIVE FLASHBACK

In theory, you could start with a flashback from any strong turning point in the story, but generally the most powerful (aside from the end) opens at the end of Act Two. Thus, we first meet our protagonist at one of his lowest moments, when all seems lost. Flashing back to the beginning, we retrace his story to find out how he got here. In due course, we find ourselves back at the end of Act Two, and he still has Act Three to redeem himself.

A flashback from the end of the second act can thus be very useful if you want to underline the redemptive nature of the story. It can also help you if you have a large jump of time within the second act itself. In *12 Years a Slave*, we first see Solomon Northup at his lowest point. He has almost given up hope. He has been enslaved for many years, his life is harsh, and there are few comforts. The film flashes back to his previous life as a free man, to show how he came to be a slave, and retraces the story to where we began – at the end of Act Two. From here, we continue into the third act to see whether, and how, he can escape.

The Act Two flashback allows the film elegantly to compress the many years of slavery that take place in the middle of the story. And the drama and dark tone of the opening compensate for what would otherwise have been a very slow, undramatic start.

3 INCREMENTAL FLASHBACK

The incremental flashback is a very powerful and evocative technique. It's particularly useful if you have a powerful inciting incident that took place much earlier. The script opens with a brief impressionistic glimpse. Something dramatic is happening, but we can't yet tell what. As the story evolves, we keep returning to this flashback, each time adding a little more clarity, until at the end of the film we finally understand what it was that started the whole story going.

Throughout the movie of *Catch-22*, we keep returning to a moment when the protagonist, Yossarian, was on a bombing mission. Gradually, we learn that a fellow crew member has a minor injury, and Yossarian is trying to bandage him. Near the end of the film, the bandage is in place, and then, to his (and our) shock, Yossarian discovers that the man has been dying from a less visible and massive injury all along.

This realization of futility is the incident that, we now understand, underlies the entire plot. By highlighting it, screenwriter Buck Henry has placed it at the film's thematic heart.

 Key idea

An incremental flashback puts the inciting incident at the screenplay's heart.

 Snapshot exercise

If you feel you need to begin with a flashback, examine the three types above to see which works best for your story.

Take a scene from your script (or create a new one) and try it out at the start. You'll almost certainly need to make some adjustments. Does it work for the story you want to tell? Is it strong enough to draw an audience in? Is there enough atmosphere, enough mystery, enough dramatic action? Does it need shortening, so as to keep the momentum?

Now look at where you return to the scene. Does the return have resonance and power? Does it give the script the meaning you want, or send it in the wrong direction?

4 EXPOSITION FLASHBACK

An exposition flashback is a scene that the writer has inserted purely to give information and, as with all information and setting up scenes, should be avoided if at all possible.

Inexperienced screenwriters imagine that, if a character describes something in the past, we must automatically see it on screen. The problem comes when that previous event is itself undramatic. In most situations, it's more effective to stay in the present scene, and build the drama there.

Key idea

Exposition flashbacks tend to be undramatic and are generally best avoided.

If you absolutely must write an exposition flashback, then make sure that the scene itself is as dramatic and involving as possible – high stakes, high action. In *The Usual Suspects*, Verbal (a small low-life criminal) is being interrogated by a policeman who's trying to catch Turkish master criminal Keyser Söze. Kint's version of the story is told in a number of flashbacks. In one short exposition flashback near the end, for example, we witness Keyser Söze becoming the cold-hearted criminal he now is. The scene works because our interest in the man has been built up over 92 pages – but, more importantly, because the scene itself is inherently dramatic, cruel and emotionally affecting.

Unless you can create an exposition scene that's as strong as this, find another way. (See Chapter 23.)

Write

Take an event that's currently referred to in dialogue in the script and write it as a flashback scene. Make the new scene as dramatically strong as possible, using all the techniques we've mentioned.

Now turn back to the original dialogue, in which the event is mentioned. Make that scene as dramatically strong as possible.

Does the new scene add something, or does it interrupt the flow? Does the dialogue gain something from the interruption or is the exposition scene merely hammering home a point that had already been made? Which works better? Have fun playing around.

5 IRONIC FLASHBACK

A tongue-in-cheek variation of the exposition flashback, the ironic flashback flashes back to show the audience that the past is *not* what we supposed it was. If a character announces that her presentation was a massive success, we immediately cut back to show us her audience looking bored.

The ironic flashback is almost invariably very fast – the moment we've got the gag, we return to the present. It has also become very predictable and, unless you have a stunningly fresh and original variation, is also best avoided.

The movie *Memento* uses an unusual variation of the ironic flashback to reflect its main theme. We start at the end, with the protagonist killing a man he suspects murdered his wife. But he has amnesia, so as the film unfolds the question that powers it becomes: did he kill the right man? Writer-director Christopher Nolan elects to tell the main story backwards so that the audience is constantly being placed in a similar position to the central character, unable to 'remember' what went before. So each short sequence starts a few minutes earlier than the previous scene, and often turns our previous understanding around.

 ## Tim Bevan, co-chairman, Working Title Films

'You've just got to know what all the tools are, and you've got to know how to use them and when to use them. Now that can only come from experience, but you've got to accept that there are tools. And that flashback, for instance, is a very handy tool. And flash forward is a very handy tool. And voice-over is a very handy tool. But if you use it all the time, then you're probably being lazy. It has to be part of your construction.'

6 PARALLEL TIMELINES

Sometimes a script feels totally unbalanced, the acts don't match, and plot points can't be made to arrive where they work best. This may be a candidate for parallel timelines.

By running two or more different timelines alongside each other and intercutting throughout the story, you can balance sequences that are very different in tone. *The Usual Suspects* alternates between two timelines using multiple flashbacks: Verbal Kint is being interrogated by the police while we see the story he's telling. By intercutting the two timelines, the film balances the slower, more thoughtful interrogation line (present) with a faster, more suspenseful action line (past). Furthermore, each flashback becomes a new clue in the detective story, ensuring that we, the audience, can play our part in working out what happened. Told in chronological order, the interrogation would have come as an anticlimax to the action that preceded it.

In Stephen Greenhorn's five-part supernatural drama *Marchlands*, we follow the stories of three families living in the same house in 1968, 1987 and 2010. Each is haunted, in a different way, by the spirit of a young girl who died mysteriously in 1967. As the three stories unfold, so the truth of what happened to the girl begins to emerge.

7 FRACTURED TIMELINE

The most extreme method of reorganizing time in a script is to break it up altogether, into fragments that intercut against the narrative logic, giving a fractured timeline.

There are many ways to fracture the timeline of a film and, as with the other kinds of flashbacks, you need to find which is appropriate according to the story you want to tell. In the ground-breaking Kurosawa movie *Rashomon* (co-written with Shinobu Hashimoto), we see four different versions of a murder, from four witnesses (including the ghost of the murdered man). In the German movie *Run, Lola, Run*, written by its director, Tom Tykwer, we are shown three different ways a situation might develop – one after the other; while Tarantino's *Pulp Fiction*, which he wrote with Roger Avary, begins and ends at the point which in 'real' time would be the middle of the story. It then flashes back to the start and jumps forward to the end before finishing in what is (chronologically) the middle once more!

Each structure has a different effect – highlighting, for example, questions about the nature of truth, fate or violence. Perhaps the most dramatically fractured film, *21 Grams*, is based on a classic three-act story, rearranged in an order that feels random on first viewing. The film follows three characters: a woman whose husband and children are knocked over and killed; the driver of the mini-van that killed them; and a severely ill man who is hired by the woman to wreak revenge. However, there is still a glimpse of three acts beneath it all. The first half-hour introduces the characters and the main story, the central hour develops them, and the final act leads up to the climax and final confrontation.

In a fractured timeline script, the writer still has to ensure that the audience has enough material (and incentive) to put the story together in their minds and enjoy the experience.

Brian Dunnigan, Head of Screenwriting, London Film School

'A lot of so-called non-linear is just reshuffling the pack. Just now, it's fashionable. However, non-linear is as old as storytelling.'

Snapshot exercise

Does your story have acts that rise in energy, or do the climaxes come at awkward times? Does the story start slowly or fade away at the end? Can the climaxes be moved, even if it means being ruthless with your scenes? If moving them is logically impossible, then can the problem be fixed by creating parallel or fractured timelines?

Cut up the scenes (or write them on cards/Post-its) and move them around so that the climaxes come at satisfactory places.

Try looking at how the scenes link together. If the story has a new energy and the links feel right, continue and see whether the new shape works throughout.

Key idea

Parallel and fractured timelines are worth exploring if you have a story that can't be easily balanced.

Playing with time on TV

It's rare for extremely fractured narratives to be seen on TV, but that doesn't mean it's not possible. Television often tends to play safer, assuming that audiences are not as sophisticated as cinema audiences, but the boundaries are always shifting, and new forms are constantly being tried. A series with a complex narrative structure might be more of a challenge, as you have to ensure that the viewers remember where they are from episode to episode, but if you take care it should be quite possible.

Key idea

Complex timelines can work strongly on TV if developed with care.

Dennis Potter's series *The Singing Detective* experimented with parallel storylines. The protagonist, a writer of crime novels, is fighting an obscure and dangerous skin disease, while at the same time we follow the story of the book he appears to be writing in his head – a very noir pulp crime novel. This is complicated by fantasy music scenes around his hospital bed. And to cap it off, Potter gives us a series of incremental flashbacks that are clearly building to a major emotional event that defined his childhood.

What could feel difficult to follow is made very watchable through a combination of humour and stylistic fun. The noir episodes are very enjoyable as parodies. At the same time, Potter makes it clear that everything relates back to the central question – will the writer recover? In a subtle way, we are made to feel that solving the crime, as well as digging out the writer's real-life childhood, will be crucial to ensuring that he lives.

More recently, the US series *Alcatraz* used flashbacks regularly to keep the audience off-balance as it interwove stories of a group of hardcore criminals who come back from the dead.

Making your time jumps work

Choosing your time structure is only the start. Every cut in time threatens to break the flow of the film and lose the audience. The more unusual the time leap, the greater the danger.

A jump forward of many months or years, – or any jump backwards at all – risks jerking the viewer right out of the story, never to be retrieved. Experienced writers know this, and build flash-forwards, flashbacks and fragmented time with great care.

For time jumps, use the following sequence:

1 **Prepare a time anchor.**

2 **Build to a cliffhanger.**

3 **Jump ... to a new cliffhanger.**

4 **Go straight into story.**

Focus point

Set each jump in time with care.

1 PREPARE A TIME ANCHOR

It's very easy for an audience to lose track of the time on screen. A novel can give you simple narrative clues (*Last night ... Two days later ...* etc.) that are denied to a film-maker, unless she uses the devices of voice-over narration or title cards. There's nothing wrong with using voice-over or titles to show the time; however, they aren't always appropriate and can feel heavy-handed, especially if there are a number of jumps in the story.

A more elegant method is to set an image or symbol to fix the time. This will be repeated after we jump back again, so that the audience knows we've returned. It could be a location, a character's position, a prop, anything that will make the situation clear.

Quentin Tarantino's first film, *Reservoir Dogs*, uses a flashback very early. After a prologue, the main story begins moments after a jewel-store robbery. There is immediate tension. One of the jewel thieves (Mr Orange) lies in the back of a car covered in blood. He's been shot and one of the other members of the gang, Mr White, is driving him fast to a warehouse, where he hopes to find help. The warehouse itself will be the time anchor, when we need it later in the movie ...

Key idea

It's easy for an audience to lose a sense of time. Give them anchors to ensure they know *what the time is.*

Snapshot exercise

Take your outgoing scene and set a time anchor that we'll see when we return. Remember the rule of description: make sure that it's an essential part of the drama, or it might get dropped. There's no harm in having two anchors or even three. Some audience members are slower than others. You want them all to be able to follow.

2 BUILD TO A CLIFFHANGER

The scene before the jump must end with suspense. The stronger the question left in the audience's mind, the easier it will be to make the jump. Build the jeopardy as powerfully as you can. The bomb is about to go off … The bride is about to reject the groom … The spaceship is about to crash …

The stronger the cliffhanger, the easier you'll make your return to that timeline, later in the story.

Key idea

Cut on a cliffhanger when you jump:

… At the warehouse, a third gang member arrives, Mr Pink. The three argue over when to get a doctor and whether they were betrayed. As Mr Orange lies bleeding, desperate for medical help, we cut back in time to …

Write

Create a strongly suspenseful ending to the outgoing scene. If necessary, cut the last lines or actions to leave even more uncertainty. But ensure that the jeopardy is high.

Jane Wittekind, ex-Head of Development, Enigma

'Flashbacks can make a script static. I like it when the pieces of a jigsaw fall into place, but you have to be careful not to create a static narrative. You must always be driving the story forwards.'

3 JUMP … TO A NEW CLIFFHANGER

After the jump in time, the audience will be disoriented and easily lost. Grab them immediately. Start the new scene with an urgent need or danger, as in Reservoir Dogs:

… From the warehouse, we cut back in time to Mr Pink, running down a street with a gun, chased by police. Without time to breathe, we are thrown into fresh jeopardy.

And immediately …

4 GO STRAIGHT INTO STORY

The new scene must draw the audience in with an immediate and strong narrative. This is not the place for a pause. The shift of time needs to be supported by dramatic action – that is: a central protagonist with GOATS, a Goal, Obstacle, Action, Tactics and Stakes.

The nature of this action will vary according to the genre. A comedy will give the audience comic action, wit, humorous character interaction and physical comedy. A legal drama will dive into a high-stakes legal confrontation. A more gentle, thoughtful story will have more gentle, thoughtful action, but the questions raised will still need to be strong and the emotional stakes high.

At the same time, ensure that the audience knows what the new time is. Either the context, or the content, of the new scene must make it clear *when* we are. The *Reservoir Dogs* flashback continues with fast physical action:

… Mr Pink hijacks a car and has a shoot-out with three cops. The dialogue before the jump sets the context, making it likely that the scene we're watching comes from the aftermath of the botched robbery, and the action confirms this.

Key idea

Grab the reader with new tension and questions immediately after the jump.

Edit

Now turn to the incoming scene and cut any introductory material. Make sure that we are plunged right into the middle of the action. Hook us right in. If necessary, you may need to do some new writing here to bring the new scene up to speed.

Check that you've clearly shown us what the new time is. Once more, feel free to show us in two or more different ways, through context, visual cues, dialogue and so on. Try to find fresh and original ways to show us the time, which fit the story and the genre.

Ending the time jump

At the end of the flashback or section of time, the same rules apply. Whether jumping back to the original time or cutting to a new time, you must build a new cliffhanger to go out on or a new cliffhanger to come in on (or a return to a previous cliffhanger).

And there should be no delay into pushing ahead with strong dramatic action:

… Mr Pink shoots at least one of the cops, possibly killing him, and accelerates away.

On this, we cut to the warehouse – our time-anchor, which tells us we've returned – straight back into the cliffhanger question of who betrayed the gang, and whether they will be able to save Mr Orange's life …

Key idea

Returning to the present is the same as flashing back: end on a cliffhanger, plunge us straight back into tension and action, and make sure that we know that we're back.

 Edit

Look at the scene, before we jump back, and the return scene and do the same as before – ensure that the outgoing ends with strong tension and that the return starts with strong tension. Trigger your anchors so that we know we're back.

Are we immediately grabbed again? If not, cut anything that's getting in the way.

Workshop

Read through the sequence, from before we jump in time to after we return. Does it work? Do we follow clearly where we are at all times? Does the momentum hold up, or are we distracted by the shift in time?

What's good about what we've created? What could be improved to make it work even better?

Where to next?

The more fractured the timeline, the more important it is for the scenes to be engaging and relatively simple to set up. The audience needs to concentrate hard to follow the story. That means you need strong characters and action to ensure that they want to bother, and to make it easier for them to grasp.

However, these all essentially remain within three acts. The trade-offs become even more important as we move away from three acts and deal with stories that demand other shapes.

In the next chapter, we move even further into unusual structures, and look at those instances where you might need to find different act structures altogether – five acts, seven acts, a hundred acts, no acts at all …

20

Series, multiple-act, no-act and other unusual structures

Being simple in structure, three acts are normally the strongest shape, both for action and also for developing more complex themes. With little to distract them, the audience can concentrate on subtleties of plot and subplot, complex characters and thoughtful dialogue. However, there are times when the three-act structure isn't right for your story. And even if you never intend to use non-standard structures, it's useful to know about them, to strengthen your understanding of how structure works.

First we look at the advantages and disadvantages of the main alternative structures available to you; then at some methods you'll need to make them work successfully.

Possible reasons not to use three acts

There are at least four possible reasons why three acts might not be right for your story, from hidden agendas to genre:

- **Hidden agendas** – three-act structure tends to imply that the protagonist needs redemption. You may not want to say this.
- **Awkwardly shaped stories** – some stories don't come neatly packaged. True stories, especially, can suffer if you try to squeeze them into three acts.
- **New angles** – breaking the rules can bring freshness to a story and add an ironic perspective.
- **Epic** – epic stories simply don't work in three acts. Three acts are too restrictive – an epic needs time and space to work.

And, of course, any TV or cinema series is, by its nature, going to need more than three acts. *Lord of the Rings* – three epic films of four acts each – totalled 12 acts. Even a short TV drama series of seven one-hour parts, each of three acts, comes to 21 acts.

Approaching unusual structure

For a single film or episode, your first plan should always be to see whether you can fit your story to the classic three acts – it will make life easier all round. For one thing, unusual structures are much tougher to write. An alternative structure is not a get-out clause for avoiding the hard work of making a story work properly. An unusual structure will demand time and energy that might be more usefully devoted to important issues of character and theme.

Secondly, don't fool yourself into thinking that an unusual shape is a good thing in itself – no audience ever came out of a movie exclaiming at its wonderful nine-act structure! The reason for choosing an unusual shape should, as with flashbacks and fragmented time, always be because it's better for the story.

 Key idea

If at all possible, stick to three acts. But sometimes an alternative structure might be the only one for your story.

There is no limit to the number of alternative structures, but in normal practice you'll find yourself choosing between:

- **Multiple acts** – five and seven are the most usual for epics although, as we've seen, *Lord of the Rings* comes to 12.

- **Two acts** – missing either Act One or Act Three.
- **Episodic** – some films avoid act breaks and are structured in individual episodes.
- **Mosaic** – the story is structured out of a number of short films that create a whole.
- **Thematic/circular** – the structure is based on thematic connections rather than dramatic ones; it may also circle round the story rather than moving forwards.

Paul Ashton, senior film executive, talent development, Creative England

'If you can make an alternative structure work, fine. There has to be a good reason. But you have to understand about structure in order to make an alternative work. If you're just doing it for effect, it's not going to work. It needs a true meaning and purpose. You need to be able to master the form, before you can turn it on its head.'

Multiple acts

If you are writing an epic, then you should certainly be thinking about a multiple-act story. Three acts is too short to contain the epic genre. The compact focus on three acts, which is normally such an advantage, now works against you. *Gladiator* is a would-be epic that suffers from this. Struggling within a conventional three-part shape, the script ends up feeling lightweight, its attempt to portray the struggle for democracy and freedom in ancient Rome undercooked.

Key idea

You can't tell an epic story in three acts.

By contrast, *Lawrence of Arabia* tackles the struggle for Arab independence during the First World War in seven acts, with a short prologue and epilogue at the start and end (see box).

While the script does not explicitly divide the film into acts, the act divisions are clear if you look for them. Each act focuses on a specific project, except the first, and each rises to a climax, with a surprise, a challenge and a new decision. The prologue is a classic flashback from the end, showing Lawrence's death, and setting up the question of who he really was.

Lawrence of Arabia – a seven-act structure

PROLOGUE: T.E. Lawrence dies racing his motorbike along country roads. At the funeral, many characters (who we will meet again later) disagree over his character – this leads into a flashback which runs for the rest of the story.

ACT ONE: Cairo, January 1917. Lawrence is underused, restless and disgruntled. A British attaché in the Arab Bureau, Dryden, sees his potential and sends him to Arabia to find Prince Feisal and discover his long-term plans.

ACT TWO: The journey to find Feisal. Lawrence meets Sheikh Sherif Ali Ibn el Kharish, who kills his guide, but Lawrence still finds his way to Feisal, who is himself under attack by the Turks. In a moment of inspiration, Lawrence realizes that the Arabs can seize a great opportunity. Despite opposition from his commanding officer, Colonel Brighton, he advises them to attack the key town of Aqaba – from a direction no one will expect – the land.

ACT THREE: Feisal lets Lawrence take a group of 50 men across the Nefud desert. Overcoming terrible obstacles, they cross the Nefud and overrun Aqaba, routing the Turks.

ACT FOUR: Lawrence returns to Cairo and reports on his success. Despite the doubts of others – and his own self-doubts – he is promoted and sent back.

ACT FIVE: Lawrence leads his Arab fighters to terrorize the Turks in a series of raids, reported on by American reporter Jackson Bentley, who turns him into a hero. Even when injured, Lawrence increasingly believes the myths of his invincibility. The Turks put out a reward for him.

ACT SIX: Making a recce of the town of Deraa in disguise, Lawrence is caught and cruelly tortured. However, he is not recognized and is thrown out. Deeply disillusioned, Lawrence returns to Cairo and begs to be allowed to give up. He is manipulated by Dryden into leading the Arabs for one last 'big push' against Damascus.

ACT SEVEN: Leading his Arabs to Damascus, he exacts fierce revenge on a Turkish column that has massacred an Arab village, but still reaches Damascus before the British. However, the Arabs are as divided as ever and Lawrence's hopes of Arab self-government fail.

EPILOGUE: As he leaves Damascus in a jeep, a motorcyclist passes – an omen of his death and a reminder of how the film began.

Issues

Whether an epic or a TV serial, when you have multiple acts you sacrifice the solidity of three-act structure. The story can all too easily become bitty and incoherent, a series of events without a spine holding them together. Instead of beginning, middle and end, you have beginning, middle, middle, middle, middle, middle, middle, and end, and an audience can grow weary, or even lost. (For ways to deal with these and other issues, see below).

Two acts

Two-act stories generally miss the first or final act, often with a very strong break in the middle.

Full Metal Jacket misses out the third act. The first half of the film takes place at army boot camp, showing the training of a group of raw recruits. In the second half, we follow the recruits to war in Vietnam.

A conventional three-act structure would have probably broken the story into Act One – boot camp, Act Two – war, Act Three – final conflict and resolution. By denying us the final resolution, the screenplay removes any chance of redemption and presents a very bleak view of war.

Issues

Two-act structures, by cutting either the normality of Act One or the resolution/redemption of Act Three, are very difficult to pull off without leaving the audience feeling either rushed at the start or let down at the end.

Key idea

Two acts make a statement either by not showing normality (Act One) or redemption (Act Three).

Snapshot exercise

Does your story feel as if it would work better in multiple acts? Would the meaning be clearer in two acts? Or would the story be stronger in three acts? What changes would you need to make to ensure that your chosen structure works?

Outline where you would place the act breaks and the act turning points, with a surprise, a challenge and a new decision.

Episodic structure

By contrast, an episodic structure abandons acts altogether. You might choose this, for example, if you want to say that your story or characters are too complex for simple redemptive storylines. It often suits true stories, which rarely work in neat shapes.

Woody Allen's *Radio Days* follows a series of semi-autobiographical episodes in the life of a New York Jewish adolescent, set against the popular radio programmes of the time. There is almost no central storyline, just a series of almost individual tales of growing up and coming to terms with the passing of time and the end of an era. Similarly, Fellini's autobiographical *Amarcord* (co-written with Tonino Guerra) and Scorsese's *Goodfellas* (screenplay by Nicholas Pileggi) create their stories out of individual episodes to give an unconventional view of a life.

A very different use of episodic structure can be seen in *All is Lost*. Here, the story of a lone yachtsman marooned in the Indian Ocean is told in a series of episodes whose deliberate lack of a conventional arc adds to the feeling of increasing desperation as he struggles to survive.

Issues

The challenge with an episodic structure is similar to multi-acts – how do you stop the story falling apart into a succession of 'middles' without a coherent frame to hold them together?

Key idea

An episodic structure removes the overarching storyline to show that life can be more complex.

Snapshot exercise

If you're considering working in episodes, divide up the story into its episodic parts. Ensure that each episode is a strong story in its own right. Give each its own premise and see how each premise relates to the whole.

Ensure that each episode is strong enough to belong in the screenplay and that they are in the right order. Reorder, cut, paste and invent new episodes as necessary to give yourself a satisfying overall shape.

Mosaic structure

In a mosaic structure, the story is constructed from individual fragments, each a story in its own right. As the mosaic builds, so we gain a multi-faceted picture of an event or character. In Alan Ayckbourn's three-part TV series *The Norman Conquests* (based on his trilogy of plays), each episode follows the same characters in a house over the same weekend, set respectively in the dining room, the living room and the garden. Each works on its own and also fills in important gaps left by the others to create the complete picture. (They can also be watched in any order.)

Mosaic structure works particularly well in TV, for example each episode telling the story from a different character's point of view. However, cinema versions include Kurosawa's *Rashomon*, which depicts the same event as told by four conflicting witnesses, and *Thirty Two Short Films about Glenn Gould*, which evokes the life of pianist Glenn Gould through 32 fragments mixing drama and documentary.

The German movie *Run, Lola, Run* demonstrates a different kind of mosaic structure, showing the same story three times, but with different outcomes.

This structure often highlights the difficulty of ever really knowing the truth.

Circular structure

Finally, a circular or thematic structure might be right for you if your story circles around a theme or idea, viewing it from multiple angles. This is a particularly challenging structure as it moves away from the idea of a central dramatic spine, and is often more suited to art-house, avant-garde movies or documentaries.

Terence Mallick's *Tree of Life* adopted a circular structure for its impressionistic exploration of war, loss and grief through the death of a soldier and its effect on his brother and parents. The film spirals out into contemplation of many issues, including, as the title suggests, the meaning of life. This loose, intellectual structure is not for everyone but can produce powerful and thoughtful movies if planned with care.

La Grande Bellezza (*The Great Beauty*) draws on two previous circular narratives, *La Dolce Vita* and *8½*, to explore the life of a once-promising novelist as he looks back on the success he could have had. Circling around his meetings with various characters and reflections on his life and lost love, the structure allows the film to present a more open-ended and less prescriptive view of what makes a man.

Key idea

Mosaic and circular structures present a more fragmented view, for example showing stories from different angles or giving higher priority to the theme.

Snapshot exercise

Thinking about a mosaic or circular structure? Be clear on the theme that underlies your story. Then lay out your scenes and sequences on cards or Post-its and arrange them in an order that feels right. Look for links that give extra meaning or surprise – contrast, reinforcement, irony. Ensure that each scene or sequence has its own intrinsic value, dramatic or otherwise. Be as ruthless as with any other structure: if a fragment doesn't belong, or distracts from the whole, cut it or make it work.

Brian Dunnigan, Head of Screenwriting, London Film School

'Dramatic principles are just simply what seem to work for an audience, who want to know what, who, when, where … and be surprised.'

How to write alternative structures successfully

As with flashbacks, any deviation from the norm creates a distance between the film and the audience. The great screenwriters and directors have always flirted with breaking conventions but built their scripts in such a way as to ensure that the audience is held, and not lost, in the process.

A film's structure has five primary roles to play:

1 **To keep the audience watching to the end**
2 **To ensure that they know where they are in the story**
3 **To hold all the elements together in a coherent whole**
4 **To prepare the audience for what they're going to get**
5 **To give a satisfactory experience.**

However, the moment you deviate from standard story shapes you risk fatally weakening all five. A screenwriter who deviates from the standard structure must find other ways to achieve these five aims.

1 KEEP THE AUDIENCE WATCHING TO THE END

Three acts, properly written, provide you with a strong spine – the power of the story question established at the end of Act One energizes the whole story. The Act Two Project drives the audience through to the final battle of Act Three.

With a more complicated story spine, you risk losing that energy. You should add to the narrative drive by strengthening the story goal, the obstacles and the stakes. Multi-act stories, in particular, need to have large goals that we can identify with – liberating Arabia, defeating evil – formidable obstacles – the Ottoman Empire, the Dark Lord Sauron – and the highest stakes.

Second, keep the momentum up by ensuring that each act or episode is strongly constructed. Acts Two, Three, Five and Six of *Lawrence of Arabia* have very strong goal, obstacle and stakes built into them. In *Radio Days* and *Rashomon*, each episode drives forward with its own individual story question.

 Key idea

With an unusual structure, you must work harder to hold the audience's interest and attention.

2 TELL US WHERE WE ARE

Without a standard structure to guide them, the audience can easily become lost. And if they get lost, they won't blame themselves; they'll blame the writer. It's therefore vital to give the audience signposts so that they know where they are.

Dialogue signposts include lines like 'This is just the beginning...' or 'It all has to end tonight'. In *Lawrence of Arabia*, Dryden calls the battle for Damascus the 'big push', as clear an indication as any that we're approaching the final act.

Non-dialogue signposts have a similar effect, but usually have to be set up in advance. Having established Damascus as the place of the big push, a road sign to Damascus becomes a literal signpost to the beginning of the end.

Large events often act as signs that the story is reaching a major turning point: in *Radio Days*, the final episode is signposted by a large New Year's Eve party, which prompts a look forward to a new decade and a glance back at the era about to disappear.

A **ticking clock** (literal or symbolic) can also be very useful in helping the audience mark the passage of time.

The TV series *24* was built specifically on the idea of a ticking clock, each episode set over one hour in a single day. Other props can stand in for clocks in a more oblique way: if the oxygen is running out in the submarine, we know where we are by watching the gauge drop. A map can show us how close we are to our destination. Daylight and darkness, the changing seasons, a growing tree, all can usefully mark the passage of story time.

> ## Key idea
>
>
> Use dramatic verbal and non-verbal signposts and ticking clocks to help the audience find their way through the story.

3 KEEP THE STORY TOGETHER

The third danger in a non-standard structure is that the different elements cease to feel that they belong in one story. Without three acts to hold them together, the scenes can begin to fall apart. To counter this, build up theme, patterns and repetitions.

A strong theme can bind quite disparate story elements. In *The Tree of Life*, Terence Malick continually emphasizes the dominant theme of life and death, grief and mourning, to give a coherence to a very fragmentary circular narrative. The theme of greed and human frailty runs through all three films in *Lord of the Rings*.

Repeating and varying patterns – visuals, scenes, characters, motifs, ideas – are important to hold any story together, especially one that uses a non-three-act structure. However, at the same time you must vary the tone and pace.

The central motif in the Danish political TV series *Borgen* is the meeting – formal and informal, indoors and outdoors – each moving the story forwards in a different way. The structure of *Lawrence of Arabia* is created out of a pattern of journeys, battles and political confrontations.

Repeating, yet varying, motifs in this way gives a feeling that the different pieces of the story work as a single whole.

Focus point

Use theme and patterns of repeating motifs to pull the story together as a coherent whole.

4 PREPARE THE AUDIENCE

When breaking any rule, it's a good idea to warn people to expect the unexpected and prepare them for what they're going to see instead.

Titles prepare audiences in many rule-breaking films and series: *The Great Beauty, The Tree of Life* and *Radio Days* herald films that are likely to be theme rather than plot-led. If you have a 24-act structure, then why not call the series *24*?

Visuals and sound and plot reversals early in the screenplay can prepare viewers for the unexpected. And, as with signposts, the dialogue itself can act as a guide, stating, for example, that this is 'no ordinary case'.

The first scene of *Goodfellas* is filled with such signs and reversals. From the opening shot, which shows a car driving on the wrong side of the road, to a strange noise, to the discovery of a man in the car's trunk, to the apparently benign driver of the car announcing, 'As far back as I remember I always wanted to be a gangster …'

Key idea

Prepare the audience for your chosen structure with internal cues, from the title to visuals, story elements and dialogue.

5 REWARD THE AUDIENCE

An unusual structure is a challenge for cinema and TV audiences. So reward them for their extra work by adding extra compensations elsewhere, such as strong narrative, fascinating characters, engaging action, wit and attractive visuals.

In *Lawrence of Arabia*, the energy and complexity of the central character is one of the primary attractions, while a strong narrative drive and exotic desert settings give the director the opportunity for a powerful story and stunning visuals. All these help an audience cope with what otherwise might be a long seven-act haul.

The French indie movie *Blue is the Warmest Colour* compensated its audience for its slow exploration of teenage love and 'difficult' lesbian themes by providing scenes of explicit sex – sparking much media discussion and considerable box office and critical success.

Key idea

Compensate the audience for the extra work of a non-standard structure by giving them something else, such as a strong drive, strong feeling, interesting characters or powerful visuals.

Workshop

If you feel that your story doesn't work in three acts, discuss which best suits your storyline and characters. Brainstorm as many techniques as you can for ensuring that the audience is still engaged with the story and is prepared for what they are going to receive.

Go through all the tools at your disposal – character, scene narrative, dialogue, visuals and sound – to see what signposts you can add. Look for what you can use to keep the story together. How can you prepare the audience for the structure you've chosen and what can you give them to compensate for their extra work?

Then be bold. Rewrite the treatment for the new structure and make every element work as strongly as you can.

Where to next?

You've made one pass through the script for structure. However, important as the structure is, the structure edit won't solve everything. It's time to revise the characters.

21

Revising character – increasing audience engagement

Once you've been through the draft, adding and editing for structure, it's time to turn to the characters. Characters, as we've seen, are the heart of any story.

In this chapter we look at more advanced levels of character development and how to troubleshoot the character problems that often arise.

The character redraft

Start by reading through the revised script but now solely for character. Look at the protagonist's journey, from her first entrance to her final exit. Then read it through a second time, purely looking at the role of the antagonist. Break down his role in the story, the number of times he appears, his goals and obstacles. Analyse his journey.

Do the same for each character in turn, large and small.

(Of course, if you see a few structural tweaks that you missed – go ahead and do those, too.)

Focus point

When approaching the character edit, it's very valuable to look at each character's journey in turn.

Snapshot exercise

Take a given character and analyse her journey from start to finish.

What role or roles does she play? Does she appear often or rarely? Does she disappear too early or hang around too long?

What do you want the audience to think of her? Is it clear what her motivations are? Is she active? Does she act believably? Does she have contradictions? An inner life? Are you pushing her too far to be believable? Or not far enough to be interesting?

How to develop character

Crucial methods for developing character are:
- making the character more active
- strengthening the obstacles facing them
- sharpening the character's point of view
- developing character detail
- clarifying the character's growth.

ACTION AND OBSTACLES

As we've seen, most stories suffer irrecoverably from a central character who is too passive and reactive, especially in early draft scripts. However, this can also apply to subsidiary characters.

Any character is only as strong as the obstacles that face her and the action she takes. You must create good, credible obstacles for each of your characters – large and small – and force the characters to confront them with all the powers at their disposal.

If you want to strengthen involvement in any character, give her an opportunity to make her own decisions and take her own actions. The fewer areas of action available to her, the harder the writer has to work.

Ernst Lubitsch, screenwriter, producer and director

'It is the task of the scenarist to invent little pieces of business that are so characteristic and give so deep an insight into his creatures, that their personalities clearly and organically unfold before the eyes of the audience.'

Key idea

The first step in developing character is to give her more obstacles and actions.

Edit

Choose a character that you feel needs further development and ask yourself whether you've provided strong enough obstacles. Strengthen the large ones and put more small obstacles in the way. Ensure that the character takes positive action to attempt to overcome each obstacle.

CHARACTER DETAIL

Characters often remain flat or clichéd because you haven't thought them through enough. Now is the time to fill in the background detail and get a sense of each character – their memories, thoughts, attitudes and style.

Check that the characters are as different from one another as possible. Try to push them to extremes. Even if all your characters come from the same Nordic village or Italian family, you can make one quieter, one noisier, one more insecure, one more flamboyant and so on.

Key idea

Know your characters so that they can come to life.

If you haven't already, now is the time to round out each character's background in detail – see Chapter 5. Starting with the central character, get them to answer questions about themselves, in the first person, to help you develop each point of view and individual voice.

Do this for all the other major and support characters in the story, and for any smaller character who you feel is not coming to life on the page. Ensure that each is significantly different from the others.

CHARACTER GROWTH AND CHANGE

Now look to see whether a problem character changes enough during the course of the story. Not all characters need to change, either because they appear for only a short time or because it wouldn't be appropriate.

An antagonist may not change at all, although some antagonists can and do. You can also breathe fresh life into a script by having an antagonist change sides, or having one of the protagonist's allies shift over to the enemy.

Other characters who have a major role may feel flat if they have no arc at all. Check that they have at least one moment of realization along the way. If not, show us why not. If the 'change' feels too forced, think of it not as transformation but growth … gaining a new skill, or a new understanding. Also, don't make it too sudden or dramatic. Plant seeds of the new growth early, and, if necessary, end on a hint rather than a fanfare.

Rainer Werner Fassbinder, director, screenwriter and actor

'Women think in [Douglas] Sirk's films. Something which has never struck me with other directors. None of them. Usually women are always reacting, doing what women are supposed to do, but in Sirk they think. It's something that has to be seen. It's great to see women think. It gives one hope. Honestly.'

Edit

Look at each character's growth. Do they change, deal with their flaws, or indeed become worse? Are they stuck? Is that right for the story, or should you give them at least one moment of change or realization? If a character grows, is that growth credible? Should the growth be less … or more? Are you providing us with surprises and reversals?

Cameos and walk-ons

After the main roles of protagonist and antagonist and the subsidiary support roles, you'll probably have a host of small roles, right down to walk-on parts with no more than a single line – characters such as the security guard who inspects the lead character's rucksack or the nurse who changes a drip bag. They can very easily fall into cliché.

Large or small, look for a way to give that character a little something special – though not so much that he or she distracts from the main story.

In *Boogie Nights*, a fleeting and otherwise unremarkable appearance by a night-club doorman is made memorable simply by being outrageously camp.

In *Psycho*, Hitchcock and writer Joe Stefano made very few changes to Robert Bloch's original novel. However, in the book, the detective hired by Lila Crane, who takes up just a few pages, is a stereotype: Stetson-wearing, tall and blue-eyed. Hitchcock and Stefano made the detective dumpy and middle-aged. The effect is both to add to the tension and bring an extra level of truth and believability to his scenes.

Films and TV series can benefit from short-lived but strong cameo characters who appear for a single sequence or episode – or reappear infrequently – as long as they have a strong effect on the main characters and their situation: a boss or neighbour, for example.

If you have such a character, then he must make a strong impression in his short time on screen. Give him memorable qualities, some eccentricities perhaps, or a particular style. Such, for example, is the impact of Noah Cross, in *Chinatown*, the powerful businessman who has a vivid effect, despite having relatively few scenes.

Write this part well and you may well land a big-name actor who will enjoy the chance to make a splash in a brief appearance, and help the financing at the same time.

Charlie Kaufman, *Synecdoche, New York*

'There are nearly thirteen million people in the world. None of those people is an extra. They're all the leads of their own stories. They have to be given their due.'

Key idea

Enjoy giving every role something special, even the smallest.

Write

Start a list of potential cameo and walk-on parts. Refer back to the 'worst person in the world' list you made earlier. Could some of these be useful in enriching the smaller roles?

Troubleshooting character problems

As with structure, you will almost certainly come across one or more character problems that are common to almost all early draft screenplays.

YOUR SCRIPT HAS TOO MANY CHARACTERS

If your script is overlong, even after the structural edit, it could be that it's overloaded with secondary characters. There's a limit to how many characters the audience can keep in their heads at any one time.

Start with characters who you could lift out of the script entirely without any significant change. As with subplots, if they don't affect the story then they should probably be cut or reduced to walk-on parts.

> ## Focus point
>
>
> Cut, shorten or combine any characters who perform the same role or don't affect the plot.

Next, dig out any characters who are too similar or who are performing the same role in the script. Do you have, for example, three people who are essentially all teaching the hero how to be a man? Cut two of them, or combine them into one.

Combining characters can be very effective. Not only do you simplify the story and shorten the script, but you end up with a character who may have an unexpected mix of traits. Combining the irascible violin teacher with the laid-back football coach and the inspirational uncle could yield a much more interesting uncle-mentor who is musical, irascible, laid back and inspirational by turns.

Watch out also for characters who fade out or who exist only for one scene. Such characters can profitably be cut or combined. Some of the most memorable and complex characters come from combining two or more underdeveloped characters into one who has a greater presence in the film (but see also below).

> ## Key idea
>
>
> Combining two or more individually weak characters can create a new interesting and complex one.

> ## Edit
>
>
> Look through the draft script to see whether there are characters who drift in and out confusingly, perform the same role or simply don't have time to register properly. Cut as many as you can, and cut down or combine the rest. Ensure that the audience has as much time as possible to focus on the main players.

YOU HAVE A MAJOR CHARACTER WHO REFUSES TO DEVELOP A CHARACTER ARC (1)

You may be writing an adventure story or a satire, which doesn't have room for a character arc (see Chapter 3), or you may be developing a mentor antagonist. A mentor antagonist is a character who teaches the protagonist a key lesson or series of lessons. He may be an official teacher, such as Mr Miyage in *Karate Kid*, or an unofficial mentor, such as Leo McGarry in *The West Wing*. Unlike normal antagonists, the mentor antagonist is not necessarily a bad guy and will often support the protagonist's main story goal. However, he appears in opposition to the protagonist at a deeper level because the protagonist wants to be taught the easy lessons, not the difficult ones.

This is very useful if you find yourself stuck developing a major character who is fascinating on the outside but refuses to come to life on the inside. Turn him into a teacher. With an antagonist, you don't ever need to see inside.

More subtle versions of mentor antagonists include such characters as Jonathan Mardukas in *Midnight Run*, a likeable but difficult fugitive who must be taken against his will from New York to Los Angeles by bounty hunter Jack Walsh, to face trial. In the process, he teaches Jack slowly, painfully and reluctantly to become a better human being.

In the Mexican rite-of-passage road movie *Y Tu Mamá También*, the mentor antagonist is an older woman, Luisa, who accompanies two adolescent boys on a trip to find a secluded beach and through whom they learn bittersweet lessons about adulthood.

A mentor antagonist differs from a support character in that he is primarily there to lead the way. At the same time, they will clash with the protagonist(s) over methods and goals – Luisa battles with the boys' immaturity; Mr Miyage has to fight hard to teach Daniel the inner lessons of karate.

Before the end, protagonist and mentor must part company, so that the protagonist can achieve his primary goal through his own efforts.

 Key idea

A protagonist or support without a journey can usefully become a mentor antagonist.

YOU HAVE A MAJOR CHARACTER WHO REFUSES TO DEVELOP A CHARACTER ARC (2)

Some films simply break the rules and develop a protagonist with no inner story, but who doesn't fit into one of the categories above.

Julien in *Ascenseur pour l'échafaud* (*Lift to the Scaffold*) is one. Throughout the entire film, we learn almost nothing about him except that he's an ex-Foreign Legionnaire and in love with his boss's wife. Another is Captain Phillips in *Captain Phillips*, the true story of a ship hijack by Somali pirates.

In these two very different films, the lack of an inner story builds tension with no room for emotional escape – we can't hope for redemption and character growth if there is no inner story from the start.

However, as with unusual act structures, the lack of an inner story comes with a potential cost: lack of identification. This can be a particular problem with true stories, which seem initially attractive but often lack an inner story. You could invent one, but an invented inner story may feel formulaic and false.

In the (rare) case that you feel the story is best told without a character journey, you have to use every means at your disposal to ensure that the audience identifies even more strongly than normal with your protagonist.

For Julien, this means putting him in an almost impossible situation, trapped in a lift with the evidence of his crime for all to see. For Phillips, it means life-and-death stakes, impossible odds against armed and unstable pirates, constant action and at the heart of it an apparently ordinary man caught in extraordinary circumstances.

YOU HAVE A VIVID CHARACTER WHO THREATENS TO OUTSHINE THE PROTAGONIST

One support character you should be aware of is the Mercutio character, named after the brightly burning character in Romeo and Juliet. Dramatic and intriguing, a Mercutio character vividly supports the protagonist before dying or disappearing dramatically relatively early in the story. Such a character will be energetic but short-lived.

This is one way of dealing with a character who would otherwise dominate the lead character and overbalance the story. It also allows you to include a very lively character who has nowhere further to develop and little or no inner growth. The risk, of course, is that the character may become so interesting that all the remaining characters (including the hero) seem pallid and insipid by comparison.

If you decide to include a Mercutio character, take care that he's instantly fascinating, but take equal care that your protagonist grows even stronger and more interesting/ conflicted/surprising/involving/energetic after the Mercutio is dead and gone.

Snapshot exercise

Go back to some of your favourite films and programmes and look to see whether they contain mentor antagonists or Mercutio characters. How do they function in the story? Are they satisfactory? If they aren't totally achieved, what feels wrong? Do the mentor antagonists feel fully developed or are they mere plot devices? Do the Mercutio characters overshadow the protagonist? Do they feel clichéd or fresh and true?

Not every screenplay needs such characters. Would they be useful in yours?

YOU HAVE A DIFFICULT, UNSYMPATHETIC PROTAGONIST – PLAN A

The rule is that the main character should be likeable, sympathetic and easy for the audience to support – but many protagonists are far from that ideal. Examples range from gangster Henry Hill in *Goodfellas* and the misanthropic Melvin Udall in *As Good as It Gets* to Ron Woodroof in *Dallas Buyers Club* and borderline Asperger's Saga Norén in the Scandinavian series *The Bridge*. They can be irascible, vain, empty-headed and greedy … in general, they have qualities you are told not to have in a central character.

If you find that you have an unsympathetic lead, you have two choices: you can either make your protagonist more sympathetic or deal with him as he is.

Plan A: You need to show your protagonist's strengths.

Many writers become so focused on their protagonist's flaws and character journey that they forget to show us his strengths. Go back over the character of your protagonist and ensure that he has a positive side and that this positive side is introduced early. You may know that Misha is a brilliant and caring doctor, but the audience doesn't until you show us.

Key idea

Remember your protagonist's strengths.

Snapshot exercise

Go back to the character hexagon shown in Chapter 5 and check that you've covered all six points. If necessary, add to your protagonist's strengths. Be very clear about why we should care about him.

YOU HAVE A DIFFICULT, UNSYMPATHETIC PROTAGONIST – PLAN B

Sometimes a character refuses to play by the rules. You try to force her to become likeable, but he just becomes bland and boring. All the fun goes out of him.

Plan B: You need to find a way to break the rules and get away with it.

Difficult central characters need to be constructed carefully, to ensure that the audience can engage with them. There are many characteristics that we admire, and indeed are attracted by, without them necessarily making the characters into perfect dinner companions.

Paul Ashton, senior film executive, talent development, Creative England

'People get very bogged down in making the script look perfect. I'd rather a more "rough-hewn" script with interesting characters. People get too into smoothing the edges off, blandifying the characters and that's the last thing you want to be doing.'

If you have a difficult character, try giving them some of the following attributes:

- **Skills** – we can't help but admire those with good skills, however dreadful they may be. The violent killer can be brilliant at planning his assassination attempts.
- **Power** – we like watching people who have power, whether it's physical or political power, or the self-confidence to do precisely what they want, whatever the odds.
- **Honesty** – we are attracted to people who speak out, however unlikeable they are in other ways. We especially like them if they say things we wished we could say, or had the guts to say.
- **Humour** – funny, acerbic, witty, sarcastic and sharp-tongued characters engage us strongly.
- **Suffering** – we automatically find ourselves empathizing with any character who is in pain, however flawed they may be. However, the deeper the flaw, the greater the suffering needs to be, to appeal to our innate sense of justice. Which brings us to …
- **Victim of injustice** – nothing succeeds like injustice. However unpleasant a character, we care if she is a victim of an unjust hurt.
- **Someone likes her** – having other characters love, like or, at least, admire your difficult character gives us a way in. We conclude that, if someone can see the good in them, maybe we can, too.
- And, most of all, **energy** – Goal, Obstacle, Action. We cannot help caring about someone trying enormously hard to achieve a goal.

Key idea

Faced with difficult characters, give them attributes we can relate to: skills, power, honesty, humour, energy … and make them suffer.

In John Sayles's movie, *Passion Fish*, May-Alice is – in her own words – 'a bitch on wheels'. We first come across this self-absorbed soap actress in a hospital bed, paralysed from the waist down after a hit-and-run accident. She is rude, abrasive and refuses to work on her rehab exercises. But at the same time she is sharp-tongued, honest and funny, and refuses to buy into the medical staff's platitudes, so we can't help warming to her. She is also suffering unfairly (she will probably never walk again). And just when we're expecting her to be rude to two admiring fans who ask for her autograph, she suddenly shows a warmer side.

Gregory House is an example of a character who constantly surprises us with his refusal to be nice. His social skills and emotional intelligence seem to be almost zero. And yet we watch him, week after week, in *House*. Part of this is because he's good at his job and his team admire him, even as they fight him, as do those higher in the system. He has one close friend, whose loyalty to him is important to the series. And, of course, he saves lives.

 John Lithgow, actor

'The most exciting acting tends to happen in roles you never thought you could play.'

 Edit

Examine your protagonist and then the other major characters in turn. Do their roles suffer if we don't like them? If so, should you make them more likeable?

If not, should you use some of the techniques above to ensure that the audience cares?

YOU HAVE MULTIPLE PROTAGONISTS

The standard structure has a single protagonist, yet many films and series work perfectly well with multiple protagonists. As with difficult protagonists, you need to structure the characters with care.

There are three kinds of multiple-protagonist stories:

- **allied**, fighting for the same goal together, such as a buddy story or caper movie
- **opposed**, such as in a romantic comedy or tragedy
- **individual**, following different stories altogether.

Allied protagonists

In allied protagonist stories – from *Thelma and Louise* and *The Bridge* – to *Ocean's 11* two or more protagonists act for the bulk of the main plot as a single protagonist, while fighting each other in subplots. However, it's essential that each protagonist carries equal weight.

Be careful that you don't shift the interest unwittingly towards one of the central characters and away from the others. In particular, in a twin-protagonist story it's only too easy for one of the two protagonists to become more interesting or more active than the other. In this case, you either have to promote the lesser character to balance the story, or demote him to a support role with a single protagonist leading the plot.

There are obvious gains to having multiple protagonists, as well as obvious dangers. With an ally in the story, the protagonists now have at least one other major character with whom to share their thoughts, hopes and fears.

However, with the script divided between them, you dramatically reduce the time to establish them. As a result, you have to be bolder in your characterization, without falling into cliché. It's very important to ensure that they have very distinctive characteristics and character arcs, as different as possible, while remaining fresh and truthful.

> ## Key idea
>
> In a dual protagonist story, it's vital that the two protagonists carry equal weight.

In Series 2 of *Homeland*, Carrie Mathison and Nicholas Brody are allies in the fight against the arch-terrorist Abu Nazir. In Series 3, however, Brody almost disappears for long stretches of time, leaving the story feeling very unbalanced. Carrie's story takes the burden of the plot, but the third series would have been stronger if Brody's action line had been given equal weight.

By contrast, the Scandinavian police series *The Bridge* achieves a more consistent balance, setting Saga Norén, a clever detective with a marked lack of emotional intelligence, against Martin Rohde, warm-hearted yet with a trail of failed and failing relationships in his wake. Each is given equal prominence and screen time, both within the main plot and also in their own relationship-line subplots.

Larger groups also share the same primary goal – robbing a bank, saving a village, winning a football match.

However, although they may each have their own quite different inner stories, dealing, for example, with bravery, overconfidence, emotional attachment, greed and so forth, it is important to search out the common theme that unites their struggle. This common theme will always bring up the question of the survival of the group.

> ## Key idea
>
> Multiple protagonist stories will always bring up the survival of the group.

Before we leave the topic of allied protagonists, be aware that many romantic stories fall into this category – with the two lovers united in their fight against the world that opposes them.

Opposing protagonists

With opposing protagonists, the central characters have opposing goals. In other words, each protagonist is the other's antagonist. This could occur in a thriller, where we find ourselves following, and to some extent caring about, both sides. For example, the motor racing biopic *Rush* is equally divided between the two bitter rivals, James Hunt and Niki Lauda.

Key idea

With opposing protagonists, each is the other's antagonist.

When romantic protagonists are not allies, they become opposing protagonists. In *Pretty Woman*, Edward Lewis's goal is to make street-walker Vivian Ward into someone who he'll be happy being seen with. Vivian's goal is to remain herself. The story revolves around the comedy and drama of their attempts to reconcile these two opposing desires, while they slowly realize (and fight against) their growing feelings for each other.

The same issues apply here as with allied protagonists. They have to be developed fast, as very distinct yet credible characters, while being given equal importance in the story.

It is also essential to give the pair a shared goal – if only in a subplot – to provide a reason for them to stay in the same room as each other. In *Pretty Woman*, Edward hires Vivian as his escort to help his business trip. They share the (subplot) goal of ensuring that she doesn't embarrass him in front of his business contacts.

Individual multiple protagonists

Individual multiple protagonists each have their own goals, and are most usually found in a multi-stranded story (see Chapter 11). In the most extreme case, they may be following different stories entirely – for example *Nashville* or *Crash* (the 2004 film) – with relatively small areas of overlap. As with the multi-stranded story 'nutshell', individual multiple protagonists will also reflect a common theme, which may not be obvious at first. Find what they share – which may be issues relating to guilt, for example, or spirituality, greed, ambition, honesty and trickery – and each may well embody different approaches to that theme.

Key idea

If you have multiple protagonists, give each a distinctive look, and repeat it in the script, so that we recognize each character very quickly as they appear.

With individual multiple protagonists, as with group protagonists, ensure that your characters are very distinct, with highly memorable characteristics – for example the clever one, the cocky one, the indecisive one – while at the same time remembering to retain freshness and subtle complexities.

The French horror TV series *Les Revenants* (*The Returned*) follows the interlinked stories of a number of people who have come back from the dead. Seemingly alive and normal, they seek to pick up their lives again, stirring mixed emotions in those in the small mountain town who have to deal with their reappearance. The theme that unites all the disparate characters, alive and dead, is that of secrecy; everyone has something to hide, and slowly those secrets begin to emerge.

Multiple protagonists pose an additional problem on TV as they may not appear for one or more episodes, and yet they must be recognized by the audience when they return. The writers must work hard to ensure that the audience can follow this complex pattern week by week.

Edit

Review the character constellation you developed in Chapter 6. For each of your multiple protagonists, be sure that you've made them as distinct and different as possible.

For each, choose at least one immediately visible attribute (style of hair or clothes, physical type, social background, prop, etc.).

Give them reasons to admire (or love) one another, albeit reluctantly, and something to share. Even the bitterest enemies often share more than they realize – a belief in their ideals, a dedication to duty and so on.

Make sure that characters are being developed every second that they're on the screen, using obstacles, subplots and inter-group conflict to allow you to show different traits.

If you find one of the protagonists taking over the story, you need to choose carefully between rebalancing the story or demoting the others to a support role. In many cases, the latter will be the strongest solution.

YOU HAVE AN UNMOTIVATED, PASSIVE PROTAGONIST

You have a serious problem. A passive protagonist is the one rule-break you can't get around. He'll suck the energy from your story. Audiences will forgive anything, if the writing is good, except passivity. The only solution for an unmotivated, passive central character is to give him a goal and ensure that he takes positive and continual action to try to achieve it.

Macon in the movie *The Accidental Tourist* withdraws from life after the death of his son. His passivity makes it difficult to identify with the story at any level and, despite the film winning awards, the reviews and audience response were mixed. A novel, such as the one on which the film was based, can get away more easily with a passive central character, as novels have other means at their disposal – language, stream of consciousness, a personal engagement between writer and reader – but films cannot so easily get the audience inside a character's world without motivated actions.

Almost as difficult is a protagonist with a negative motivation – a desire *not* to do something. One example is the American indie movie *The Station Agent*. In this film, Finbar inherits a disused station from his late employer. Without a job, he moves in, with the sole desire of being left alone. This negative goal leaves the story with nowhere to go and, notwithstanding some moments of humour, the film drifts.

If you find you have a protagonist with a negative goal, turn it into an equivalent positive goal. If he wants *not* to get married, then what *does* he want (e.g. leave the country, convince his fiancée that he doesn't want to marry her, find a better man for her himself …)?

 Focus point

A passive or negative character will kill your screenplay. You must make them active.

Workshop

Select one of your characters and read through a selection of their scenes in the workshop.

- Can you follow an arc? Are they flat, difficult or passive? Discuss the degree with which the readers engage with them or not.
- What part do they play in the story? Is it distinctively different? Are there other characters carrying out the same role? Is he believable? Interesting? Surprising?
- What are the character's strengths? What would you not want to lose?
- What techniques could be used to improve them, or should they be cut or combined with another?

Where to next?

With the character edit under your belt, you can safely turn to revising the individual scenes. In the next chapter we look at the scene-by-scene narrative of your screenplay, and how to make it flow strongly.

22

Redrafting scenes – building story energy

Once you've revised the draft for the characters, it's time to look at your individual scenes. However great the overall structure of any script, it's the individual scenes and sequences that provide the power. It's here that the audience engages with the story moment by moment.

With the scene edit, you focus on the moment-by-moment narrative and ensure that it has the right forward momentum and emotional energy.

If the script is long, you may need to consider cutting or combining scenes. It's easier to do this once you've made each scene work as well as it can. Finally, in this chapter, we'll look at undramatic scenes and when they might have their uses.

Starting the scene edit

Read each scene in turn. In particular, check that you are clear on who the protagonist of the scene should be. The audience will normally watch the scene from the psychological point of view of that character, so ensure that you've chosen the character with the most at stake. Also, take care that you're not inadvertently switching to another character's point of view during the scene. This risks diffusing the dramatic energy. Keep it clean.

Remember, a scene is a unit of story in which something changes. Be sure about what that change is, and adjust if necessary.

Next, are you clear on the GOATS – Goal, Obstacle(s), Action, Tactics and Stakes – for your main character? If any of the five are missing or weak, the scene will falter. Strengthen them. These form the dramatic spine of the scene.

Now look at any other characters in the scene. Each one needs their own goal, obstacles, actions, tactics and stakes.

Key idea

Every character in a scene needs to have GOATS – Goal, Obstacles, Action, Tactics and Stakes.

In the opening scene of *Passion Fish*, May-Alice wakes to find herself in a hospital bed. Her goal is to get up. However, she can't move her legs; she accidentally turns on the television instead of pressing the buzzer for a nurse; the nurse tries to calm her down rather than helping her get up (obstacles). Her actions are to try to call the nurse and insist on being helped. Her tactics are to argue, complain and generally throw her weight around. At stake is the fear that she can't control her own body.

The nurse (the only other person in this scene) has her own GOATS – she wants to calm May-Alice down (Goal); however, May-Alice is difficult (Obstacle); she tries to speak soothingly (Action); her tactics are to avoid the issue and, if possible, get a doctor to sort May-Alice out; and at stake is the well-being of a badly injured patient.

Edit

Take your first scene. Determine who the protagonist of the scene is, and whether the point of view remains consistent. Write down his goal, obstacle, actions, tactics and stakes. What has changed by the end of the scene. Has he changed? Do you need more change during the scene? Do the same for the other characters.

Now revise the scene to make the dramatic spine clear.

Starting and finishing scenes

A typical mistake that beginners make is to write scenes with too much introduction and too much tying up of loose ends at the end.

Forget all the hellos and goodbyes. A good scene starts and ends in the middle of things. Dive in where the story is hot. Start immediately with goal-obstacle-action and get out as soon as matters begin to cool again. You don't need to hang around while they shake hands and leave.

Key idea

Get in late – get out early.

Most scenes in a cinema screenplay should be focused on one dramatic beat (change). A few scenes will run longer, and have two or more beats, but they should be kept to a minimum or the script will feel slow. If the scene contains more than one beat, ask yourself whether you need all those beats. If you do, consider cutting after the first beat, and creating a new scene.

Viki King, in *How to Write a Movie in 21 Days*

'A scene doesn't need a beginning, middle and end; it needs to take care of business and be done.'

TV scripts have traditionally had more beats per scene than cinema, but now tend to follow the cinema model, especially with more action-based stories. Social drama and comedy, especially sitcom, still lean towards multi-beat scenes, often because they are shot faster and with fewer sets. Soaps classically get round this by intercutting between two storylines, which keeps the pace up.

Resist the temptation to tie up each scene with a neat ending, a tag line or action. Often, these read well when seen in isolation, but they round off the scene too completely. A good scene leaves something important unfinished and makes the audience want to see what happens next.

Key idea

If in doubt, cut it out.

The May-Alice scene could have dwelt on her sleeping, waking slowly, looking confused. Instead, it starts as she opens her eyes. Immediately she reaches for the buzzer. No preamble. The scene could logically have gone further than it does – with a doctor arriving to explain the situation, but instead we cut to May-Alice receiving rehab treatment in the hospital pool and any explanations are left until later.

Keeping focused on the heat of the action, however, doesn't mean that the scene must be narrow and predictable. However, any complications should relate directly to the main spine of the scene or the protagonist's inner story.

Having accidentally turned on the television, May-Alice finds herself watching herself starring in a daytime hospital soap. At the end of the scene, she complains that the director gave the other actress her close-up, setting up a theme of self-centredness that will run throughout the film.

Key idea

Leave the audience wanting more.

Edit

Revise the scene, trimming the start and finish. If in doubt, cut it out. Now focus on the action of the scene, to avoid repetition and distraction. If appropriate, though, allow complications to stop the scene becoming predictable. However, ensure that the complications relate back to the main spine of the scene, or to the character's inner journey.

Cutting and combining scenes

One common cause of an overlong script comes from two or more scenes doing the job of one. In such cases, you must either cut them or combine them into one scene that does the job of the rest.

REPEATED SCENES

In a first draft, you are exploring and experimenting, and often that leads to scenes which contain variations of the same idea in different contexts.

Suppose that you've written a sequence in which the protagonist buys a Valentine's Day card, red roses, chocolates, food for a special dinner, candles and a secret present. Do you really need all of these? Is anything really changing?

You're treading water and slowing the story down. You must be ruthless. If they are all great scenes, it can be a wrench, but you have to be cruel to be kind. If they are delaying the story, they go. Remember – kill your darlings. Or, to be more precise, cut them and keep them for another script.

If in doubt, choose the scene that is most dramatic, most unusual, most moving or poses the strongest question, and delete the rest.

Less obviously, you may have a number of scenes that look very different at first sight, but are still essentially doing the same job. For example, you might have five scenes that establish your protagonist's bravery. Again, choose the best and delete the rest.

Repetition can also apply within scenes. You will often find that a scene performs the same task two or more times. You may have been exploring the idea in the first lines, finding a better angle in the second part and encapsulating the whole action differently in the final third.

Decide which part is best, and cut the rest.

REVISING TO CUT

Sometimes you find half-repeated scenes, each of which does part of the work but not fully. The problem is that you can't cut one without losing something you need.

In three successive scenes, you show Tariq's fundamental honesty: the first has a clear goal but suffers from a lack of action; the second has action but isn't very believable; while the third has action and credibility but lacks a clear goal. You need to cut two, but they are each supporting the others, albeit weakly.

One answer is to revise one or more of the scenes so that they each work strongly. Once you have a strong scene that you're happy with, it's clearer that you don't need all three, and you can cut two of them without any qualms.

COMBINING SCENES

As with characters, you may find you have a number of partially developed scenes, which together would make one more interesting and surprising scene. In this case, the answer might be to combine them.

Create a single scene that has the strengths of the three combined and works properly.

Edit

Find scenes in your script that repeat the same idea or develop the same plot point. If they are strong, choose which is the best to keep. If they don't work, decide whether to strengthen one or more, or combine them into a single strong scene.

Layering

Good dramatic scenes carry out more than one purpose in a script. This adds to the interest and complexity of the story, and keeps the flow moving.

Thus, a scene whose main purpose is to advance the plot will also have other layers. These might include planting an idea for the future, paying off an idea that was planted earlier, developing one of the themes, showing new or changed character traits, or reminding the audience of a subplot.

Key idea

A good scene is multi-layered.

The short opening scene from *Passion Fish* has many functions. As well as starting the main storyline – May-Alice's struggle to cope with her inability to walk again – it establishes where we are and the fact that she is a soap star, develops her character, plants the idea that the doctor will be visiting, tells us she had an operation previously that she's forgotten, and leaves us with three major questions (what happened to her, what's going to happen next and will she be able to handle it?)

Joe Eszterhas, screenwriter, in *The Devil's Guide to Hollywood*

'Don't write a "leggy" script. Even though character-driven scenes will be the first ones to be edited for time and budget reasons, these are the scenes that will give depth to your script. Give it some heart; otherwise, as they say, your script will be "all legs"– all plot, racing from one point to another.'

Variety

At the same time, a well-structured narrative will vary the pace. Each scene should be significantly different from the scene before, in pace, tone or mood. Often, having left the audience wanting to know what happens next, the next scene will develop a completely different aspect of the main storyline or subplot, only returning to the previous strand once it, too, has set up questions that will be left hanging for a short while.

Key idea

Vary your scenes: pace, tone, mood. Keep the audience on their toes.

The opening scene with May-Alice answers none of the questions it raises. Instead, it's followed by a rather quieter, shorter scene in the hospital therapy pool, with less dialogue and a different focus.

Edit

Take any scene in your screenplay. What is its main function in the story? What other functions could it perform: developing character, adding humour or diversion, reminding us of an important fact, adding suspense, creating questions, keeping a subplot going, planting something you'll need later ...?

Add layers without distracting from the main reason for the scene – a comment here, an action there.

Now look at the scenes before and after. Make sure that they are noticeably different from one another, in pace, tone or mood. If not, how could you adjust them to add variety to the narrative?

Undramatic scenes

An undramatic scene doesn't mean a gentle or thoughtful scene; it means one without the dramatic basics – goal, obstacle, action, tactics, stakes. The gentlest scene still needs to have these – watch the films of the great Japanese director Ozu, such as *Tokyo Story*, and see how the drama builds powerfully beneath the apparent calm of the surface.

In most cases, the solution to an undramatic scene is to go back to GOATS and simply make the scene work. However, very, very occasionally you may want to leave the scene deliberately undramatic.

Undramatic scenes are rare (at most three or four per script) but they have their uses. Why might you want deliberately to write an undramatic scene? There are three possible reasons you might put a no-scene scene in your script:

1 tension or aftermath

2 descriptive/evocative/impressionistic

3 exposition.

TENSION SCENE

We've all seen it: the killer is out there. A policeman stands guard. The scene dwells in detail on every tiny action, from lighting a cigarette to investigating a dripping gutter ... Tension mounts.

A scene in which very little happens can be very effective in building suspense – the slow seconds before the big fight, the preparations for the parachute jump, the silence before the tornado ... Audiences know instinctively that a no-scene scene promises something big. But make sure that you deliver on your promise. Undramatic scenes that are not followed by significant action will leave your audience flat and disappointed.

Key idea

If nothing happens, the audience begins to expect something big – so make sure that you deliver.

AFTERMATH SCENE

This is the exact mirror of a tension scene – after a major shock or emotional climax, you're allowed a scene or two of non-action, to change the pace.

After a bomb explodes, people wander around numbly. After a climactic courtroom row, the protagonist simply slumps.

Aftermath scenes only work if they follow a genuinely strong emotional moment – the larger the climax, the more undramatic the aftermath can be.

DESCRIPTIVE/EVOCATIVE/IMPRESSIONISTIC SCENE

A short descriptive, evocative or impressionistic scene can help enrich the world of your story (this is not the same as exposition; see below). Whether it's approaching the slowly revolving space station in *2001* or tracking through the urban jungle in *Taxi Driver*, a moment taken away from story to establish atmosphere can be valuable. Such scenes can also be used to link or establish locations.

An impressionistic scene, as the name suggests, gives an impression of an emotional state. Examples include drug trips, dream sequences or romantic interludes in the park. The danger with such scenes is that they can not only become cliché but fatally slow the pace of the script. Keep them fast-moving and original.

The film *Witness* features a scene where the farmers build a barn. There is little dramatic action. It holds the audience's interest for a time because of the intrinsic interest of watching skilled craftsmen at work. However, without a dramatic spine it outstays its welcome.

Keep any such scene interesting, and short.

Key idea

Keep non-dramatic scenes short, interesting and moody.

EXPOSITION SCENE

An exposition scene (like an exposition flashback, Chapter 19) is one that is written purely to give the audience information and is therefore to be avoided at all costs. If you find yourself writing an exposition scene, either turn it into another kind of scene or cut it entirely and find another way to get the information to the audience. With the exception of the 'map scene' (see Chapter 23 on exposition, below), audiences hate exposition and informational scenes will sabotage your writing. Be ruthless.

MULTI-PURPOSE UNDRAMATIC SCENES

As with dramatic scenes, many undramatic scenes also carry out more than one purpose. Thus, a documentary scene may also be a tension scene and an atmospheric scene at the same time. An aftermath scene might also slip in some exposition.

In *Psycho*, Marion Crane escapes with the money she has stolen on impulse, to meet her lover and elope with him. In a three-minute scene, we watch her driving cross-country.

The scene is an aftermath scene (following the drama of the theft), descriptive (the detail of a long drive), impressionistic (we have little more than an impression of other cars, changing weather, nightfall), linking (it links Phoenix with the Bates Motel, and makes it very clear that she has travelled for many hours and that the motel is a long way off the beaten track) and tension (promises something dramatic will happen at the end of it … and it does).

Workshop

Read through a short sequence of scenes in the workshop. Look at the movement of the story scene by scene. Does it build? Is there variety? Have you given the scenes more than one purpose? Is there repetition, or are there scenes which only partially do their job?

Are there any undramatic scenes? Can you make them work dramatically? Have you tried to combine functions?

Where to next?

Now that you have a firm grasp on your structure, characters and scene-by-scene narrative, we can begin to polish the dialogue to ensure that every word is spoken to maximum effect.

23

Rewriting dialogue – clarifying and sharpening

You have a strong structure, well-developed characters and a powerful narrative drive; it's time to turn your attention to what the characters say. This gives you a chance to concentrate on their speech, without being distracted by the shape, the characters or the order of the scenes you've chosen to tell your story with.

The dialogue edit

As we saw earlier, screen dialogue mimics everyday dialogue, but is not the same.

Let's go into more detail this time. Polished screen dialogue needs to be:

- **Realistic** – which is not the same as 'real'. The job of a good dialogue writer is not to mimic the precise tics, confusions and meanderings of real dialogue but to give a tidied-up impression of the rhythms and music of how real people speak. We want the sound of real people, without the boring bits.

- **Oblique** – in life and in films people rarely say what they mean, but the meaning is 'between' the lines – in the 'subtext'.

- **Precise** – notwithstanding the above, dialogue should not be vague or unintelligible. It should generally be clear about what the characters are intending to say, even if they don't succeed. And avoid too many lines which trail off into …

- **Motivated** – in other words, people (in scripts as in life) only speak when they want to have an effect on someone: to impress them, to persuade them, to convince them.

- **In character** – you should be able to cover the names of the character and still know who's speaking from the way the dialogue is written.

- **Short** – whereas in real life people blather on for ages, in scripts you must distil down. Follow the 'rule of thumb' – cover the dialogue with your thumb, if it extends below, then the dialogue is too long! Allow yourself only a few longer speeches in an entire script, and then only for special effect.

- **Forward-moving** – often first-draft dialogue repeats the same pattern over again: 'I want to go out', 'I don't want to', 'Well, I do', 'I don't', 'Why not?', 'Because I'm tired'. Jump this to 'I want to go out', 'I'm tired.' Look hard for instances where the dialogue has fallen into a rut, or is stating the obvious, and cut, cut, cut.

- **Aesthetically pleasing** – we all like to hear entertaining and well-written dialogue that enhances the genre and style of the movie or TV drama. Wit, unusual turns of phrase, well-honed put-downs, a clearly observed epithet and thought that has been expressed in a particularly striking way are all good value in a script. Different characters will have different styles, but even illiterate or rough-hewn characters can sparkle with an appropriate yet strongly phrased line. Conversely, try to avoid having your characters express themselves in worn-out or obvious sentences. It bores the audience and weakens the originality of the characters you have developed.

Edit

Read through your first scene, and this time focus on the dialogue above all else. Mark and adjust any dialogue that fails to observe the rules.

Now that you know your story better, you'll be better equipped to cut unrealistic speech, change lines that are too obvious or vague, ensure that they are being spoken for a reason (goal/obstacle). Now that you know your characters in more depth, you can ensure that they each speak with their own voice, using the vocabulary, thoughts and rhythms that are right for them. You should also eliminate repetition and long-windedness and keep the momentum moving forward.

 Raymond Chandler

'The challenge of screenwriting is to say much in little and then take half of that little out and still preserve an effect of leisure and natural movement.'

Dialogue ping-pong

A typical early-draft fault is dialogue ping-pong. That's when a conversation bounces repetitively between two characters, like a table-tennis rally.

An interchange like this rapidly becomes monotonous. Liven it up by breaking up the rhythms. Vary the lengths of the lines. Cut answers and leave the questions dangling. Cut questions, and leave the answers as non-sequiturs. In this way, you free up the rhythm and give the audience the pleasure of filling in the gaps for themselves.

Audiences hate being told everything, and love being credited with the ability to work things out (even if you subtly have to lead them by the hand).

Take this exchange from *When Harry Met Sally*. We're in the Shakespeare and Co. bookstore, and Sally is with her friend Marie.

```
Marie looks up for a moment for a new book, sees
something.

                    MARIE (CONT.)
          Someone's staring at you in Personal
          Growth.

Sally glances over to the Personal Growth Section.
It's Harry.

                    SALLY
          I know him. You'd like him. He's
          married.

                    MARIE
          Who is he?
```

                    SALLY
Harry Burns. He's a political
consultant.

                    MARIE
He's cute.

                    SALLY
You think he's cute?

                    MARIE
How do you know he's married?

                    SALLY
Because the last time I saw him, he
was getting married.

                    MARIE
When was that?

                    SALLY
Six years ago.

                    MARIE
So he might not be married any more.

                    SALLY
Also he's obnoxious.

                    MARIE
This is just like in the movies,
remember, like The Lady Vanishes,
where she says to him, "You are the
most obnoxious man I've ever met" —

                    SALLY
                (correcting her)
—"the most contemptible"—

                    MARIE
And then they fall madly in love.

                    SALLY
        Also he never remembers me.

                    HARRY
        Sally Albright—

                    SALLY
        Hi, Harry—

                    HARRY
        I thought it was you.

                    SALLY
        It is. This is Marie …

Marie is exiting down the stairs. She waves goodbye.

                 SALLY (CONT.)
        … <u>was</u> Marie.

Sally turns back to Harry.

                    HARRY
          How are you?

(scene continues)

Figure 23.1 From *When Harry Met Sally*, screenplay by Nora Ephron, Rob Reiner and Andrew Scheinman

Look at the way in which Ephron varies the tempo, answering a question with another question, shifting the subject, using non-sequiturs and interruptions to keep the dialogue on the move. Short lines are interspersed with long, and every line is there for a purpose – to achieve a goal.

Snapshot exercise

Go through the example above, and note the variations. Seek out the goals behind each line. Note what the logical replies would normally be in an everyday conversation, and how rarely the characters give them. Mark the shifts and changes of subject, the places where questions are deliberately left unanswered. Look at the little speech about *The Lady Vanishes*. What point is it making and how might another writer have said it more prosaically? Why does Sally correct her? What do we learn about Sally and Marie in this scene?

Paddy Chayefsky, screenwriter

'First cut out all the wisdom; then cut out all the adjectives.'

Style and aesthetics

Craft your dialogue with an appropriate style to your story. This doesn't mean elegant overwritten wordiness, but just because your speakers are, say, down-to-earth or even unpleasant, it doesn't mean that they have to speak in low-life clichés.

Some of the greatest screenwriters (Ring Lardner, Nora Ephron, Woody Allen, Harold Pinter) have unearthed truthful yet rich language from unexpected characters.

Of course, dialogue must always serve the story, the characters and the emotions you want to create, but you can often find ways to make it interesting and aesthetically pleasing at the same time.

Revising for subtext

In real life, people rarely say what they're really thinking. This is the case, too, in the best scripts. Audiences like to feel that there is subtext beneath every line of dialogue – thoughts and feelings going on under the surface. It makes the characters feel real and believable. It also draws viewers into your story.

Conversely, if the lines are 'on the nose', the audience will become bored and dissatisfied. In fact, actors find it almost impossible to speak lines that lack subtext. The very best actors will try to invent a subtext for themselves. Less experienced actors will simply make your writing sound bad.

Look at the following:

```
                    MARY
           Do you love me?


                    FRANK
           I have to admit that I don't really
           love you very much.


                    MARY
           That makes me feel very unhappy, but
           I'll just have to get on with it,
           even though my heart is breaking.
```

Every line here is right on the nose, and even the greatest actors would have difficulty making this scene work. However, we can do better. The first line stays the same – sometimes under extreme emotional pressure, people do blurt out exactly what they mean. Even then, we suspect, there are further, hidden, reasons for Mary's sudden question.

```
Mary toys with her food. She looks up at Frank.


                    MARY
           Do you love me?


Frank says nothing but stares at his plate.
```

> **MARY**
> I'll get the dessert then. It's
> trifle. Your favourite.

In the redraft, Frank says nothing at all, but his silence speaks volumes. Mary understands that, and her reaction is to change the subject. Her emotions are too strong. She has to lose herself in distraction.

Go through every line of your script, ensuring that there is some element that the character is not saying. Context is important here. Inferences and innuendoes are more eloquent than speeches.

Key idea

In dialogue, what is not said is often more powerful than what is.

Write

Invent a new scene. For each line of dialogue, write down the character's thoughts, as if you could read their minds.

Now go back over the scene, turning every single thought into a line of dialogue or wordless action that attempts to hide that thought. See how the very attempt not to express a thought will reveal it, through subtext.

Viki King, in *How to Write a Movie in 21 Days*

'Dialogue is not conversation ... dialogue is a function of story. Three words can tell a whole story; all you have to do is choose their context.'

Troubleshooting dialogue

I HAVE SOME LONG SPEECHES – HOW CAN I MAKE THEM WORK?

Start by doing your best to cut all long speeches back to four lines (or even shorter). In most cases, this will improve the dialogue enormously. You rarely need as many words as you think you do.

If you still have one or two long speeches, you have to work hard to make them work. The first problem with a long speech is that the reader loses sight of what's happening on screen. Having been ruthless in cutting the speeches down to the shortest that will satisfy the script's needs, you should break it up with action so that we can 'see' the speech.

The action should preferably be dramatic but, if necessary, you can fall back on 'business' – have the speaker pick up a glass of water, stumble over a word, stare for a moment out of the window.

Keep the audience engaged – giving the speaker a strong goal, placing obstacles in her way (interruptions, distractions, anything that makes it difficult for her to get her message across), forcing her to adopt new tactics and, if necessary, raising the stakes.

 Key idea

If you have long speeches, try to eliminate them or keep them to a minimum. Then increase the dramatic context, and break them up into shorter segments to make them easier to read.

AM I ALLOWED TO WRITE VOICE-OVER?

For some reason, many writers seem to think that having an off-screen narrator is against the rules. So let's be clear: there is absolutely nothing wrong with writing voice-over, as long as you understand how.

The reason that voice-over has had such a bad press over the years is less to do with using voice-over itself – many great movies have a narration – than with how it's been used. The big mistake with voice-over is to employ it as a crutch, to tell the story rather than show it. If you're using narration as a means of telling the story, then don't.

The rule of voice-over is straightforward: the story should work without the voice-over, and work even better with it. The voice-over shouldn't carry the work of telling the story, but bring out aspects that we wouldn't otherwise be able to see. It should be as economical and brief as possible. And you must always make it clear what we'll be seeing on the screen at the same time. Otherwise, the script begins to read like a radio show.

 Key idea

If you're using voice-over, your script should first work well without narration – and work even better with it.

Voice-over can be used for many reasons, but it's particularly valuable when you have a character who doesn't easily express her feelings to other people, either because of who she is or because of the situation she's in. A voice-over narration then becomes a good tool for getting inside her head.

In *Juno*, written by Diablo Cody, Juno's sassy voice-over sets the tone for her character, while allowing the pictures to tell the story. From time to time, the voice-over returns to underline her cool alienation from those around her, with a dry wit that is never allowed to slow down the pace of the film.

Little of the story would be lost without it. All the important plot points are already there, in dialogue and visuals, and her character can be seen through her actions. But we'd miss much of the flavour and subtext of Juno's sharp-eyed view of the world and her struggle to discover her softer side.

I HAVE A CHARACTER WHO SPEAKS IN A STRONG ACCENT OR DIALECT

Writers often get unnecessarily hung up on how to deal with characters who speak with a strong accent or dialect. In fact, the rules are very simple:

- **Keep the dialogue as close as possible to standard English.** If you've told the readers that a character is (say) Serbian, African-American, Brummie, Chinese … they can be relied on to fill in the rest. Often, the character's name alone (Pieter, Indira, Zhu Ling) is enough for us to 'hear' the accent.

- **Keep spelling variations and words of dialect to an absolute minimum.** They are very wearing to read. Use a very few to indicate the general gist of the accent if absolutely necessary – but often no spellings need to be changed at all. This is particularly true if the speaker's English is supposed to be fairly good.

- Instead, what you do need to do is **find and bring out the authentic rhythm or music of that accent or dialect.** Some accents have a very specific lilt, a distinctive rise and fall. Take these lines from Spike Lee's *Do the Right Thing*:

```
               MOOKIE
Wait a minute. Wait a minute. I just
got here. You sweep, I betcha Sal
asked you first anyhow.
```

- We certainly 'hear' Mookie's New York Afro-American accent when we read this, but most of the effect derives from his name and the syntax: the repeated first sentence, the truncation of 'I just got here', the final 'anyhow'. Just one word is respelled – 'betcha' – for emphasis. The rest is all in our minds.

- **Research the character's voice and vocabulary.** If they would use certain words, use them sparingly, and avoid cliché. And if you use non-standard words, make sure that it is clear what they mean from the context. Never include footnote 'translations' of non-standard English – it looks amateurish and makes the reader feel patronized. Not a good idea.

I HAVE A CHARACTER WHO SPEAKS A FOREIGN LANGUAGE

If a character has to speak in a foreign language, then there are essentially four possibilities.

1 If you have a long exchange, you can write the dialogue in English (with an appropriate rhythm as necessary) and tell us the language up front:

```
Ricardo and Luisa speak Portuguese:

                    RICARDO
          Show me the way to the church or I
          shoot.


                    LUISA
          Don't be such a fool …

     … etc.
```

2 Alternatively, if the language is changing more rapidly, indicate the relevant language in parenthesis before each applicable line.

```
                    RICARDO
                (in Portuguese)
          Show me the way to the church or I
          shoot.


                    LUISA
                (in English)
          Don't be such a fool …

     … etc.
```

3 If we don't need to know what's being said, you can simply leave the lines in the appropriate language. (However, don't include too many lines like this and do get the lines checked by a native speaker before you send the script out.)

4 Finally, you can summarize the whole exchange in description, as in:

```
The two old men argue angrily in Turkish as Ryan
nervously looks at the clock.
```

You don't need to be consistent. If necessary, you can use all four methods in the same script, choosing whichever works best at the time.

I HAVE TO GIVE AUDIENCE INFORMATION THEY NEED TO KNOW – HOW DO I DO THIS WITHOUT APPEARING TO GIVE 'EXPOSITION'?

The audience need information to understand your story. But exposition – lines of dialogue that only exist to give information to the audience – spells screen disaster.

Take this speech:

> BILL
> Hi, Karen. It's good to see you here in the Seattle office on a Tuesday, a day you don't normally come in, because you're normally needed at home, helping your aged mother, who's been suffering from Alzheimer's and fell and broke her hip last week, after she escaped and went hang-gliding with her seventy-five year-old boyfriend, Gerry, who ….

Horrible. As always with screenwriting, the rule is *show, don't tell*. So, Plan A would be to find a way to show this information to the audience, through action and visuals. But what the books don't often tell you is that sometimes it's just not possible. To show all the information in the speech above would take far too long. Sometimes, you have to tell, not show.

Key idea

Sometimes you have to tell, not show …

The problem is that there is no credible reason why Bill would say any of this. He's telling Karen what she already knows, because the writer doesn't know a better way to get this information to the audience. Furthermore, the dialogue is totally undramatic (no goal – obstacle – etc).

So, Plan B is **to give Bill a goal** – a reason to speak. And, because this is drama, a goal means also providing something to overcome (obstacles). Then the information can come out more naturally as part of the conflict.

                    BILL
          Who's that?

No one answers.

                    BILL (CONT)
          Karen?

Karen puts her head round the door.

                    KAREN
          I'm not here.

                    BILL
          Good. I need you on the other side
          of Seattle in thirty minutes.

                    KAREN
          Bill! It's Tuesday.

                    BILL
          I know. It comes after Monday.

                    KAREN
     My mother ... ... etc.

However, drama takes time, and you don't always have the time to develop it, so Plan C
is to impart the information during an unrelated dramatic or tense situation.

Bill and Karen slide quietly away as their boss continues to yell at everyone in the room.

>   BILL
>   I love Tuesdays! Peace comes to
>   Seattle.

>   KAREN
>   I shouldn't even be here.

A stapler bounces off the wall. They flinch.

>   BILL
>   I know. How's your mother?

>   KAREN
>   OK, when she can remember where
>   she is.

A door slams.

>   KAREN (cont'd)
>   They've got a new Alzheimer's drug
>   they're going to try … … etc.

Plan D is **to distract the audience with something else to watch,** to make things moody and cinematic – moving characters, smoke-filled rooms, anything that takes the edge off the information being smuggled in. Aaron Sorkin, developing *The West Wing*, pioneered what Hollywood rapidly dubbed 'walkposition' – long passages of exposition passed on as the characters walked rapidly through the corridors of the White House. Look out also for 'sexposition' – where two or more characters impart vital information in a club while lap-dancers gyrate in the background of shot. Strong emotion helps, too.

Bill races down the stairs, talking as he goes.

                    BILL

         I hate Seattle, Karen! I hate
         it that you're hardly ever here
         on Tuesdays. I hate it that you
         spend the best years of your life
         looking after a woman who can hardly
         remember her own daughter's name,
         and can't wait to get away to break
         parts of herself -

                    KAREN
         It was only a hip -

                    BILL
         - going hang-gliding, for God's
         sake, at her age, and with that
         Gerry …
         (… and so on)

Meanwhile, Plan E is **not to tell us at all.** As a writer, you will have researched your characters, you'll know their backstory, where they live, the history of the place and all kinds of other fascinating facts that you're bursting to tell us. But do we *really* need to know? Most stories work just as well without the audience knowing that the heroine was scared by spiders when she was ten, and that the hero achieved a starred first at Cambridge. Indeed, audiences, as we've seen, often resent having everything spelled out for them.

Be disciplined. If you really do have some fascinating facts to impart, choose the most enthralling, and bin the rest. See how much you miss them: it will be less than you'd think.

BUT WHAT IF I STILL HAVE EXPOSITION THAT I CAN'T HIDE?

After you've used dramatic action, distractions and moodiness, and cut ruthlessly, there may well still be a chunk of exposition you need and can't hide.

You create what I call a 'map scene'.

The map scene originates from war movies. A typical war film opens with a scene of high-octane action, before the hero is flown back to meet the commander in a tent. Here the CO pulls out a map, points to the goal and tells our hero what he has to do and why. So a map scene more generally is *any* scene which tells us up front what the story is going to be about.

Almost all films and series in all genres have a map scene (with or without an actual map) into which all the remaining exposition is swept. This may be the scene where the two lovers first discuss the obstacles they will have to overcome. Or it may be the scene where the bank robbers lay out the details of their cunning plan.

Key idea

Sweep all your remaining crucial exposition into a map scene.

- In *Tootsie*, it's the scene in the agent's office where Michael Dorsey explains why he needs a part and his agent lays out just why no one will hire him.
- In *Schindler's List*, it's the scene in the factory where Oskar Schindler and Itzhak Stern tell each other (and us) why they're going employ Jews.

Audiences understand that stories need a moment to pause and make sure that everyone understands what the story is going to be about. As long as the map scene is interestingly written and there aren't too many such scenes in the script (one is usually quite enough), they accept it happily and move on.

Snapshot exercise

Reread the opening of one of your favourite screenplays, and mark all the information that you've been given without realizing it. You'll be amazed how much detail an expert screenwriter can hide inside the dialogue without you ever feeling you've been given 'exposition'. What techniques does the writer use to distract you (drama, movement, mood, etc.)?

Find and mark the 'map scene'. Does it work? What techniques does the writer use in this scene?

Finally, ask yourself how much information you have *not* been told. How much did you not need, how much did you work out for yourself, how much could be safely left until later in the story, when you wanted to know?

Workshop

Invent a scene in which a character overcomes obstacles to achieve a goal. Now decide on five pieces of apparently irrelevant information that must be planted in the scene.

Examples might include such details as the make and colour of a character's car, what he did the night before, the last three digits of his phone number, the name of the town he was born in, etc.

Insert these details into the scene without the reader or audience noticing that they have been 'told'. Any of the above techniques can be used, but try to vary the approach rather than using the same technique five times.

Work as a group, or work individually and compare notes at the end.

Where to next?

Having tried to make the dialogue as good as we can, we will now try our best to cut it all out. In the fifth edit, we move from the spoken word to the visuals.

24

Rewriting descriptions – adding screen values

By this point, the structure, characters and dialogue should be looking much better. But during the editing process the original energy of the first draft often begins to leak away. However, energy is the one vital element a script must have. Thriller or gentle comedy, it must push you along through the sheer vigour of its writing. In this draft, you'll begin to replace that energy – through images and sound.

The description edit

For the sixth run, read through each scene in turn, looking for visual (and aural) ways to express every dramatic beat. Your aim is to replace as much dialogue as possible with images and sounds that tell the same story.

 ## Focus point

How much of your story can you tell without words?

 ## Write

Before finishing her screenplays, veteran Italian writer-director Lina Wertmüller writes one draft in which she removes every single line of dialogue and rewrites the story as if it were a silent movie. Having done that, she will replace only that dialogue that is absolutely essential.

Try it – it's a very powerful exercise that will greatly strengthen your visual storytelling. Start with the first scene in your script and replace the dialogue entirely with visuals and non-verbal sound. Be creative. What visual could replace that fierce argument, in such a way that the audience would know what was going on? What sound effect might tell the story as clearly as a character calling out that she's home? Take everything out, and then replace only that which is absolutely essential.

 ## Eugene Vale, screenwriter

'The writer who wants to learn how to use dialogue in the motion picture should try to make his story understandable without the spoken word.'

Reworking the descriptions

As we saw when we were preparing to write the first draft, all description should be dramatically relevant at the time (see Chapter 14). The most basic fault in screenplay description is to write descriptions that belong to literature (mind-reading, editorializing, failing to advance the drama) or theatre (too mechanical, too prescriptive, in the wrong place).

Other faulty descriptions are just plain wrong (wrong tone, untrue, forced, out of character, predictable, flat, distracting).

Revising for energy

Most draft descriptions rapidly improve in energy and pace once they are pruned down. In all cases, cut:

- **repetition**, whether it's the overuse of the same words or repeated similar actions – watch out in particular for favourite words and phrases; we all have them

- **stating the obvious** (for example, if it's cold, you don't need to tell us everyone's wearing thick coats)

- **unimportant details that can't be easily arranged during filming** – such as specific weather conditions, unless they are crucial to the story

- **distracting details that lead nowhere**

- **names of pieces of music, works of art** and so on – unless again they are vital to the plot and you know they're in the public domain or you can afford the copyright.

And, of course, cut anything that **can't be filmed** because it's inside someone's head.

> ## Key idea
>
>
> Use the description edit to put energy back into your script.

Descriptions should be totally understandable and unambiguous. This is not a place for poetic vagueness. Descriptions should be readable, visual and active. Read good short stories to develop a sense of how language can be used to create rapid effects.

As we saw with treatments, precision works better than vagueness – especially because it forces you, the writer, to think clearly about what you mean.

Keep each paragraph short – one to three sentences. Anything longer will begin to look overwritten, so consider cutting down. If necessary, break up longer paragraphs to keep the pace going.

If you're unsure about the basics of grammar, punctuation and style, find out. Language is your tool, in the same way that paint is the painter's and melody and harmony the musician's. You owe it to your craft to know how words can work best for you. There are books on language, style and grammar and there are websites that deal with many common (and not so common) questions that writers ask.

Avoid abstract or long words, and cut down on adjectives and adverbs. They slow a script down and create distance between you and the reader. Direct language has more impact (Change 'She looks angry' into 'She's furious' and 'She is approaching' into 'She tiptoes closer'.)

Look for fresh language and strong verbs, and avoid the passive mood ('She kissed him' rather than 'He was kissed by her'), impersonal phrases ('he has to…' rather than 'it is necessary for him to …'), overuse of the verbs 'to be' and 'to have' ('it shines' rather than 'it is brightly lit' or 'it is shining') and all clichés.

Clichés weaken a script because they're vague and unspecific. They don't give the reader a clear, fresh image. A line such as 'He works his butt off' shows me very little. Compare this with: 'He drags the logs down to the river, his T-shirt soaked with sweat.' Your aim should be to create a stream of vivid images in the reader's mind.

Look again at the style you're using – should you be shortening the sentences to give more punch, or finding more poetry to evoke a quieter, more contemplative approach?

Key idea

Weak language and cliché weaken your writing. Use words that are active, specific and vivid.

Edit

Revise a scene for style. Check for clarity, specificity and cliché. Are you using the simplest, most direct method to communicate what you want? Can you find a clearer, more vivid way to say it?

Is the tone right? If you marked passages that you liked in the screenplay, refer to them once more to remind yourself of the style. Can you bring some of that tone into this scene, now?

Making picture and sound descriptions work for you

To strengthen your descriptions, look first at:

1 using movement and action
2 making the most of settings, décor and locations
3 choosing the right props.

1 USING MOVEMENT AND ACTION

TV or film, moving pictures should move. Physical action by your characters will bring your script to life – whether it's an exotic action adventure or a witty and urbane comedy. Find ways to get your characters moving and find movements and actions that develop character and tell the story.

Instead of asking for a drink, make your character walk over to the bottle and pour for herself. Instead of saying he's sad, have a character fling himself face down on to his bed, put on his favourite CD, run in the darkness for half an hour until he's exhausted or sit alone in his room and channel-hop aimlessly.

If you have a necessarily talky scene, search for ways to make it mobile. Can your characters talk while running down flights of stairs, cycling up the street, shouting at each other as they kayak through rapids or while simply working on adjacent cross-trainers in the gym?

Key idea

Moving pictures should move.

Write

Take any scene from your treatment and imagine what actions your character could take to achieve his goal.

Pretend, for the moment, that you're not allowed sound. Can you dramatize the scene in such a way that we're drawn into the story without hearing the dialogue at all?

Or, if the dialogue is essential, can you find an interesting and imaginative way to keep it on the move?

2 MAKING THE MOST OF SETTINGS, DÉCOR AND LOCATIONS

Descriptions set the scene, creating emotions in the audience – or failing to. Don't always accept the first location you think of. From the very first scene in the script, be aware that your choice of location can make or break the reaction of a reader or an audience.

Too many writers choose the first location that comes into their heads, but a visually uninspiring setting can sap energy from a story. On the other hand, a new and interesting location can bring a scene to life.

Ask yourself what the visual possibilities of the scene could be. Does a meeting have to be in an office, or could it be set in a lumber yard, beside a canal or in a disused library? Look for settings with the right emotional resonance: will an argument be more effective if it takes place on a beach? Or during a New Year's Eve party? Do you want the setting to play along with the emotion (a romantic split in an empty house) or bring ironic counterpoint (a romantic split at a wedding)?

Settings can also provide their own obstacles – for example setting a big emotional scene in an aeroplane, where the two characters have to keep their voices down even as the emotional temperature rises.

A predictable location can also be made fresh with a twist of décor. An office could be made entirely of scrap iron. Or piled high with boxes of perfume. Or squeezed into the back of a theatre while rehearsals are taking place. Or it could overlook a wrestling match …

Key idea

Find settings that bring something special and resonant to the story.

And don't forget sound. Different locations also have their own resonant sound atmospheres – the soft breaking of waves against the shoreline, the whine of jet engines at an airport. A highlight of *The Third Man* is the climax, set by Graham Greene in the cavernous, echoing sewers under the streets of Vienna.

Snapshot exercise

List the locations for the scenes mentioned in your treatment. Next to each, write down the resonance of the setting and then the emotions you want to achieve with the scene.

Now write three *different* possible locations for each scene. Which of the four do you prefer? If you stick with the original, how are you going to ensure that you maximize the value of the setting to underpin the emotions of the scene?

Richard Russo, screenwriter

'I have to constantly remind myself to see the story as clearly as I hear it. The physical world in which these characters live is as important as what they're saying and doing.'

Remember, film isn't only visual; it can also be very physical. Heat, cold, sweat, weight, height and depth can all be used to powerful effect.

The heat in *Body Heat* oozes out of the script and adds a tragic intensity to the noir story of a small-town lawyer who is drawn into committing murder, while in the British film *Buried* the suffocating, claustrophobic interior of the coffin that's the single setting for Chris Sperling's screenplay drives the movie forwards.

Key idea

Remind the audience of the physical reality – use heat, cold, height, space and so on for emotional effect.

3 CHOOSING THE RIGHT PROPS

Don't underestimate the value of the props that your characters use, when it comes to developing the screenplay. For our purpose here, props include any item that is owned, borrowed, handled, worn or otherwise made use of during a scene. They, too, can reveal story and character.

In *The Seven Samurai,* the Samurai fight with long and short swords, the villagers with wooden staffs and farm implements. That simple choice of props speaks volumes about the fault-lines within the village and goes to one of the fundamental themes of the story, the division between warriors and peasants.

In the movie *Something about Mary*, a zip, a dead dog and some unusual hair gel are drawn on for gross-out comedy, deliberately challenging the audience's preconceptions.

Look around you to spark your own insights and imagination. Any prop that has resonance with your life will have potential for adding emotional and psychological resonance to your script. Again, avoid the clichés and search for the fresh and the true.

> ## Write
>
> Choose a scene from your treatment and add props for your characters to use. Try to select props that carry meaning and aren't too predictable or cliché. Or see if you can use conventional props in an unusual way.

Introducing places and characters

A vivid and concise introduction can bring a scene to life. When you introduce a new place or character, your first-draft description will probably say far too much. Now is the time to cut it down. It should be brief and to the point, and yet evocative and distinctive.

Introduce a new location or character with a single, memorable – and *visible* – trait and then move rapidly into action or dialogue. Only bring in other details as and when they become dramatically relevant to the viewer.

The second scene in *Bonnie and Clyde* introduces the main street of the town where Bonnie Parker lives, and also, by implication, the life that both protagonists want to escape from. Newman and Benton sketch the main street in two sentences, before moving straight into action:

EXT. MAIN STREET — DAY

They are now on a small-town street of barber shops, cafés, groceries, etc. At the moment, it is deserted. They continue walking down the empty street, talking.

This early location in the romantic comedy *Moonstruck* (screenplay by John Patrick Shanley) is immediately active – bringing the place to vivid life:

INT. BUTCHER SHOP — DAY

WE SEE a cleaver whacking an oxtail into section. Now WE SEE Loretta, a few feet away, tabulating on a chopping block that is partially obscured by a row of hanging rabbits, unskinned.

The first time a character appears in description, their name is written in capitals, to mark their entrance. (Some writers will put character names in capitals every time they appear; this is also acceptable.) As with locations, a character introduction is best given briefly and then immediately expanded by actions that add further to the characterization. Back to *Bonnie and Clyde*:

```
Extreme close-up of a woman's mouth. She is wearing
bright red lipstick. The camera pulls back to reveal
BONNIE PARKER. Blonde, somewhat fragile, intelligent
in expression, she is standing in front of a mirror
putting on make-up.
```

The writers take us straight into a vivid image of Bonnie's lips, before giving us no more than a half-sentence of character blurb – *Blonde, somewhat fragile, intelligent in expression* – then directly back to action again. This is the only description of Bonnie in the script. Everything else we learn about her comes from her actions and dialogue.

Dennis Potter introduces us to a major character in the TV series *The Singing Detective* with similar economy:

```
Suddenly into view comes a well-dressed man in a good
overcoat. MARK BINNEY. He stops. His eyes narrow.
```

When a new character is brought into an episode of *Hustle*, writer Matthew Graham creates a little climactic bustle of phrases that echo the activity around the character herself:

```
A flurry of excitement heralds the arrival of a
statuesque New York lady in flowing designer clothes.
She is limping on a cane and trailed by a coterie of
admirers. MEREDITH GATES.
```

(from *Hustle*, Season 1, Episode 3, 'Picture Perfect')

By now, you should be getting the point. Writers agonize over how much they should tell the reader about a character on first appearance, and the answer is very little. Name and the briefest of first impressions are all that's required at this stage.

 Key idea

Introduce locations and characters in one sentence, followed by action.

Note that in none of these three examples are we given their ages. Putting every character's age (usually in brackets) is an obsession with beginner screenwriters, but it is rarely necessary, and can get rather monotonous. Most often, the age range becomes rapidly clear from the context.

Similarly, at no point are we told that anyone is beautiful or handsome. This would, for one thing, be amateurish and unnecessary. Most films and TV programmes star attractive people. It would only be relevant to mention if they *weren't*!

Write

Write an introduction to a new location and an introduction to a new character. For each, give one or two sentences of description and an action that shows what kind of place or person it is.

Settings to avoid

Three situations that challenge all writers are restaurants, phones and computers – partly because they are so familiar and overused, and partly because they tend to render the characters boringly static.

Restaurant scenes trap the characters in their seats. If you must have a restaurant scene (and they are admittedly difficult to avoid), then either make the static nature of the scene work for you, or try hard to find an interesting way to stage it. Or make the scene so rivetingly strong that we forget where we are.

Phone conversations have at least become somewhat easier to keep moving now that most people have mobiles. However, the physical lack of connection between the actors limits their range and the scenes can become rather flat and predictable. Again, keep them short and try to find a fresh approach.

Computers pose many problems. They seem attractive at first, but almost always involve a number of people standing in front of a screen, reading. Not only is it difficult for the director to stop the scene becoming static, but you also either have to make the audience read the screen (which only works for very short sentences at a time) or have one of the characters read or explain for us. The alternative, that the computer reads the message aloud, is hardly any better.

Again, try your hardest to find another way to stage your scene and, if all else fails, make such scenes as dramatically interesting (and short) as possible.

Creating the right images

Look carefully at the pictures you're conjuring in the reader's mind. Are they interesting and do they help the style or drama of the story? Are there any images that might create the wrong impression? For example, a banal image in a moment of tension might sabotage the mood.

Key idea

The right or wrong word can have a powerful effect on the reader, for better or worse.

By contrast, choosing precisely the right image can condense swathes of dialogue down to a powerful story moment – illuminating plot or character like the sudden flash of a camera in the dark. These are known as **flash-bulb moments**.

In a late episode of *The West Wing*, Donna and Josh are on the campaign trail and growing closer, but have not yet taken their relationship that step further. One night, Donna announces she's going to have an early night, quietly leaving her hotel room key in front of Josh. Before he can move, a colleague snatches up the key and runs after her, thinking that she's left it behind accidentally. Josh sits motionless, showing no visible emotion.

The whole moment takes far less time than it takes to write, but contains at least three flash-bulb moments: the surreptitious leaving of the key; the colleague finding it and jumping to the wrong conclusion; Josh's dilemma, unable to show his reaction.

Look for such moments in scripts and make note of them. How do they work? Can you think of a place where you could use that idea? You'll doubtless spot many clichés – the pregnancy test that shows positive, the candlelit dinner that the lover doesn't turn up to. Can you find a way to revitalize the cliché and make it fresh?

 ## Snapshot exercise

Invent a few situations, and try to create at least three different flash-bulb moments for each one that show the audience what's going on, if possible without any words at all. Avoid the clichés and find images that are fresh and original.

Here are some situations to start you off:

- Dani is pregnant.
- Grock is opening a new restaurant in an hour's time, and he's run out of a key ingredient.
- Ursula's credit card is maxed out.
- Zizi is planning to break with tradition and propose marriage to her boyfriend.

 ## Focus point

Look for flash-bulb moments in your script – moments where you can encapsulate a thought or a dramatic beat in a single image.

Camera tricks – and how to use them

In general, you must avoid writing in anything that could be seen as a camera direction. Nothing will show you to be an amateur as fast as writing in the camera shots or moves. Your job is to tell the story, simply and without technical distractions.

You may well find scripts that break this rule. In most cases, they will be older films (early films were often written this way), shooting scripts or scripts that have been written up after production by film buffs. Don't follow their example.

However, that doesn't mean that a writer shouldn't have a view on how a story should look on screen. In fact, a screenwriter *must* develop a strong visual sense of how the programme or film is to look and find *non-technical* ways to express this on paper. But to do this, you have to be a little sneaky.

The trick is in the way you use language. Write it as you see it, not as you'd film it – give us the *impression* of the shots, without the technical details.

Key idea

Don't write camera directions; write how the shots appear.

For example, certain sentences automatically create the effect of size and distance. Others create a mental image that has to be small and close.

So you don't need to write:

```
WS: Empty hall.
MS: A security guard moves slowly along, stops by
one of the chairs
CU: The guard picks something up.
```

Instead write:

```
In the vast hall, long lines of chairs wait, empty.
A security guard walks anxiously between the lines,
a small bulge betraying a gun under his jacket. He
stops by one of the chairs, reaches down and picks
up a single blue feather.
```

In this way, you create the effect, to the reader, of a wide shot, followed by medium shot and close-up, without any technical terms being used at any point.

Having said that, sometimes a technical direction is the simplest and most cinematic way to get across a point. In that case, go ahead and use it, as long as you use such terms sparingly. (And if you do use a technical term, always write it in capitals.)

Useful terms are:

TRACK (move the camera along the ground)

CRANE (move the camera up into the air or back down again)

ANGLE ON (to emphasize that you've shifted to show a different person, or a different area of the locale, within a scene)

POV (when you want to underline that we are seeing from the point of view of a particular character)

INTERCUT (when introducing a sequence where you want to cut continuously between different locations without having to keep saying it throughout). For example:

```
INT. GARAGE — DAY

Josephine dials on her mobile. We INTERCUT with

EXT. FUNFAIR — DAY
```

Ahmed is on a big dipper. He answers.

                    AHMED

            This is not a good time.

Josephine examines the monogrammed handkerchief.

                  JOSEPHINE

            We need to talk …

(etc.)

Complex visual effects are fine, if they are dramatically necessary (and appropriate). As above, describe them in layman's language. So don't write:

CGI will SUPERIMPOSE starships moving towards camera against BACK-PROJECTION …

Leave the technology to the technicians. Go for the emotions:

Starships swoop down from out of the night sky …

Workshop

Take a scene from a favourite produced script and workshop it – are there any words that could be cut or improved? Discuss the pictures and sounds it creates in your mind. Does it create the appropriate mood and emotion? Are there any false steps? Surprises?

Now select a scene of your own. How does it compare? Are there any techniques or tricks you can apply to yours?

Are there words you could cut or improve? Different images or sounds that would create a stronger effect?

Where to next?

You've given your script five detailed edits, for structure, character, scene narrative, dialogue and description. By now it should be almost finished. But there remains one final, and crucial, stage. This sixth edit can make the difference between failure and success. In the next chapter, we look at the final polish.

25

The final polish – the difference that makes the difference

Don't underestimate the time a script takes between almost right and finished. This stage can feel very frustrating, especially if you believe you have a cracking good idea and can't wait to get it out to the industry. But producers and agents are busy. They'll only read your script once. You owe it to yourself to present the best possible work that you can.

Emotion, premise and genre

With all the editing that's taken place, it's easy to forget the basic purpose of your script. Go back once more to your premise. Ask yourself again whether the script reflects the fire that originally lit up your idea.

Be honest. What needs to be added or taken away? Have you lost sight of the dramatic incident that sparked the story? Do your main characters spend enough screen time with each other? Has the tension somehow gone missing in the effort to make the story work?

If necessary, revisit the chapters on structure, characters, narrative, dialogue and description, until you've fully diagnosed the problem.

Emotion is often the most important element to be forgotten in the struggle to get the words down and edit them. Remind yourself of the primary emotions you were aiming for – fear, comedy, horror and so on. Are they there on the page? What could you do to increase them?

 Focus point

Push the emotions in your script further, deeper and truer than before.

Be clear about what genre/genres you are working in. The patterns that come with those genres will help you develop the emotions you need. If you're writing a noir, for example, have you included the key noir motifs – deception and betrayal, dark city streets, lone characters with little to live for, violence, guns, sex...?

Revisit films and programmes in your genres and remind yourself of their primary motifs. Are you missing a few tricks here? Look at what's out there, and what you can learn from them. Remember, too, that genre means surprise. Are you delivering something fresh and new?

Don't underestimate the power, energy and precision that needs to go into any successful script.

 Paddy Chayefsky, in *The Craft of the Screenwriter*

'The writer's job is to take charge of the script, to take full responsibility for the script. Don't depend on anyone else to get it done for you. Don't count on the director covering holes for you; don't count on the actors covering for you. Get the script done yourself. Be constantly responsible for it.'

What have you left undone?

Before you move on, give yourself one more moment to pause. What have you still not done? I guarantee that there'll be one thing you've been putting off.

Maybe it's a character you've left in who you know in your heart should really be cut. But you love him, and you've been trying to convince yourself that he really works … Now is the time to face facts and cut him out.

Sometimes a writer hangs on to what I call 'eggshell'. This is a piece of the original idea that may have been needed to develop the project but has outlived its usefulness. Watch out for any remaining eggshell, and discard it now.

Often, however, the problem is more urgent. It's a key scene that you've been avoiding writing. You know it's needed but somehow you never got round to it. Possibly, the emotions are too close to home. Or some other difficulty is stopping you. Now is the time to be brave and write it.

The change you've been avoiding, however small it may seem, will very often turn out to be the very element that takes the screenplay to an entirely new level.

Write

What have you been avoiding?

What's stopping you?

Do it now.

Raymond Chandler, *The Long Goodbye*

'There is no trap so deadly as the trap you set for yourself.'

Typos, format and spelling

When you have the draft as good as you can make it, read it through for one last time, checking thoroughly for any last errors.

Presentation is one way the industry sorts would-be professionals from amateurs. By laying the script out correctly, you're saying that you care about doing the job right and will be easy to work with. Why would you not do that? (Details of professional script format can be found in Appendix 2.)

At the same time, double-check for spelling errors and typos. Don't rely on your spell-checker; it will miss words that are properly spelled but wrong in context, such as 'here' instead of 'hear'.

Key idea

Presentation is one of the ways the industry sorts the professionals from the amateurs.

Examine the most important words extra carefully. For some reason, writers are more likely to miss mistakes that concern the things they care about most – such as the title, your main character's job or the counterfeit painting at the very heart of the plot.

If your story is all about a stolen Ferrari, then make doubly sure you've put all those *rs* in the right place.

Edit

Print out the whole script and read through it carefully. Don't rely on checking on screen. Somehow, errors which are invisible on the computer become glaringly obvious in print.

This final reading is also a safety net for other mistakes. By this point, there shouldn't be too many large errors, but you may well spot misnamed characters, inconsistencies or even lines that can be quickly improved.

Of course, if you see anything larger that needs fixing, go back and sort it out. It's always painful to spot a weakness in the script, but better to spot (and deal with) it now than after you've sent it to a dozen important producers.

Simon Williamson, agent

'Don't send it out if you're in two minds. Fix it.'

Getting feedback

You've proofread your draft in detail and are doubtless impatient to sell it. However, you're still not finished. Before you send a script out to a producer or agent, you absolutely must obtain feedback, just as you did when you tested the premise.

No writer, not even at the peak of their career, can see all the strengths and weaknesses of their own work. It's only too easy to send out a script that has a crucial, but easily fixable, flaw. You might think that it's the job of a producer or agent to help you find that flaw, but they're not in the business of developing you as a writer. That's your responsibility.

The first stage of screenwriting is one that you undertake more or less on your own. Now it's time to involve your network, or start building one.

Step one is to give your script to two trusted friends. If you don't already have a workshop group, choose two friends who will be gentle with you.

Focus point

You must get feedback on your script – from friends, then from professionals.

Reading a draft script takes much more work and imagination than reading a novel, so if they're not in the industry give them some guidance. Suggest that they imagine their favourite actors playing the roles (feel free to cast the roles for them). Explain that a script must give only the bare bones and that they must create the scenes in their minds.

Ask them to tell you what they liked about the script (sometimes people forget to do this). Tell them that you don't expect them to know how to solve any problems they find, but you still want them to be honest with their criticisms.

It can be very useful to provide them with a list of questions to answer as they read, especially if you have specific issues or doubts. For example:

- *Stop at page 10. Do you know what the story is about yet? Who is the main character? Do you care what they want?*
- *Page 30. Does this scene slow the pace? Or is it a useful comic interlude?*
- *Page 59. Do you remember who Dr Oosterhuis is? Do you need me to provide a reminder?*

When you receive their comments, feel free to take the praise personally, but not the criticism. However harsh it may feel, they are trying to help you make it better. The tiniest criticism will appear devastating at first. The gentlest suggestion will sound life-threatening. Don't be tempted to argue back. Simply listen to what they have to say, and thank them for their time and effort.

Key idea

The tiniest criticism will appear devastating at first.

Give yourself time for your anger, depression, grief and so on to die down, and then get back to work.

How to take and use criticism

One of the most important skills of a good writer is the ability to listen to criticism and turn it into constructive action. Screenwriting is a collaborative art. Like it or not, you will be listening to comments and criticisms all your writing life. Moreover, you already have been. The first, and most important, critic of your work is yourself. Now it's time to get good at turning all that criticism to good use.

Laozi, in *Tao Te Ching*

'The truth often sounds paradoxical.'

There are three possible kinds of criticism you may receive:

1 **Right on the button** – some criticisms are just obviously right. You knew it and have been trying to ignore it. You may get angry, go into denial, punch the wall, but in your heart you know they're right.

2 **Totally wrong** – other comments are so obviously wrong you almost laugh. I once tried to sell a film to a distributor who announced she never bought a film with a snake in it! Feedback of that nature can be safely ignored. (Unless a large number of people say the same thing – if all distributors had said they hated snakes, I'd have needed to listen.) However, if you find yourself becoming angry or defensive, then look more closely. There may be an important issue here that you're avoiding.

3 **Scattergun** – often, however, readers don't know what the real problem is. Even experienced readers may not be able to unpick what is causing them to react in the way that they are. You may even receive a number of comments, all of which scatter around a particular area but might all be missing the true target. For example, three different readers may separately find fault with Scenes 4, 5 and 7. However, it could be that Scenes 4 and 5 look wrong because they build to a climax that's expected in Scene 6 but doesn't happen. And Scene 7 doesn't work because it should follow an event that never took place. The real problem lies with Scene 6, which nobody mentioned at all.

 Key idea

Feedback can sometimes be tricky to decipher.

Another typical situation occurs when different readers disagree. One tells you (say) that your story is not serious enough, whereas another says it needs to be funnier. Ironically, they could both be right – and both wrong. The story is stuck in the middle, half serious and half funny, and not quite succeeding at being either. The solution may be to go one way or the other: either make it more serious or funnier, but don't stay where you are.

As you can see, feedback can sometimes be tricky to decipher. But, in the end, you're in charge. Don't try to argue back, because it's more important to listen clearly to what people are saying to you. The stupidest response from a reader may reveal something you failed to communicate in your script. Take that on board. See whether anybody else shares that problem or whether it's a one-off.

It's not about winning an argument, it's about getting it right on the page. Ultimately, it will be you, not them, who decides what goes in and what comes out.

Make sure that you've allowed enough time to make the changes you decide are necessary. If there are many issues, then you may need to write a full new draft as we did before, starting with the structure and working through to the final polish.

Key idea

The only thing worse than bad feedback is no feedback.

Getting professional feedback

You're still not finished. By this point, at least two friends have given you feedback, and you've made the changes you felt necessary. But friends will generally try to be nice. A professional knows the reality – she can judge your work by industry standards and spot the flaws that can sabotage an otherwise excellent script.

Professional script reports may not be cheap, but they will save you time and money in the long run. You'll find a variety of report services on the Internet, from freelance script readers to companies. Before you commit, check out the reader's CV and, if possible, ask for a reference from a writer who's used them before.

A good service will offer short bullet-point reports as well as longer reports, and possibly also custom-made feedback and personal consultations. The bullet-point reports give you the main strengths and weaknesses, with constructive suggestions for how to address the latter, and they can be an economical way to try out a service first. In longer consultations you can set the agenda and discuss your work with a consultant at greater length.

You may see the term 'coverage'. In the industry, this usually means a one-to three-page summary report, usually a set of tick boxes with a brief synopsis, ending with a suggestion to pass (decline), consider (there are strengths but also issues to be addressed) or recommend (a strong script that is recommended for production without reservation). If offered coverage, make sure that it also includes constructive suggestions for how to deal with any problems, as coverage would not normally include them.

 Edit

Every time you ask for feedback, allow time to make use of it. Decide which points you want to use, and write another draft. Again: scripts aren't written, they're rewritten.

Be flexible. Know your script's primary goal and be prepared to change anything else to make that goal achievable. Keep all your drafts in a special folder for reference and try everything sensible that's suggested – if it doesn't work, you can always go back to a previous draft.

Hearing your script read

One of the most powerful methods of obtaining feedback is to hear your script read, out loud. This might sound scary (it is) but it's well worth it, and you'll progress faster as a writer than in almost any other way.

The simplest, and often most effective, method is to gather a group of friends or fellow writers and allocate one or more roles to each. If possible, have a separate person read the descriptions and on no account take a part yourself. Your job is to sit, listen and (if you wish) make notes. Ask that the script (or a selected section) is read through without interruption.

You'll get more unspoken feedback by listening to the words than a hundred discussions can give you. It helps if the readers are somewhat similar to the roles, but it's not essential. Nor do they have to have any acting skill for you to hear how the script works.

You'll immediately hear where the story flags and where it lifts; where the tension rises and where a scene goes on too long. Only interrupt if a reader has so completely misunderstood a part that it's throwing the entire story off course. In this case, start by praising what they have done so far, and gently ask whether they can readjust as appropriate.

Afterwards, allow the readers – and audience, if there is one – to discuss freely. Don't try to explain or defend. What you're after is their honest first impressions, which will be more valuable than gold dust.

If your friends have time, and especially if there is someone with directing experience, you can organize a rehearsed reading. This gives each reader a chance to dig a little more deeply into the characters. You can also arrange readings (cold or rehearsed) with experienced actors. If you don't know any, contact a local amateur or professional acting group or a local theatre. You may have to pay a token fee for their time, or they may be happy to read for the fun of it.

A few organizations even offer script readings as a service. Rocliffe New Writing Forum, in London, runs regular events where writers can submit a script extract. If selected, the scenes are rehearsed and performed by professional actors, under a director, and then discussed by the audience and a panel of industry experts. Even if you don't have a piece chosen, it's well worth going to watch those that are and listening to the critiques.

Finishing

At some point, however, the job is done. Set yourself a deadline. Too many unsuccessful writers spend too long on each script before moving on, or never finish at all. It's too easy to be seduced by the idea that the next rewrite will transform your script into a winner.

 Key idea

Scripts are never finished, they're abandoned.

Some screenplays grow as far as they can. It's as important to accept that you've done as much as you can as it is to know that you have to bust a gut to write a new draft. If you keep rewriting the same script for three years, you end up with one script, which probably still has flaws. And you still have only one script to sell. In that same time, you could have written 12 different screenplays, using what you've learned, and have 12 times the chance to make a sale and take the next step of your career.

Philip Roth, novelist

'The road to hell is paved with works-in-progress.'

How do you know when to stop? There are no hard-and-fast rules, but here are a few guidelines:

- If you've gone through the stages of depression and elation and can now see good and bad in it at the same time, it's probably finished.
- If the feedback on new rewrites doesn't improve dramatically, you've probably done as much as you can, and should move on.
- If you've listened to feedback, polished, put back the energy that was lost, and are totally confused as to whether it works or not, it's almost certainly finished.
- If you're making changes and almost immediately changing them back again – stop! You've definitely finished.

Some scripts just are what they are, so take what you've learned and start selling it.

Workshop

Organize a reading of part or all of your script. If appropriate, prepare questions beforehand, to help focus the reading, or tell the workshop which areas you are most concerned about.

Listen with the script and a pen in your hand. By all means note the odd duff line, but most of all get a feel for the general shape. Mark the points where the readers, or listeners, laugh, or grow particularly engrossed. Notice in particular where you, yourself, are swept along by the story and where your mind wanders on to other issues. If you find yourself distracted at any point, make a note on the script. That scene may not be working so well.

Afterwards, discuss it with the readers. Say as little as possible, but listen carefully to their responses. Remember, you don't have to win the argument. Ultimately, you are the one who'll eventually decide what goes in and what comes out.

Where to next?

By this stage, you'll have received a large amount of feedback and been surprised by how much you've managed to improve the script you thought was finished. You may have written anything from four to 40 new drafts or redrafts. You've tightened, enhanced, revitalized, and you couldn't rewrite another comma.

It's time to send it out.

26

Preparing to go to market

Here we look in detail at what you need to know in order to sell your script. What do you want to achieve? Who are you selling to? What do they want and where do you find them?Then you'll need to know how to approach them – and the pros and cons of having an agent.

Why do you want to sell your script?

This may seem a strange question. Indeed, the answer may seem so obvious it isn't worth asking. Or is it? Here are some possible reasons, given by writers at my workshops:

- to make money
- to get my film made
- to tell a story
- to educate
- to entertain
- to get a credit
- to develop my career
- to give myself confidence
- to work with others
- to make connections in the industry
- to gain a track record
- to change the world
- to learn
- to set up the next film
- to get into TV
- to become rich
- to become famous
- to impress my friends
- to become a director
- to communicate a message
- to prove I can.

You could probably add many more. However, not all goals can be attained at the same time. And some producers and agents may be better for one than another:

- One producer may be likely to get your film made, but not offer you any money.
- One producer may have money, but may not get your film made.
- One producer may have money, and get it made, but it'll probably change from the story you wanted to tell.
- One producer will probably get it made, but has a reputation for bringing in her own writers.

If you don't know why you're selling, how can you know whether you're pitching to the right person?

Snapshot exercise

Write a list of the reasons why you want to sell your script. Be honest with yourself. Make sure that they're *your* reasons, not goals that you feel you ought to have.

List your reasons in order of priority, and highlight the top three. These are the aims you'll need to focus on most, as you plan your campaign.

Who are you selling to?

As a writer, you're likely to be talking mostly to producers and agents. The producer lies at the heart of the industry. She raises the money, finds or commissions the script, hires the director, the actors and the crew, pays for the production and sells the film for distribution. She may be independent, and have relationships with the distributors, studios or TV channels, or she may work in-house, in a studio or TV station, where her 'market' is made up of her colleagues, but the job is essentially the same.

You may also find yourself talking to the people who deal with producers – film distributors, TV commissioning editors or development funds (such as those granted by the BFI) who have specific funding for finding and developing screenwriting talent. Or you may be talking to assistants or development executives, who act as gatekeepers, filtering out the dross and sending recommendations on.

At the same time, you'll doubtless be thinking about finding an agent to represent you. But, as we'll see at the end of the chapter, an agent is not essential and certainly won't do all the work for you. Indeed, many successful screenwriters have no agent at all.

They all, however – producers, executives, agents – need you as much as you need them. Without good scripts, they have nothing. Approach them professionally, with an understanding of what they require, and expect to be treated professionally in return.

 ## Julian Friedmann, agent

'Make it clear that you welcome change and desire to improve and you'll be welcomed back. Make it your business to know the producer's problems and make it clear you know them and you'll be loved.'

What do producers want?

Having asked why you want to sell, it's appropriate now to ask why a producer might want to buy.

What everyone in the film and TV business ultimately wants is to be excited. If people get excited, they sign cheques, beg to star, direct and crew, sign for less than their normal fee, put in their best work, design great posters and do all that's needed to make your story hit the screen.

 ## Jane Wittekind, ex-Head of Development, Enigma

'Even after reading hundreds of scripts, I open every new script with a real anticipation that this one will be a real goodie. A script that will make me nod with recognition because there's something truthful, that strikes a chord, even if the situation is alien. A ring of truth.'

But, however excited a producer gets, she has five unavoidable questions in her mind. If those questions aren't answered to her satisfaction, then your pitch won't succeed, no matter how good it is. These five questions are:

1 **Appropriate?**

2 **Budgetable?**

3 Cinematic?

4 Different?

5 Employable?

1 APPROPRIATE?

If your idea doesn't fit with her career plans or those of her employers, then your pitch will fail immediately. You must do your research. Don't waste your time, or hers, pitching a star-led comedy to a company that makes only low-budget horror. Don't pitch an offbeat romantic indie series to an agent who represents only mainstream crime writers.

Focus point

Before approaching a producer or agent, you must do your research.

Of course, not all the information is publicly available. People and companies change. Look to see whether she's quoted in *Screen* or *Variety* as saying that she's starting to look for different genres or move into new markets.

And, if you're not sure, ask. Phone or email and check whether your genre is right for her at the moment.

Snapshot exercise

Search online or use an industry directory (see Appendix 5) to find companies or freelance producers that seem appropriate for your project. List the comparable projects they've developed and the reasons why they seem right for yours. Search trade and professional websites to see whether the producer has any recent interviews that might show what she's planning now. Begin to create a list of potential targets, in order of likely interest.

2 BUDGETABLE?

Can she produce it for less than she's likely to make in sales? The true budget of any cinema film or TV programme isn't what you can film it for; it's what you can sell it for. As a writer, you don't need to know the details of budgeting – but you do need to know the market.

Adult cinema (i.e. not children's) has traditionally been divided into four markets – or quadrants:

Male under 24	Female under 24
Male 25 and over	Female 25 and over

Figure 26.1 The four cinema quadrants

While audiences have been shrinking and changing in recent years, the model still remains essentially valid. The top two quadrants roughly comprise the main multiplex audience. They watch stories with wide appeal. This means your script will need to offer accessible emotions (thrills, fear, justice, romance, etc.) and roles that will appeal to stars, although these can include antiheroes and cameos.

Films for these two quadrants would include *Gravity*, *The Hobbit*, *Mamma Mia !* and *Bridesmaids*.

The over-25s are more difficult to sell to. They go out less frequently and are therefore more choosy when they do. They read the reviews and may gravitate more to the independent, art-house or specialist cinema screens.

It would be a mistake to think that films in the lower two quadrants are simply those that failed to make money in the multiplexes. This more mature audience wants films that are different: with more challenging themes or an unusual style, revealing subcultures or offbeat characters. It tends to be attracted by star directors rather than star actors. However, this is a much smaller market, so a script for the indie market will need to be cheaper to make – with cheaper locations, a smaller cast and fewer (if any) special effects.

This sector would include movies such as *All about My Mother*, *Philomena*, *Pan's Labyrinth* and *Nebraska*.

 ## Elliot Grove, founder of the Raindance Film Festival

'*Every now and then I meet a screenwriter who has a well-written story and who understands the commercial realities of getting their words off the page and on to the screen.*'

In television, there is a more graduated spectrum, but with similar issues. The equivalent to the multiplex would be a primetime slot on BBC1, ITV and Channel 4 in the UK, and the networks in the States. These offer wide appeal and star roles in dramas, comedies and series such as *Prime Suspect*, *Doctor Who*, *Homeland*, *Downton Abbey*, *EastEnders* and *Outnumbered*.

While budgets are generally lower than for cinema, there is also a thirst for larger stories, which may be financed by co-producing with other countries.

Programmes for smaller audiences, of any age, would go to off-peak slots on BBC1 and ITV, the smaller terrestrial, cable and online channels such as BBC2 to 4, much of Channel 4 and 5, Sky, HBO in the States, and on-demand services such as Netflix. As with the indie film sector, such slots would attract stories with a more specific 'niche' appeal. A niche might be a specific age group (young or old), shared interest or theme, as well as any programme with an abrasive or unusual style, and challenging content or language.

Examples include *Skins*, *Fresh Meat*, *The Politician's Wife*, *Curb Your Enthusiasm*, *Queer as Folk*, *Last Tango in Halifax* and most single dramas.

To confuse matters, some movies and TV programmes cross over, appealing to all four audiences. In the film industry, such films are known as 'four quadrant' movies. However, they are rare, and while producers dream of them they can't be guaranteed. Experienced producers will generally aim for a specific market with a view to building on wider success later. *The King's Speech* was always thought of as a small movie until it crossed over to the mainstream. Many TV series begin on the more specialist channels before they've proved they have wider appeal. *The Office* began this way, as did *The Wire* and *The Sopranos*.

Key idea

Screenwriting is both an art and a business – so know your market.

Snapshot exercise

Ask yourself whether your story is multiplex/prime-time or indie/off-peak. Research other films or programmes that are close in genre, style and subject and find out where they played. If cinema, what screens? How many countries? Did they go straight to DVD or video on demand? If television, what channels and what times of day?

3 CINEMATIC (OR TELEVISUAL)?

No matter how strong the idea, the producer will pass if she doesn't feel it would work on screen. Any pitch, query letter or treatment you give her must bring out the visual, as of course must the script itself.

If feedback suggests your story would be more suitable for another medium, you may need to look more closely at ways of creating a more cinematic, or televisual, style.

Sometimes producers find that a screenplay intended for cinema feels more like television. (The complaint is rarely made the other way around.) Should you receive this response, look again at the movies in your chosen genres. What is it that they have that yours doesn't? 'Cinematic' may not necessarily mean big, expensive scenes, but it does generally mean a larger emotional vision, shorter scenes, less dialogue and strong imagery.

Skip Press, screenwriter

'Too many screenwriters somehow miss the idea that writing a script is so a film can be made from it.'

Snapshot exercise

Compare adaptations for cinema and television, and note the similarities and the differences. Many stories are adapted from novels and theatre and can be compared directly. There are also some stories which have been adapted from TV to cinema or vice versa. Look, for example, at the cinema and TV versions of *MASH*, or the movie *Traffic* and the original British mini-series it's based on, *Traffik*. What has remained the same and what has not, when changing medium?

4 DIFFERENT?

Many otherwise well-written scripts fail to sell simply because they add nothing new. You must show how your idea is different from all the rest.

A good producer will know the market and the competition. You need to know your niche as well as she does. Study the competition in detail. Know what it is that you bring that's different. And be prepared to deal with the question, should it come up.

Simon Williamson, agent

'When there's so much competition, you've got to find a way for your script to stand out. It's so difficult to get a movie made or a TV script accepted, you've got to find an angle that makes producers choose yours.'

Write

Redo your research. Go online and ask everyone you know for examples of films or series similar to yours. Read everything you can on the genres in question. Keep up with the latest reviews and discussions.

Write a one-page dossier on the niche you're working in, with examples and brief analysis of similarities and differences from your own script. As new comparisons come in, keep your file up to date.

5 EMPLOYABLE?

Why should she employ *you*? Why should you be the right person to write this script and work with her on future drafts? What do you bring to the table?

At the least, this means: are you professional? Do you understand the basics of the industry? Can you communicate and collaborate? After all, this is a relationship that will last at least as long as it takes for you to write any new drafts she may find she needs – and probably the years that she'll take to raise the finance and shoot the film. You don't have to be best buddies, but you do need to be able to work together and understand each other's needs.

Hilary Wayne, agent (quoted by Blake Snyder in Save the Cat!)

'Every sale has a story! The story is you.'

Key idea

Know why you are the best person to have written this script.

At best, you bring something special to the script that she wants – not merely writing skill but also a personal connection with the story. First-time screenwriter Rob Dawber worked with producer Rebecca O'Brien to write *The Navigators*, a movie for Ken Loach, based on Dawber's knowledge of working on the railways. Do you have personal experience or contacts that will help sell your script?

Use your writing skills to build your CV. Start a blog based on the subject of the script, or even consider pitching articles to newspapers or magazines. Many local newspapers and radio stations are keen to take interesting items by local writers. It all helps.

Snapshot exercise

Write a short paragraph about yourself, focusing on any details that are relevant to this screenplay. Make it personal. What's the story behind you writing this script? Is it based on a passion of yours?

How long did you research and how deeply? How many personal contacts do you now have? Include any experience in the media, writing credits, competition success, articles or stories that have been published or broadcast.

At the end, list the possible ways you could build your CV in future months – a blog, articles, spin-off projects.

Kevin Dolan, Film London

'For low-budget, I want writers who know the world they're talking about. The closer you are to your subject matter, the more authentic your voice will be.'

Finding producers, agents and development executives

Before you can talk to an industry professional, you have first to locate her. There are essentially eight ways. They range from directories, trade magazines and festivals to networking events, film funds and personal contact, and you'll need to use all eight.

Landing a deal is a combination of hard work and luck. You can spend a year or more sending out query letters and then meet your future producer standing in a queue at your local supermarket. However, you never know in advance which route will work for you.

1 PRINTED DIRECTORIES

There are a number of books printed annually which list production companies in different countries, although their number is diminishing. Prime among them, in the UK, is *The Knowledge*. The listings are not exhaustive, but you'll find many production companies and their contact details, as well as directors, agents and screenwriters. (You can get yourself listed, often for free.). *The Artists' & Writers' Yearbook* is the main reference work for agents, and also for ways to develop your writing career, such as writing articles. Directories can be bought or sometimes obtained free, and they can be found in local library reference sections. (For these and other sources mentioned below, see Appendix 5.)

2 ONLINE DIRECTORIES

Many directories have gone exclusively online, and offer the same services, generally kept up to date. The printed directories also have online versions. You can also subscribe to receive newsletters by email.

3 TRADE MAGAZINES

Trade magazines such as *Screen*, *Hollywood Reporter* and *Broadcast* give information about who's doing what in film and TV, in print and online. A subscription to at least one is a wise, if not essential, investment. They will keep you in the flow of industry developments and give you news (and often pictures) of producers who might be worth approaching. Knowing the latest names and trends will be essential in meetings.

Some newspapers specialize in media coverage, often interviewing key players. In the UK, *The Guardian* particularly covers media, TV, film and writing news.

4 CREDITS

Note the producer credits on films and TV programmes that are closest to your script and search online for the producers and production companies named. You can also search online databases, such as the Internet Movie Database (IMDb) and ScreenBase, the database run by *Screen*, the trade magazine. IMDb is free to use in its basic form, but IMDb Pro and Screen Base are worth paying for, to obtain fuller information and contact details.

5 FILM FESTIVALS AND MARKETS

Producers, and their staff, emerge blinking into the light of day from time to time, in particular when their films appear at festivals. There are now more film and TV festivals on the planet than there are days in the year, and each has its own specific flavour. Start by checking out your local festivals, and those targeted at your genre or audience (short films, sci-fi, comedy, female, black, Jewish, etc.).

The larger film festivals now have an attached market, where the buying and selling takes place. These often provide opportunities for producers to meet and talk to writers. Less formally, the festivals may offer Q&A sessions with producers, where you have a chance to make contact. Particularly good festivals include:

- **Rotterdam** – a medium-sized market with a friendly atmosphere and a section devoted to arranging meetings with industry professionals.
- **London** – a festival aimed more at showing films than developing new ones, it nevertheless attracts producers from all over the UK and the world.
- **Birds Eye View** and **Underwire** – specifically for women writers and film-makers.
- **Cannes** – this is *the* film market; try to get to it if you can, even if you have to borrow the EasyJet fare and sleep on the floor of a shared apartment. Be there between the first Thursday and the following Wednesday and that week will be worth a year's film school anywhere else.
- **Raindance** – Europe's largest indie film festival, which also runs networking and training events in London during the year (see below).

6 SCREENWRITING FESTIVALS, PANELS AND NETWORKING EVENTS

From time to time, producers and agents speak at panel events. Screenwriting festivals are dedicated to helping new writers and offer rare opportunities to interact with the industry. Best is the London Screenwriters' Festival. It's not the cheapest, but the cost is balanced by the chance to attend high-level seminars and make contact with professionals at all levels. National and regional bodies such as film agencies, and independent organizations such as Euroscript and Raindance, also run free or nominally priced networking events with invited speakers from the industry.

Building relationships with other writers at any events will help you build a support network, and share news of producers who may be useful to approach. There are increasing numbers of online networking opportunities too, from Twitter and Facebook to LinkedIn forums and screenwriting blogs. Shooting People is one of the leading indie sites, offering news, discussions and notices of training and events, for a small annual subscription.

7 FILM FUNDS AND AGENCIES

Most countries have funds and development agencies with executives devoted to helping writers. In the UK, these include (at the time of writing) the BFI, along with regional and national organizations such as Film London, South West Screen and Creative Scotland. Check out which apply to you, and what they're doing. They often run events and consider projects for development assistance.

8 PERSONAL CONTACT

Don't underestimate the value of personal relationships. They are the foundation of the industry. Building a network means that you will be able to share information and also contacts, so take an interest in everyone you meet. You may get a valuable introduction from a friend of a friend of a fellow writer, or a contact through a make-up artist that your cousin once went out with. You never know.

Elliot Grove, in *Write and Sell the Hot Screenplay*

'The film business is a people business; it's not what you know, it's who you know.'

Snapshot exercise

Start a list of places where you can find producers. Aim, over the next two to three months, to use all eight methods: visit your nearest reference library, go online, consider subscribing to the trades (or persuading your library or nearest arts organization to do so), start networking and check out your local festivals and agencies.

Making the approach

There are four rules here:

1 **Never send a script out cold.**
2 **It's about building relationships.**
3 **(Almost) never pitch a script before you've finished it.**
4 **Approach individuals, not companies.**

Let's look at each in turn.

1 NEVER SEND A SCRIPT OUT COLD

Nobody likes a pile of paper that arrives on their desk unannounced and unasked for. You should always aim to prepare the way.

Your aim is to get them to ask for the script. Check their websites to see whether they have rules for submissions. If they ask for you to send work in a specific way, then that is *exactly* how you submit it. Don't write: 'I know you ask for a one-page outline, but my story is too good to tell in fewer than three pages…' You want to show that you are capable of working professionally to a specific remit.

2 IT'S ABOUT BUILDING RELATIONSHIPS

If you haven't met, then phone or email a query letter to ask whether they're interested in knowing more. See the next chapter.

If you make contact at an event, don't pitch there and then. Producers like to be treated as human beings, not targets! Have a conversation, if there's time, and use the opportunity to ask about them, not talk about yourself. Ask whether there's anything they need. If there's a bar, offer to get them a drink.

If they're being mobbed, and you have only a few seconds, tell them that you admire their work and ask politely how they like to be approached – by email, on the phone, or should you come to see them? Offer to swap business cards (so that you get their contact details).

Don't be pushy. Be professional. It's about establishing relationships. You're in this for the long haul and there is always a next time.

Focus point

Print a set of business cards designating yourself as screenwriter. Keep the layout simple and clean. Don't try to be clever with multiple fonts or pictures. You want to be remembered for your writing, not your cards.

3 (ALMOST) NEVER PITCH AN UNFINISHED SCRIPT

It's very tempting to pitch a script you're still writing. Otherwise, it can feel as if you're working for ages with no support or confirmation that someone will want to read it at the end. A positive response can give you extra energy and confidence at a crucial time.

However, tempting as it is, this is not a good idea. If your pitch is successful, the producer will want to see it now – not in three or six months' time. By the time it's polished, the producer may have changed priorities or even left the company. At best, you're wasting your time, and theirs.

At worst, a negative response may throw you off track and diminish your confidence in the middle of writing the script.

The exception comes at a very early stage, when you'll want to test that your project is really worth developing. At that point, it is essential to pitch the story, and often. But be clever. Don't pitch to producers and executives you might sell to later. Try your ideas on the people they deal with – distributors, financiers, directors, script editors. You'll find them in the same places that you find producers.

If the script is *very* close to being finished, you may be able to get away with saying you'll be ready to send it in two weeks. But if you say this, you must deliver.

4 APPROACH INDIVIDUALS, NOT COMPANIES

Do your research and make a list of the most appropriate producers for your script. Note any productions that are relevant, films or programmes that you admire and are in your genre.

Always approach a producer or development executive by name. Try, if possible, to speak to her first in person, either at an event or on the phone. Tell her how much you admire her work, say you have a project you feel she'd like, and ask whether you can meet to talk about it. You may find that she invites your pitch there and then, so be prepared.

 ## Key idea

Always approach a specific producer (or agent) by name.

Often, you won't get past the PA who asks you to send an email. Clarify what's wanted, and send it. More often than not, it will be a treatment (ask how long!) with a covering letter. Whatever is asked for, be rigorous in complying with their request and do it quickly, ideally the same day. This is a test to see how professional you are.

Finding an agent

Approaching an agent is an almost identical process. The only significant difference is that a producer is concerned only with the one project, while an agent is interested in your long-term career. But an agent also has to sell to producers, so everything that applies to producers applies almost equally to agents, too.

You'll need to research agents' lists for writers you admire and who work in your genre. If it's a large agency, don't send a blanket application but decide which agent will be most suitable. When you approach him, you'll mention the writers on his personal list and why you feel your work could fit right in.

 ## Key idea

Having an agent is useful, but not crucial.

However, having an agent is not essential and won't solve all your problems. A good agent will represent you, possibly advise on how to improve your script (yes, more feedback). He will know the best people to send your script to, and have it read. Some producers say that they only read scripts that have come from agents. He may arrange meetings with producers looking for writers. He will negotiate contracts for you – and ensure that you get paid.

The downside is that he takes a percentage, up to 15 per cent, of all money that comes in (even if you found the producer yourself). He will also have his own strengths, weaknesses and priorities. He will have other clients, probably larger and more lucrative at first, and be very busy. He will not act as a writing tutor. He won't be available every minute on the phone, and you will still need to get out, network and sell your scripts for yourself, too.

By all means look for an agent, but don't feel it's the end of the world if you don't get one. The wrong agent (like the wrong producer) may be worse than none at all. You're better off without him if the chemistry doesn't work or he tries to push you in a direction that's not right for you. Many writers cope perfectly well without an agent. They find their own producers, maintain their network and negotiate their own deals (or hire a media lawyer – see below).

You should also join the Writers' Guild of Great Britain, or the equivalent in other countries. They will advise members on contracts and support writers in disputes.

Finally, in this respect, beware of any agent who says you need to pay him to read your script. Reading is part of his job. No reputable producer or agent will ever ask you for money to read your work.

Workshop

Prepare your marketing plan. Make lists of appropriate producers and/or agents and where you're going to find them.

Be clear about your target audience, what's different and why you are the right person to have written this script.

Brainstorm with your workshop colleagues to see whether there's anything you've missed.

Where to next?

You've worked out why you're selling and who you want to sell to. Now, what do you say? We look next at how to pitch and what to do if you're asked to send a query letter.

27

Pitching and query letters

In Hollywood mythology, as satirized in Robert Altman's movie *The Player,* a writer holds a producer spellbound for minutes as he unfolds a story from start to finish. It's a bravura performance, after which the producer is supposed to say, 'I want it. Here's a cheque.'

Maybe this happens sometimes. The reality, for the rest of us, is that you have one sentence, maybe two if you're lucky, to catch a buyer's attention. And that applies whether you're speaking face to face or sending a query letter.

Word of mouth

At the heart of your campaign to sell your script is your 'elevator pitch', or logline – a few short words that encapsulate your story in one or two dramatic sentences.

Why so short, when it was hard enough cutting the screenplay down to its current length? Because ultimately films and TV programmes are sold not by advertising, or clever PR, or even by star names, but by word of mouth. For all the marketing effort that goes into opening a cinema film or launching a new series, in the end it comes down to a friend saying – at a bus stop or over the office photocopier – you should watch this. And he doesn't have 15 minutes to describe the complexities of the character development or the clever plot twists. He has about two sentences to say what was so brilliant about it, before the listener says, 'My bus is coming', 'My boss is calling me' or, if you're in luck, 'Tell me more.'

When you deliver your pitch to a producer, whether face to face, on the phone or in a query letter, she's thinking about delivering it in turn to her boss, the star actors she wants to hire, the director, the marketing department, the sales agent, the distributor, the exhibitor, the chat show host… everyone visualizing one friend telling your story to another – in a few seconds in the street or over coffee – and asking themselves whether the friend will say, 'Tell me more.'

The good news is that you've already done the groundwork. Your pitch is your premise. All you need to do is polish it up.

The second piece of good news is that you don't have to be clever at public speaking, or particularly silver-tongued. Your producer is listening for the quality of the idea, the spark not your ability to perform.

And the third saving grace is that your pitch has one very simple goal to achieve, and no other. And it's not to sell the script. (If you don't have a track record, you're very unlikely to make a sale on the basis of a pitch alone.) The single goal of your pitch is to hear the words, 'Send me the script.'

Key idea

The ideal outcome: the listener says, 'Send me the script.'

Your secondary goal is for her to say, 'Tell me more.' This gives you a chance to impress with a very few more choice details… so that *then* she says, 'Send me the script.' (Sometimes she'll say 'Send me a treatment', which is why you need to have treatments of different lengths standing by on your hard drive.)

In other words, you don't have to sell the entire story in your pitch, but quite the reverse: you only have to hook their interest enough to make them want to read the real thing. In fact, the point of a pitch, as with a treatment, is not how much you can squeeze in to get her to read the script, but how much you can cut out.

Key idea

It's not how much of the story you need to tell to get a producer to read your script, it's how little.

Write

Go back to the premise you created at the start, and have been refining as you wrote the script. Does it do the job? Has it got enough in it to hook a producer and make her want to know more? Does it answer her five key questions: appropriate, budgetable, cinematic, different, employable?

If not, it's time to revise and polish it, with the extra knowledge you've gained.

Polishing the pitch

The best pitch is natural and conversational. Remember the two friends at the bus stop. Some writers are urged to create pitches that are too condensed to be easily understood. They are told, for example, that they must be '25 words or fewer'. The rule is a myth, based on the belief that TV listings are limited to 25 words. If they ever were, they aren't now. You can take longer, as long as you don't go over two conversational sentences.

Key idea

A pitch is just another word for a conversation.

There's no need to be clever; the simplest sentences are the best. Follow this template – it sounds natural and will work 999 times out of 1,000:

> 'It's a (genre) about a (flawed protagonist) who (goal or obstacle), only to find he/she (big ironic character change).'

Let's unpick that and see how it works:

- **Genre** – by stating the genre up front, you leave no doubt as to the emotional impact you're aiming for.
- **Flaw** – this sets up the inner story and tells us how the audience will be engaged.
- **Protagonist** – don't give a specific name at this point. You want the listener to concentrate on the essentials. (The exception would be if this were a true story and the protagonist is famous.)
- **Goal or obstacle** – one usually implies the other. If the goal is to escape from prison, the obstacles are probably obvious. Similarly, if the protagonist is being threatened by a murderous poltergeist, the goal doesn't need to be outlined.

- **Ironic character change** – this relates directly to the flaw and shows you understand the character journey. An ironic twist helps fix it in the listener's mind. It's ironic that Sarah Connor, in *Terminator*, herself becomes a killing machine. It's ironic that, after being betrayed once, Solomon Northup has to relearn who he can trust in order to escape from 12 years of slavery.

SAMPLE PITCHES

> *Little Miss Sunshine* – It's a satirical comedy about a squabbling, dysfunctional family who set out to help the seven-year-old daughter enter the beauty competition she's set her heart on.

This pitch goes to the heart of the story's comic idea. It avoid any temptation to dwell on the set-up. No subplots or subsidiary themes are brought in. They are not necessary at this stage. Remember, the aim is to get the listener to ask for the script or want to be told more. However, it makes it clear that much of the humour will come from the interplay of the family. As well as stating the genre, the pitch should give a hint of the appropriate emotion through the way it's phrased. In this case, the ironic twist is implied at the start – clearly they will need at some point to stop squabbling – so it doesn't need to be made so explicit.

> *Mandela: Long Walk to Freedom* – The true story about Nelson Mandela's struggle against apartheid. After supporting armed resistance, Mandela is forced to continue the fight from jail, only to realize that he must reverse decades of violence if he's to win.

This is the essence of the idea, in which the writer has resisted the temptation to go into the set-up, the twists and turns of the plot or even mention the other characters.

> *Line of Duty* (Series 2) – It's a police procedural about a team of detectives investigating a wily and experienced policewoman whose colleagues have been murdered in cold blood … but who find their investigation increasingly hampered by mistakes in their own personal lives.

Here again, there is no attempt to detail the complexities, twists or subplots of a rich and complex six-part crime serial. The team's flaws are left to the second half of the pitch, to make the sentence easier to understand.

OTHER PATTERNS

While the pattern I've given you is the simplest and most powerful (and probably the most used in the industry), there are others.

The *when* pattern:

> 'When (dramatic event) happens to (flawed protagonist), he/she has to (set off to achieve goal) and learn (character improvement) in the process.'

As in:

> *Gravity* – When her space shuttle is catastrophically damaged by space debris, a first-time astronaut finds herself marooned in space. Still grieving over the death of her young daughter, she must rediscover her determination to live if she is to survive and return to Earth.

This model can give a powerful start to your pitch, but be careful that it doesn't become too wordy.

Some people like to start with a *question*:

> *Gravity* – Did you know that satellite debris is such a risk now that it will soon be too dangerous to go into space? Well, my story is an action-thriller about…

A variation begins 'Imagine …' or 'What if …?'

> *Line of Duty* (Series 2) – Imagine hitmen attacked and killed a convoy escorting a protected witness, but for no apparent reason one police inspector survived…

One variation you may be tempted to use is the list. This was briefly in fashion a few years ago among Britflick writers trying to sound slick. Lists like: 'A comedy-thriller about two men, a car and a bucket of fish.'

Aside from sounding rather smug, it's vague, tends towards cliché and tells us nothing about the story. Avoid.

Pitching an episodic series

As with a series premise (see Chapter 3), you need a series pitch, and also individual pitches for sample episodes. Your series premise was designed to reassure you that the idea not only struck sparks but also had 'legs'. Now, as a pitch, it has to do the same for a producer.

Design your series pitch in a similar way to a single-story pitch. If there's a single protagonist, focus on his flaw, and the typical goals and obstacles that will confront him in each episode. If there are multiple protagonists, find the theme that unites them.

Your pitch must hint at enough tension between the characters, or between the characters and their environment, to yield at least a dozen or more varied and different stories, with the potential of many more to follow.

If your pitch is successful, you'll be asked to send a full series proposal bringing these strands out more strongly, including sample treatments and pitches for individual episodes together with a sample episode script (see Chapter 10).

SAMPLE SERIES PITCHES

> *The Good Wife* – A legal and political drama series centring on a former lawyer whose state's attorney husband is jailed for corruption, forcing her to go back to work – at the firm run by her ex-lover.

> *Fawlty Towers* – A sitcom about the irascible owner of a small hotel and his attempts to deal with his bossy wife, hapless waiter and a succession of odd and demanding guests.

> *Spooks* – A fast-paced action series about a group of MI5 agents working with the latest technology to fight the enemies, of the modern British state both from outside and within.

Snapshot exercise

Read at least 50 pitches. You'll find them whenever someone summarizes a story in a sentence – online in databases such as IMDb, in television and cinema listings, in trade magazines, in reviews and in interviews – essentially anywhere that people talk or write about film and TV. Which are the strongest and which are the weakest, and why? Which would make you go and see the movie or programme? Which would make you think there was a definite audience?

Analyse how they work and the different patterns. Experiment with them to create different pitches, then try your pitches out on friends and colleagues to see which catches fire.

Stacking the pack in your favour

As you refine your pitch, there are a number of things you can do to make sure it has the maximum impact on your listeners.

Be specific and avoid cliché. Whichever pattern you use, every word has to count. Vague and abstract or clichéd language wastes energy and fails to stimulate the listener's visual imagination. Be specific and you'll spark strong visual images in the listener's mind.

Should you reference other productions? Long ago, there was a vogue for mash-up loglines, such as '*Star Wars* meets *Gone with the Wind*' ... They are out of fashion now. Referencing previous movies or TV programmes in your logline is not necessary. You can do it, but there are two strict rules:

1 **They must have been financially successful.** However artistic the original, your producer still has to balance the books, and comparing your project to a financial failure is not a good starting point.

2 **They must have been made within the last 18 months.** The industry moves fast. A year and a half is ancient history. No matter how successful an older movie was, someone will say your story sounds stale ... Why take the risk?

There's a third danger – you may mention a film that the producer hates! You don't need to compare with other stories, so unless there is a great reason to do so in your pitch, don't. That is not to say you can't ever discuss other films. Do it in conversation, before or after the pitch. Find out what the producer likes, and mention sources of inspiration. But keep movie references outside the main pitch.

Focus point

You don't have to reference other movies or programmes in your pitch, but if you do they must be recent and in profit.

Snapshot exercise

When you have a pitch you like, practise it out loud until you can say it naturally and conversationally without wandering. It doesn't matter if you change the odd word. It shouldn't sound unnaturally rehearsed, like a poem. But it does need to sound as if you mean it.

High concept/low concept

The idea of high-concept and low-concept movies was popular in Hollywood in the last decades of the twentieth century. The phrase is somewhat less fashionable now, but the idea is still powerful, if misunderstood. You'll find some writers asserting that high concept means plot-driven, as opposed to character-driven. But you can have character-driven high-concept stories. Others say that high concept means a story that can be expressed in a single sentence. But a single sentence is no guarantee of success.

In reality, a high-concept idea is one that is essentially so strong that it will attract a large audience regardless of how it's put into practice. This may be because of the essential strength of the dramatic premise, or because it has an element of mental real estate – a famous book, character or event that people will flock to see (for more on mental real estate, see Chapter 3). A low-concept idea might still be a good one, but to gain an audience it will need to be well executed – in terms of script, casting, acting, photography, design and editing.

High-concept movies would include *Superman*, *Alien*, *Harry Potter*, *Gone with the Wind*, *The Sound of Music*, *Gandhi* and *12 Years a Slave*. High-concept TV might include *Heroes*, *Homeland* and *Fawlty Towers*.

Low-concept stories might cover *Let the Right One In*, *Little Miss Sunshine*, *Goodfellas*, *Curb Your Enthusiasm*, *Fresh Meat* and *The Killing*.

If your story has elements that people will queue round the block to see, then great. It's nice to have, but don't give up if you don't have one. A low-concept premise can work well if it has strong elements and forms the basis of an excellently written script.

The title

Your title is one of the most important elements in attracting attention, yet many writers are content with a makeweight title that adds nothing to the script. The best titles have a resonance; they draw you in and make you want to know more.

Key idea

A good title is a crucial part of the script.

Titles fall into three types – great, awful and good.

- **Great** is rare. Great would include such titles as *Last Exit to Brooklyn* and *Fried Green Tomatoes at the Whistle Stop Café*. It's nice to have a great title, but not essential.

- **Awful** is disastrous. Awful is flat, uninteresting, vague or even impossible to remember. There is one film whose title I can never remember. It's a list of names that have no resonance and put me off seeing the movie for years (it turned out after all to be an amusing romcom). More often, titles are simply dull. If your title doesn't create excitement, change it.

- **Good titles have resonance.** They wouldn't necessarily win prizes for literary merit but they draw viewers. They are specific yet at the same time evoke a mood or theme.

Frank Cottrell Boyce, screenwriter

'*A great title can make a big difference. The musical* Oklahoma, *as it was initially called, famously flopped in the provinces, but became a massive hit after they added the exclamation mark.* Orson Welles *said* Paper Moon *was such a great title they wouldn't need to make the movie, just release the title.*'

Snapshot exercise

List the titles of recent films or programmes in your genre. Are they long or short, literary or unsophisticated? Which work best? What patterns can you see?

Here are six ways that writers use to create strong, attractive titles. Many good titles draw on more than one at the same time. Try each in turn and in combination.

1 BIG PROMISE

Promise the audience a special experience or emotional journey. Superlatives help here – *greatest, first, most* – special people, places, times, events, or the suggestion of strong feelings:

The Greatest Show on Earth, The Big Lebowski, The Last Picture Show, The Good Life, Life on Mars, Stormy Monday, The Killing, The Return, Cliffhanger, Scream, Hangover, Fresh Meat, The Thick of It.

2 MEMORABLE

You want your title to stay in the mind, so include elements that are memorable. Use striking turns of phrase or a twist on an old saying. A sense of humour or poetry helps here:

His Girl Friday, Skins, All about My Mother, Educating Rita, The Good, the Bad and the Ugly, Lost in Translation, Last Tango in Halifax, The Good Wife, Secrets and Lies.

3 PROVOCATIVE

Wake people up. Challenge the audience. Be politically incorrect. Stir things up. Suggest that you're going to be crossing boundaries:

Psycho, Alien, Misfits, Shameless, Stalker, Bad Santa, Queer as Folk, Sex and the City, Breaking Bad, Nymphomaniac, Slumdog Millionaire, Scum.

4 MENTAL REAL ESTATE

Use key words that are part of people's lives – names, places, issues, typical situations, experiences, and also dates, times, numbers:

Elizabeth, Mandela: Long Walk to Freedom, Sherlock, Goodbye Lenin, Welcome to Sarajevo, The Politician's Husband, Cheers, The Office, The Year of Living Dangerously, 2001, Six Feet Under, Quantum Leap.

5 RHYME AND REPETITION

You can use literary means to give the title impact – rhyme, repetition, alliteration, assonance:

Pride and Prejudice, Fast and Furious, Educating Essex, Breaking Bad, Malcolm in the Middle, The Rumble in the Jungle, Run, Lola, Run, The Murder in the Rue Morgue, Mrs Brown's Boys.

6 VISUAL IMPACT

Excite our visual imagination – films and TV stories are visual and a title that creates images in our minds will stick in our minds: landscapes, locations, set-pieces, colours, even body decoration:

Priscilla Queen of the Desert, The Bridge, Bridesmaids, Waking the Dead, Spiral, The Hunt for Red October, Blue Is the Warmest Colour, The Girl with the Dragon Tattoo.

Write

Create at least five titles for your story from each of the six categories in turn, that is, five which offer a big promise, five based on memorable words or phrases, and so on. You should end up with at least 30 possible titles for your script or series.

Take your favourites and try them out on friends. In your writers' group, read out your best six and ask the members of the workshop to put up their hands when they hear their favourite. They are allowed only one vote each.

Snapshot exercise

The time has come! Choose one of your target producers or agents. Draft a query letter. If possible, aim initially at one of your second- or third-level choices. That way, you can adjust as you go along, without ruining your chances with your prime targets.

Phone her office number, as in the role play above. Explain to the PA that you love/admire a specific production of hers (one that you've seen, or at least researched in great detail) and would like to talk to her about a project you think she'll like.

Be ready to explain in a sentence who you are. Be positive and truthful. If you're put through, repeat the above, briefly and confidently. If there's an appropriate response, be ready to deliver your pitch, conversationally and naturally. Finish by saying that you'd love to meet and discuss it further, at her convenience.

And wait to see what happens. If she says 'no', ring off politely and then celebrate! You have your first rejection. You're on the way to becoming a professional. There will be many more. If the answer is 'yes' or 'maybe', respond appropriately. (For more details, see the pitch meeting, below.)

Farah Abushwesha, Rocliffe New Writing Forum

'Opportunities only come to those who make them. If you don't have confidence in yourself, don't expect anyone else to.'

Writing a query letter

Your pitch or logline will also form the basis of any covering letter or query letter. A query letter is used if you're making contact, or following up a contact, by email.

It must be brief and to the point and no more than a page of A4, with three to four relatively short paragraphs. The same letter should be used as a covering letter if you are asked to send in a treatment. The query letter sets out your best answers to the five questions a producer wants answered and includes your pitch (sometimes known as a pitch on paper, or POP).

Always address the query letter to a specific person – never 'Dear Sir/Madam'. It may be obvious who to write to, or you may need to do more research. If a production company or agency asks you to write to their submissions department, do so for the attention of a named producer or agent.

A query letter must be brief, to the point and addressed to a named person.

- Paragraph 1 outlines why you're writing the letter and why your project is appropriate for them.
- Paragraph 2 gives your best pitch.
- Paragraph 3 tells them about you – don't boast or lie, but be confident and put yourself forward in the strongest way you can.
- Paragraph 4 ends by saying what you've attached or enclosed, if anything, and signing off.

ATTACHMENTS, REVIEWS AND ENHANCEMENTS

If you have a top-level star or star director attached, by all means mention the fact. But be clear – top level means big. In movie terms, they can 'open' the movie – that is, viewers will go to see the film or turn on the TV just because their favourite star is in it. Such marquee names are limited to no more than half a dozen at any time, often fewer.

Otherwise, forget it. The same applies, I'm sorry to say, for crew. Nobody cares if you've landed the best director of photography in the world. It won't help sell the movie.

Secondly, if you do seriously have a major name attached, you need proof. They have to sign a letter of intent, which is a promise to be involved should the terms be right. It binds them (and you) to nothing, but don't be fooled, a letter of intent is not easy to get. If you've managed to obtain a letter of intent from a major director or star, that's something to boast about.

Aside from that, kind words mean nothing. Don't tell people that X famous agent said the script was great, or that Y famous writer thinks it should be made. If they haven't offered money or work, it makes you sound like an amateur. Similarly, don't waste your time quoting favourable script reports or advice that you've been given. It's a hard-nosed industry, and producers want facts they can take to the bank.

Also, don't lie. If you fake credits on your CV, pretend to have an attached star that you don't, or pretend that you have contacts you don't have – you will be found out. It's a very small industry and news of your transgressions will spread fast. You want to be known as someone who's straight and can be trusted to do a good job.

And don't oversell. Don't tell the producer that this script is hilariously funny (that's not for you to say), will make him a ton of money or win awards.

On the other hand, don't be over-modest. Everyone has to start somewhere. Don't be shy or diminish yourself, but show confidence about who you are and what you've written.

EXAMPLE QUERY LETTER

> To: alice.astuteproducer@astuteproductions.com
>
> Subject: Out of Time
>
> Dear Ms Astuteproducer
>
> Following my telephone conversation just now with your assistant Matt, I'm looking for a production company for my cinema screenplay, *Out of Time*, a sci-fi legal drama set in space, with a similar pace and spirit to your film *Planet of the Orphans*.
>
> *Out of Time* tells the story of a well-meaning but often arrogant lawyer who suddenly finds himself in the 24th century and realizes that the only way he can get home is by ensuring that a vicious killer escapes justice. In the process, he learns about the meaning of humility from the very killer he started off despising.
>
> I have long been interested in law, especially the ethics of lawyers, and as a result of my research started a blog, the Morals of Lawyers, which now has over 10,000 followers.
>
> I would be pleased to send you the polished screenplay.
>
> Kind regards
> John Newwriter

Write

Draft a query letter. The first attempt, as with any initial attempt, will doubtless feel awkward, flat and too long. Read it through and revise it. Be absolutely ruthless.

Try to put yourself in the position of the recipient. The first sentence must tell him why he should bother to read on. Why are you writing to him? Why is this project appropriate to his needs? Are you over, or under, selling?

Does the pitch in the second paragraph strike sparks? Does it need yet another polish? Does the third paragraph set out your strengths fairly and confidently?

Keep polishing until you are sure of the letter, then put it aside and look at it after a few hours. Can you polish it some more?

Finally, send it out. Then save it as a template and revise/polish it again each time you use it.

The pitch meeting

Finally, you get to meet someone: a pitch meeting in a producer's office, or over a cup of coffee at a market, such as Cannes. This could be scary, but need not be if you know your stuff.

A pitch meeting, rather like a query letter, will also be in four parts.

It will start with a short period of informal chat, while you introduce yourselves. In most cases, it will be relatively informal, just the two of you. Many writers waste this time, either by promoting themselves or diving straight into the pitch. But this prologue can be very valuable if you approach it correctly. Use it to make contact, establish rapport and find out more about the person you're talking to.

Ask how he is and what he's working on. This is not simply a matter of politeness, but gives you a chance to update your research and confirm that you're talking to the right person. It also gives you a moment to take stock. You may end up working with him for many years, so you need to get a sense of the chemistry, if there is any.

At a certain point, depending on how busy he is, the producer will say something along the lines of 'So, what have you got?'

This is your moment. Deliver your pitch conversationally and clearly. Speak directly – never, ever read your pitch; you need the eye contact. A slightly less word-perfect pitch, spoken with eye contact, will always be more powerful than the most polished reading. This is your story. If you can't manage two sentences about it without reading, who can?

 Focus point

Never, ever, read your pitch. Look the producer in the eyes, and tell him what your story is about, conversationally.

Don't hand out any printed material, or the producer will break eye contact and start to read. Keep to your one to two sentences (don't be tempted to ramble on). And once you've said them – STOP. Wait for a response. If you're still talking, you haven't given him a chance to say 'I love it!' I've known writers talk themselves out of a positive response, merely by not stopping to listen for one!

This is the start of the third part. The other party will say one of the following:
- 'Send me the script.'
- 'Send me the treatment.'
- 'This one's not for me.'
- 'Do you have anything else?'
- 'Tell me more.'

If it's one of the first two, you say you'll be very happy to send the material immediately and finish the meeting. You may have the treatment, or a one-page 'leave-behind', with you, in which case now is the time to leave it behind. If you haven't already, swap business cards and go. Beware of the temptation to keep talking. It's still possible to talk a 'yes' into a 'no'!

If they're not interested, be professional. Don't attempt to argue back. It's a waste of your time and theirs. You can, however, ask what it was that didn't work for them, for your own education. However, don't rush off to change the whole script until you've had three or four people say the same thing.

If they ask what else you have – that's an excellent response. It means that they consider you a professional. While this idea wasn't for them, they could consider working with you on something else. It's good to have a few other pitches up your sleeve.

And then there's …

'TELL ME MORE'

If they ask to know more, your elevator pitch worked. Now you move into a longer pitch. But you still don't tell the whole story. Give them the key bullet points, almost as if you were showing them a trailer. Broadly follow the outline of the six-sentence treatment (see Chapter 10).

- **Two to three sentences:** introduce the normal world, the protagonist, her flaws and her main outer challenge.
- **Three sentences:** give three glimpses of what she does along the way – actions which reveal character, visuals and emotion.
- **Two last sentences:** tie it all up with the final confrontation and what your protagonist has learned (or failed to learn) by the end.
- And STOP. Wait for a response.

If he still wants to know more, you *still* don't tell the whole story, Instead, you discuss what's exciting (and saleable) about it, such as the central characters and what makes them so interesting. You describe your most striking visual moments; give examples of a couple of memorable scenes.

Simon Williamson, agent

'When you meet a producer or agent, they're evaluating you as a person. You need to be good in a room – confident in your ideas.'

QUESTIONS TO BE PREPARED FOR

Be ready to answer questions on:

- **Audience** – who do you see as the target audience? There's no need to go into technical demographics. An idea of the age and type, or some examples of films or programmes that your target generally watches will do the job. On the other hand, don't aim too wide. If you suggest your film will be popular across the board, you'll just sound inexperienced and over-optimistic (of course, nobody will complain if it turns out later to be the case).

- **Ideal cast** – who do you see starring? Have some realistic names in mind. If it's a micro-budget indie idea, there's no point in suggesting Tom Cruise. Know the appropriate actors who are hot at the moment.

- **Cross-platform opportunities** – be ready to talk about the possibilities for a spin-off Internet series, games, web pages on related themes, Twitter accounts for the characters, or whatever seems to make sense. It may never happen, but it shows you're aware.

- **Yourself** – whether they ask or not, make yourself a part of the package. Talk about why you first had the idea. What intrigued you? What personal experiences relate to this – either directly or indirectly? Is the story based on your own life? Or can you relate to issues it brings up? If they ask what you've done so far, be proud of what you've achieved, whether that's winning a screenwriting prize, making a short, getting an agent, or simply finishing a polished draft!

- **Anything else** – you never know what questions might come up. Be ready to improvise and think on your feet. A team player.

But, most of all, give them a chance to talk. Your aim should be to turn this into a conversation. You want the other person to become involved, to have ideas, to ask questions, to feel a part of the process and to ask to *see the script*.

Finally, whatever the outcome, at some point the other person will end the meeting. Don't overstay your welcome. Say a brief thank you and leave.

WILL THEY STEAL YOUR IDEAS?

Before we leave pitching, there's one question that always comes up with developing writers – is someone going to steal their work? I say 'developing writers' because experienced writers don't have an issue with this. They understand that the job entails going out and telling people about their ideas, and that theft of ideas is extremely rare. They're careful, but not paranoid.

 Key idea

> Most experienced writers are relaxed about pitching their ideas. They're careful, but not paranoid.

First, under UK law, every single thing written down is automatically your copyright. Assuming that it's original, and you didn't plagiarize it from another source, nobody can use it without your permission. You don't need to put a copyright © symbol on the front page, although it's OK to do so, next to the date. However, if you have concerns it's a good idea to register your script with a registration agency, primarily to prove that you wrote it when you did. The Writers Guild of America, for example, operates an online registration system and will hold your script for a time for a relatively small fee.

However, the idea itself is not covered by the law of copyright, only the development of that idea. This is one more reason why you should have developed your script as fully as you can before you start to pitch.

There is a law that covers ideas, and that's the law of confidentiality. Under that law, nobody has permission to take, repeat or use anything they've been told, if it was communicated to them confidentially.

A private meeting, a personal letter or email, even a workshop, would normally be considered to be confidential. To be absolutely sure, you probably ought to use the word 'confidential' at some point in an email or letter, but in fact that is often considered to be a sign of amateurishness in the industry – as is putting © or a copyright registration number on every page of a treatment or script.

The truth is that the risk of theft is minimal. Ask yourself why on earth they would want to steal your idea. The producer would only have to find another writer and pay them to write up the script. There would be no guarantee that the other writer could make your idea work. It would be much cheaper for them to buy your script and, if necessary, pay for rewrites.

That is not to say that many writers don't think they've been ripped off. Anyone who sees scripts regularly knows that the same ideas go round all the time. In 1994 two films were released coincidentally about Wyatt Earp. In 2005 two separate films were made about the writer Truman Capote. No theft. The idea was in the air.

Increasingly, writers are asked to sign confidentiality agreements when they submit work – this is to protect producers from being sued when the writer thinks that their ideas have been stolen. It is not, I suggest, a way for producers to steal your idea from under you. However, if you have any questions, you absolutely must check with an experienced media lawyer. The law does vary from country to country, and can change.

Having said that, very occasionally people do steal ideas. Be sensible. Don't go tweeting the premise or telling all your friends on Facebook. Don't pitch until you have a fully polished, compelling script and, when you do, pitch to reputable producers and agents. But the harsh truth is that few ideas are as enticing as their writers think they are.

Following up

Once you've sent your query letter, treatment or script, be patient. Producers and agents are busy, and have to fit reading time into an already crowded schedule. After two weeks to a month, it is perfectly permissible to email or phone politely to ask whether they've received the material, or when they expect to be able to read it.

Meanwhile, there is no reason not to send to other possible buyers. In the old days, it was considered bad form to send to more than one producer at a time, but life's too short and some producers have been known to sit on a script for six months or more – or never reply at all.

If someone asks to look at your script exclusively, that's a good sign, but insist on a strictly limited time period – one to two weeks would be reasonable.

In any case, don't carpet-bomb. Select your producers and agents with care. But keep going. You will receive rejections, of all kinds. If you're not getting rejections, you're not sending out enough. You'll know you're starting to get somewhere when you graduate from no reply, through a standard format rejection to a personal explanation as to why they aren't going to take it.

Key idea

If you're not getting rejections, you're not sending out enough.

All successful writers have had work rejected – often the very work that was praised later. However, if a script is consistently receiving the same response, it may be time to send it out for more feedback.

And while you do all that – start the next one. Build on what you've learned and make the next screenplay even better.

Tim Bevan, co-chairman, Working Title Films

'You just have to be tenacious; if you can't take no for an answer in order to get to yes, you ought not to be in the business.'

Workshop

Pair up. Each pair role plays a ten-minute pitch meeting. One of the pair plays the producer. The producer welcomes the writer and runs the meeting. Begin with some introductory conversation and then, when the time feels right, the producer asks what the writer has. After the pitch, the producer asks questions that feel appropriate.

At the end of ten minutes, the producer gives two minutes of sandwich feedback. What was good? How did the writer appear? Did he listen? Did he jump in and pitch before being asked? How was the pitch? Was it clear and short? Did he have good answers to the follow-up questions? What could be improved for the next time? What was the best thing he did?

Now swap around so that everyone has a chance to pitch to, and be pitched by, everyone else in turn.

At the end, ask for general feedback. What did you each notice when you were being pitched to? What did you notice when you were pitching?

And then ... success. What does success mean for you? And what happens afterwards? It's time to look into the future, at how you develop a screenwriting career.

28

Success – building your career

What is success? Success may initially be receiving some positive rejections for your first script, making useful contacts with your second, and having your third script praised, if not bought.

Then, one day, someone says 'yes'. If you persist, and continue to read, write, learn and listen, you have every chance of writing a script that an agent or producer will want- or that a producer likes enough to commission you to write a different one. What happens now?

Working with an agent

If it's an agent who says 'yes', she'll want to know that you have other ideas. She's not just taking on this one script, but your future career. You'll need to send her some evidence of new projects you're planning to write, or have written.

Assuming that they go down well, she'll give you an agent's agreement that outlines the percentages she takes and the terms on which you will work together. It probably won't be very long, maybe just a few pages, but if there is anything you're not sure about you ought to take legal advice (see 'Using a lawyer', below).

It should be easy to end the relationship. An agent's contract is usually open-ended, with no end date. Either side can end it, without needing to give a reason. Any contracts she's negotiated for you will usually remain with her, and she'll continue to collect her fee on any earnings from them. Any agreement that asks for more than that, such as fees from other contracts negotiated before you joined or after you leave, should be viewed with grave suspicion.

Key idea

An agent's agreement is usually open-ended. Either side can end it at any time.

Then she'll start sending your script out for you. She will know more people, and have more openings, but that doesn't mean your work is over.

First, she may well ask for another draft. There will be no money for this, of course, but you would be foolish not to do it. Someone in the industry is devoting their own time and effort to your script. You are free to discuss different approaches, but be open-minded. She has experience of what works for producers.

If you think she's misunderstood or a suggestion doesn't work, then, rather than merely blocking her ideas, come back with alternatives. She wants to see that you are professional, which means being able to work collaboratively. At worst, if after trying her ideas, you feel that the new draft really doesn't reflect what you wanted, then you can always say so. And if you can't reach agreement, you can always walk away. It's still your script.

Assuming you deliver a new draft you're both happy with, then don't expect your agent to do all the selling for you. You still need to get out, network, meet possible producers and pitch.

Hugh Laurie, actor

'Screenwriting is the most prized of all the cinematic arts. Actually, it isn't, but it should be.'

Write

Prepare a short list of pitches for further projects that you can show potential agents when they ask what other ideas you have. Between four and eight should be enough. They should be the strongest ideas you can think of. You may indeed already have a number that you've been working on, the either in early stages or even fully polished scripts.

There's no harm if they cover a range of genres, or even media, some cinema and some TV. As with a good series, an agent wants to know you have 'legs'.

Working with a producer

If a producer shows interest, there are two likely outcomes. One is that he'll ask for a rewrite before he signs an agreement; the other is that he'll offer an agreement before you rewrite. Either way, you can be sure that he'll want at least one new draft.

He'll also probably be even more prescriptive than your agent. You may think your script is finished, but no script ever is.

THE OPTION AGREEMENT

Only studios and some TV companies will ask to buy your script outright. In most cases, you'll be offered an option agreement. In an option agreement, the buyer doesn't buy the script but the exclusive right to work with the script, raising finance, and so on, over a fixed period of time. During that time, they can upgrade to a full assignment of the rights in the script, usually for a further payment, so that they can go on to make the film. However, if the time period for the option passes, the option lapses, which means all the rights are yours once more, to do with as you wish.

Never sign any agreement without obtaining advice from an agent, lawyer or writers' guild. A producer will send out a contract that's tilted in his favour, and agents and media lawyers are trained to spot anything that may work against you. However, here are the key features of a typical option:

- **Option period** – during this time the buyer has exclusive rights to use your script to raise finance, order rewrites, in effect do anything except actually shoot the film. The period may be lengthy, but one to three years would be normal.

- **Option payment** – the fee could be anything from £1 upwards, depending on how much they want to buy and you want to sell. But it is non-refundable; in other words, you get to keep the money whatever happens. If they have very little money to offer at this stage, you may decide to ask for a short option period, say six months or a year, with further payments specified for a second and third year. The second or third options may be granted only if the producer has made some mutually agreed progress.

- **Rewrites** – it's usual to ask for one rewrite to be included for free, but further drafts should really be paid for.

- **Exercise of option** – this happens generally when filming starts. At this point you should get a further fee, up to 2 per cent of the budget. You may also be offered a percentage of the net takings of the film. Accept the offer, by all means, but don't bank on ever seeing any of it.

- **Other terms** – there will be many other terms covering everything from who writes any sequels to the size of your screen credit. On your side, you will warrant that your script doesn't defame, libel, breach copyright or do anything else that may cause problems in the future. Read them carefully and get advice.

Key idea

Never sign anything without advice from an agent, lawyer or writers' guild.

Using a lawyer

If you don't have an agent, and are comfortable conducting your own negotiations, you can obtain good advice from experienced writers' associations, such as the Writers' Guild of Great Britain. But they won't do the deal for you.

Alternatively, you can hire a lawyer to represent you in negotiations. Don't try to cut corners and use your family solicitor. You need a specialist in media law, who is up to date with the latest legislation. You should find details of media lawyers in a good film industry directory (see Appendix 5).

Lawyers can be expensive, but many good media lawyers will be open to an offer if you are short of cash. Always agree a fixed fee in advance, to avoid nasty surprises. And make it clear, in writing, that they must not incur any further costs on top of that fee without your written agreement.

Nevertheless, whoever represents you, lawyer or agent, you are the one signing the contract, not them. They are acting on your behalf. So take the responsibility for ensuring that you understand every clause. Ask questions if necessary. Don't avoid asking because you're afraid you'll look foolish or like a beginner. You *are* a beginner, and their job is to help you as best they can.

Irving Thalberg, producer

'The most important person in the motion picture process is the writer, and we must do everything in our power to prevent them from ever realizing it.'

Snapshot exercise

If you're sent a contract, read it carefully and make sure that you understand all of it. You don't need to be an expert in law, but you should understand the basics of what you're signing. If necessary, ask. Don't make assumptions. And ask for any rights you want, such as consultation (see below) and first refusal over sequels. It'll be too late afterwards.

What next?

How things progress after you sign depends on the producer, the agent, the project and you. You may hear nothing for months at a time. This could be because they are developing the package, or because they keep getting turned down and don't want to give you bad news. Feel free to make contact occasionally, but don't nag. Ask how it's going and if there's anything you can do.

In other situations, you may be worked off your feet, rewriting drafts, consulting on developments, being invited along to meetings.

If you want to be consulted on who should direct or star, then ask for it up front and have it put in the option agreement. However, it's unlikely you'll get a veto, unless you've a strong track record or have helped raise some of the finance.

Some writers like to be involved, be on the set during shooting, see the rushes. Whether you can very much depends on the relationship you cultivate with the producer and director. If you are professional and a good collaborator, they may be happy for you to be around while they work – however, if for some reason they prefer you not to be, respect their wishes. Would you want them to insist on looking over your shoulder every minute while you write?

Some writers prefer not to be involved. Meetings can be time consuming, and, for all the glamour, spending time on set can be profoundly boring and take valuable time away from your writing. A good compromise would be to ask to be included in the major discussions (key cast and crew), a couple of rehearsals (if there are any), to attend key shooting days, and be invited to discuss the rough and final edits.

 Key idea

How much you're involved in the production depends on you, the producer and the director. Remember, they have their own needs and pressures, too.

There may come a point, however, when a new writer needs to be brought in. It happens to the best. No writer can do everything, and if the producer is prepared to pay for someone to strengthen the structure or add some jokes, take it as showing that your original script is worth the extra.

Your option agreement will certainly allow for a new writer, should one be needed, but, if possible, you should include the right to be consulted. Assuming that relations haven't broken down, a good producer would want to do this anyway.

Be professional and, at the same time, open-minded. You'll learn that, as a production grows, everyone has an opinion on the script – from star to catering. Smile and listen. They have probably seen more stories filmed than you have, and the assistant electrician is just as capable of having the big idea that saves a scene. Many great lines have come from other sources… and the writer still gets the credit.

David Nicholls, novelist and screenwriter

'A screenplay is really an instruction manual, and it can be interpreted in any number of ways. The casting, the choice of location, the costumes and make-up, the actors' reading of a line or emphasis of a word, the choice of lens and the pace of the cutting – these are all part of the translation.'

Developing your career

Think in the long term. It's all too easy to get caught up in the short-term impatience of the industry, but you need to plan your career as a screenwriter with care.

Farah Abushwesha, writer-producer

'Commit to a career, not to a screenplay.'

DON'T GIVE UP THE DAY JOB

Your first deal may tempt you to give up the day job. Don't. This is for at least two reasons – financial and psychological.

Financially, you are unlikely to have a steady stream of income for many years. Even if you've been clever/lucky and made good money on your first option or commission, this will probably need to be spread over the many years that you spent writing this script, and will spend writing the next. There is so much insecurity in a writer's life and the last thing you need is extra financial worries.

Another advantage of not being totally dependent on the next contract is that you have some freedom to think and create. And you can walk away from a bad deal if you have to.

There is also much to be said for having something else to think about. Without any other responsibilities, pressure grows and you can be tempted to overwork an idea. By contrast, during your day job, your unconscious can be working away and coming up with more creative solutions – and you are also observing people, experiencing new situations, meeting people and seeing the world.

Key idea

A day job can be useful in removing the pressure to deliver every day, financially as well as artistically.

What work is best for a writer may be a more difficult question, assuming that you have any choice at all. Every post has its advantages and disadvantages for a writer.

Work that involves writing could be useful – allowing you to develop your writing skills and be paid for it. However, this can use up your writing energy, leaving little for your own scripts.

A job in film or TV, if you can find it, offers the chance to make valuable contacts and learn how the industry works. However, such work is also demanding and time consuming. Having said that, the young Kurosawa held down an arduous job as an assistant director during the day, and wrote his scripts by night.

Tim Bevan, producer of many of the UK's top movies, recommends that all writers should spend time working – or at least observing – in a cutting room. Everything in your script comes to fruition there and you'll learn rapidly what works and what doesn't on screen – how a long speech can be replaced by a glance; how a simple cut can jump over unnecessary scenes.

Sometimes, the best day jobs can be those that take the least brain power. Stacking supermarket shelves or cleaning gives you plenty of time to ponder those tricky plot points or dialogue riffs. Whatever the work, remember to carry that notebook and pen at all times.

Meanwhile, if you have problems managing your time, and who doesn't, I recommend the book *Getting Things Done*, by David Allen. His system is devastatingly simple and effective – most people who read it become avid converts.

 Harlan Ellison, author and screenwriter

'Anybody can become a writer, but the trick is to stay a writer.'

 Snapshot exercise

In a spare moment, think back over the experience of the last script. What can you take away that could help you avoid the same pitfalls and progress faster with the next? Reread your journal. List a few possibilities. Maybe you'd like to try a different approach to character. Maybe you'd like to plan more at the start. Or less.

AND AT THE SAME TIME...

Whatever you do, keep writing. Whether it's an hour in the morning before work, or five hours at night before you sleep.

Try new ideas. Learn from your mistakes. Build on what you have. If you find you've struck a chord with a thriller, maybe you should consider writing two or three more thriller scripts before branching too quickly into other genres. However, if your first script is not finding traction, explore other genres. Perhaps you're more suited, at this point, to comedy. Or very personal stories. Or something else entirely.

The chances are that you'll do your best writing with the kinds of stories you enjoy watching, but that doesn't necessarily mean that every writer is best at writing what they love. You can love pulp, and write excellent and profound personal tragedies. And vice versa.

Write

Leave a suitable gap after completing the last screenplay. Then begin to jot down ideas for the next. It may be one that you listed for agents, or something quite different. You may have had an idea bubbling away while you were writing before, but you may also find that something quite new appears. Give yourself time. Don't rush into the new script, but at the same time don't delay too much either.

Toy with some thoughts. Doodle. Play with the ideas that come. Try out a premise or two. Allow one to take hold.

Jeffrey Caine, screenwriter, *The Constant Gardener*

'The more scripts a young writer can produce the better. My best calling card for years was an unproduced script — it still is not produced. Can you do a comedy, a love story, a thriller? The more varied your portfolio the better.'

DIGITAL FILMING

With the growth of digital filming and the Internet has come a large growth in ability to make short and very short films to a very high quality. Try writing films at ten minutes, five minutes and shorter. Three-to five-minute films do well on YouTube. If you have a phone and a computer, you can film one yourself. There is no experience as valuable as seeing your own work on the screen.

And you can gain from working with actors, directors, production designers, photographers, editors and musicians. Make contact with local film-makers, film students and acting groups. Many will be looking for good scripts to film.

COMPETITIONS

The Internet has also made it much easier to enter competitions. Some script competitions give cash prizes for winning treatments and scripts, while others give feedback to entrants and offer the winners time to work with a professional script consultant on their scripts. Yet other competitions offer the facilities to film an Internet short and have it publicized.

And don't underestimate the lustre a prize adds to a script, and to your own CV.

OTHER MEDIA

Equally importantly, look at other media. The structural, character and dialogue skills you're developing are in just as great demand for other platforms.

If you've been writing draft scripts for cinema so far, try creating an idea for television – or theatre.

Many of the best screenwriters refined their art in theatre. From Noël Coward and Harold Pinter to Tom Stoppard and Christopher Hampton, they have used the distinctive voice they developed as playwrights to create equally distinctive work for the screen. Theatre also offers a good writer opportunities that film and TV rarely can: for one thing, there are far more theatres taking new writing – especially if you include fringe venues. Even a small fringe production will give you two to three weeks' rehearsal and, say, a one-week run. That means you have 20-odd chances to hear actors speak your dialogue, and to adjust and rewrite as you go. That's equivalent experience to 20 film productions…

Radio drama is also a good place for you to ply your trade. While there are fewer slots in radio than there used to be, there is still a demand for good writing and well-told stories.

Finally, your structure and dialogue skills will also translate well to short stories and novels. The space available to a novelist can give you a chance to explore your characters and plots in greater depth and discover what works and what doesn't.

And if you can prove that your idea has an audience in print, you strengthen the chances of selling it to cinema or TV later.

Life as a writer

Ultimately, a writer's life is filled with contradictions.

You have to look inside, and also out. You have to write for yourself above all else, and yet never forget your audience. You have to make up lies in order to tell the truth. You have to be honest about deeply personal issues that you would probably not tell your closest loved-ones, and put them on a screen for the world to see. You have to live a full life and yet spend considerable time alone. You have to battle against your weaknesses – and yet accept them and use them to create – and this is one of the most powerful things a human being can do.

There is no one answer, and (despite the title of this book) no completion. A complete understanding of screenwriting is something you aim for, over a lifetime, while knowing it can never be achieved. Because you never stop learning. Otherwise it wouldn't be worth doing, would it?

But somehow, out of all of the paradoxes, come some of the greatest works of art that have ever existed on this planet.

It is how the human race talks to itself. And, if you put in the work, you have every right to take part in that conversation, too.

 Chinua Achebe, novelist

'The day when I am no more than a writer I shall cease to be a writer.'

Workshop

With your writing colleagues, go over your feelings about the finished script. Ask them what they feel your strengths are and how you can build on them.

Talk about what you might write next. Listen as much as you speak, if not more. You may be surprised. They may see strengths that you weren't aware of, or didn't see as being valuable. We often dismiss what we are naturally good at doing, and place more value on what takes greater effort. You need the effort, but you need to build on your natural abilities, too.

Discuss what you need to progress, and what's stopping you. What do you need to do more of? What do you need to do less of? What do you need to start doing and what do you need to stop doing altogether? Do you need to set boundaries or rearrange your time?

In any case, you are the one who'll have the final decision as to what you do next. Your fellow writers can advise and give feedback. But you're the one who will go off and write it.

Where to next?

If you haven't started, start. If you have started, keep writing.

And remember, enjoy the process and have fun along the way. Tell me how it goes via my website: http://www.charles-harris.co.uk

Appendix 1: 'Three ways' pages

When you come across a new understanding or a tip that strikes a chord with you, write it here. Underneath, add three simple, concrete actions that you can take based on this new insight. (You can, of course, add more.)
For example, if 'Writers have to put in the work' struck home, you might write:

1 Schedule a fixed time to write every morning, starting Monday.
2 Practise at least one exercise a day.
3 Mark the number of pages I write each day on my calendar (and give myself a reward).

The three actions should be specific and timed or dated, and at least one of them should be simple enough that you can be sure you'll do it. And if you reward yourself, it makes it even more likely that you'll remember next time.

Insight:

_____

_____

Action 1 _____

Action 2 _____

Action 3 _____

Insight:

_____

_____

Action 1 _____

Action 2 _____

Action 3 _____

Insight:

_____

_____

Action 1 _____

Action 2 _____

Action 3 _____

Insight:

_____

_____

Action 1 _____

Action 2 _____

Action 3 _____

Insight:

_____

_____

Action 1 _____

Action 2 _____

Action 3 _____

Insight:

_____

_____

Action 1 _____

Action 2 _____

Action 3 _____

Insight:

_____

_____

Action 1 _____

Action 2 _____

Action 3 _____

Insight:

_____

_____

Action 1 _____

Action 2 _____

Action 3 _____

Insight:

_____

_____

Action 1 _____

Action 2 _____

Action 3 _____

Insight:

_____

_____

Action 1 _____

Action 2 _____

Action 3 _____

Insight:

_____

_____

Action 1 _____

Action 2 _____

Action 3 _____

Insight:

_____

_____

Action 1 _____

Action 2 _____

Action 3 _____

Insight:

_____

_____

Action 1 _____

Action 2 _____

Action 3 _____

Appendix 2: Screenplay format

```
                TITLE OF SCREENPLAY

                        by
                  Writer's Name

                 Based on X by
                 Original Author
                 (if appropriate)


          Date (of current draft)
```

```
Your contact address
Phone
Email address
And agent's details if any
Go here, bottom left
```

This format and the planning charts that follow can also be downloaded for free from http://www.charles-harris.co.uk. together with a template for use in MS Word and similar word processors.

                                                    FADE IN:

INT. LOCATION - DAY

The text for your screenplay should be in Courier 12pt
font. Set A4 paper for European scripts (Quarto for USA)
with the left margin at 1½" (USA: 2").

Every scene must be headed by a SLUG LINE, which is all in
capitals. The slug line is primarily intended for the
production department, to help them break down the script
into different locations and lighting set-ups, so there
isn't much room for creativity here.

It begins either INT. or EXT. or very occasionally
INT./EXT. if the location is interior but also outdoors,
for example inside a car. This is followed by the name of
the LOCATION, which should remain consistent - don't give
the same location different names in different scenes.

The slug ends with instructions for the lighting cameraman -
DAY, NIGHT, DAWN or DUSK. Avoid other times, such as
"morning" or "afternoon", which don't involve changes in
lighting. You can use CONTINUOUS - but only if the scene
runs continuously, in a single camera shot, through
different locations.

Don't number the scenes until the film is financed.

Descriptions, visuals, actions, sounds, etc, should go in
the main text, as here, and be written in plain, non-
technical, English.

                    CHARACTER
          The name of the person speaking
          is placed above the dialogue, in
          capitals and indented 3½"

                    NEW CHARACTER
          Dialogue is indented 2½" from the
          left and around 2" from the
          right. Everything, including the
          speaker's name and dialogue is
          left aligned, extending to the
          right, not centred...

In the description, use CAPS the first time we see a NEW
CHARACTER. Some writers use caps for character names
throughout, but it's not necessary.

                    NEW CHARACTER (cont'd)
          ...and putting (cont'd) after the
          name of the speaker shows that
          dialogue was interrupted by
          action or a new page.

Pages must be numbered. The page number should be set top right (optional for the first page).

Use caps also for EMPHASIS, SOUND or (rare) TECHNICAL directions.

Keep the paragraphs short.

Especially in fast action scenes.

And don't put descriptions in brackets before dialogue. These should be reserved purely for instructions for how to deliver the line - and even then should be used very, very sparingly. Instead, try to make the delivery evident from the context.

                    CHARACTER
                (shouting)
            If you absolutely must describe
            how a character speaks, write it
            in brackets, as above, indented
            ½" to the right of the dialogue.

                    NEW CHARACTER (O.S.)
            Insert (O.S.) to show the
            character speaking out of shot,
            or (V.O.) for voice-over
            narration.

A transition such as FADE OUT., MIX TO: etc, is placed on a line of its own, also on the right.

                                        WIPE TO:

EXT. NEW LOCATON - NIGHT

You'll come across older scripts which use CUT TO: at the end of every scene. This is now unnecessary and looks rather dated.

Nowadays, writers use transitions sparingly and only write CUT TO: to point up a particularly sudden or dramatic cut.

Start the script with FADE IN: and, when the story's over, write FADE TO BLACK.

No need for THE END.

                                    FADE TO BLACK.

Appendix 3: Planning charts

1 Premise development checklist (see Chapter 3)

Project title	
Genre(s)	
Genre emotions	
Protagonist	
Protagonist's flaws	
Main goal/obstacle	
Irony (character change)	
Stakes?	
Visual?	
Different?	
Mental real estate?	
Copyright?	

2 Genre planning chart (see Chapter 4)

Genre(s)	
Favourite examples	
Genre emotions	
Genre patterns	
Twists and surprises	

3 Structure planning chart (see Chapter 7-9)

Act One	
Opening mood/visual	
Normality – flaw	
Taste of success	
Inciting incident	
Turning point – surprise – challenge – climax	
New decision	

Act Two	
Act Two project	
Initial denial (subplot?)	
Moment of commitment	
Midpoint	
Respite	
Downward path	
Turning point – surprise – challenge – climax	
New decision	

Act Three	
Final battle	
False ending	
True ending	
Character change	

4 Flashback planning chart (see Chapter 19)

Type of flashback (end/Act Two/ incremental/ironic/other)	
Outgoing scene	
Time anchor	
Outgoing cliffhanger	
New scene	
Immediate tension	
Indication of new time	
New dramatic line – goal – obstacle – action – tactics – stakes	

5 Balancing unusual structures: checklist
(see Chapter 20)

Structure type (number of acts/ episodic/mosaic/circular)	
Strengthened story goal	
Obstacles	
Stakes	
Momentum	
Dialogue signposts	
Non-dialogue signposts	
Ticking clock	
Theme	
Patterns and repetitions	
Methods for preparing the audience – title – visuals – sound – plot reversals – dialogue clues	
Rewards and compensations	

6 Pitching scratchpad (see Chapter 27)

Memorable title	
Genre	
Logline	
Target audience	
Comparable films/TV	
Difference	
Why this producer/agent? – strengths/successes	
What you bring – passion/experience/research	
What you've achieved (finished draft/ script competitions/other writing or relevant work)	
Your personal logline	
Exciting lead character	
Exciting antagonist/support	

Imaginary trailer	
Key character scene	
Key action scene	
Key visual scene	
Ideal cast	
Cross-platform opportunities	

Appendix 4: Glossary

ACT

A unit of storytelling at the end of which something crucial has changed. It finishes with a serious challenge to the protagonist, a surprise, an emotional climax and a new decision leading to the next act (or the end of the story).

ANTAGONIST

A character who is opposed to the protagonist's goals.

ART HOUSE

See Independent.

BEAT SHEET

Also Step outline. A longer treatment divided into individual story 'beats' or steps.

BLURB

A very brief summary of a film, drama or series, designed to hook a viewer, which doesn't give the ending.

CHARACTER ARC

Also Character journey and Inner story. The internal changes a character makes during the story or series episode.

COVERAGE

A script report made for a production company or agency, usually very brief, ending with a suggestion to pass (decline), consider (has pros and cons) or recommend (suitable for production).

DRAMADOC

A fictionalized true story.

INCITING INCIDENT

An event that takes place early in a script, or sometimes before it starts, which challenges the protagonist and sets the main story in motion.

INDEPENDENT

Also Indie or Specialist (used to be Art House). A sector that caters for audiences who want Non-mainstream films; cinemas independent of the main multiplex chains.

INNER STORY

A protagonist's internal struggle to overcome a major character flaw throughout the story, which directly affects their ability to achieve an important outer goal. See also Character arc and Outer story.

LEAVE-BEHIND

Material to leave after you've finished a meeting, usually a one-page summary of the project, including logline, short treatment and contact details. See also: one-sheet.

LOGLINE

One- or two-sentence summary of your story, ideally as stimulating and dramatic as possible. *See also:* pitch.

MASTER SCENE TREATMENT

A long treatment giving the story in considerable detail, close to the final script, except with less or no dialogue.

MENTAL GAME

Your mindset; your approach to the job of writing.

MENTAL REAL ESTATE

Names and ideas that are known across the world; key words and ideas that may attract a large audience.

MINI-SERIES

A short serial of generally two to three episodes; in the United States all serials are called mini-series.

MISE-EN-SCÈNE

All the non-verbal elements of a script, including setting, time of day, décor, visual action, sounds, etc. The way the scene is staged.

MOCKUMENTARY

A parody of a documentary.

O.S. (OUT OF SHOT)

Use O.S. after the speaker's name in a script, when a character is in a scene but talking off-camera. If the character is elsewhere, use a specific parenthesis such as (on phone), (over the Tannoy), etc. (However, don't use this for narration; *see* V.O.)

ONE-SHEET

(1) A one-page treatment; (2) A summary of the project on a single page, usually including title, logline, name of writer, one-paragraph treatment, writer's biography and contact details.

OUTER STORY

Also Throughline or Dramatic throughline. The visible external storyline, following the protagonist's attempts to achieve a filmable, concrete goal in the outside world. The driving force of a story. (not to be confused with the inner story.)

OUTLINE

Another word for treatment. See also: beat sheet

PITCH

(1) Your one- or two-sentence logline; (2) A (slightly) longer presentation giving the essential premise, theme and attractions of your project.

POV

Point of view; as if through a character's eyes.

PREMISE

The underlying idea for a project – film, single drama or series; usually expressed in no more than one or two sentences. *See also:* pitch.

PROTAGONIST

The central character of a story.

SCENE-BY-SCENE

A treatment that is broken down into individual scenes.

SEQUENCE

A series of scenes that make up a distinct step in the story.

SERIAL, SERIES

A serial (mini-series in the US) is a single screen story broken into individual episodes; a series is a succession of stand-alone episodes centring on the same characters, location or theme. There is also an increasing trend towards hybrid series in which each episode follows an individual story at the same time as developing storylines that run throughout the series.

SLUG-LINE

The line at the top of a scene in a script that shows the location and whether it's day, night, dawn or dusk (but not morning, midday, etc.). If there's been a jump of many years, the slug-line will often include the year, for clarity.

SPEC SCRIPT

A script written speculatively, not commissioned.

SPECIALIST

See: Independent.

SPEED-WRITING

Writing fast using 'writer's mind', without stopping, correcting, criticizing or reading back; first-draft writing. This may be timed or open-ended.

STEP OUTLINE

See Beat sheet.

STRAP-LINE

A line about the film or programme used in advertising, for example on a poster. Unlike the logline, this aims to give a mood or emotion, rather than the story premise.

SUBTEXT

Unspoken thoughts and ideas that are understood by the audience by reading between the lines.

SUPPORT CHARACTER

A subsidiary character who is trying to help a major character, such as the protagonist or antagonist.

SYNOPSIS

See Treatment.

THROUGHLINE

See Outer story.

TREATMENT

Also Synopsis, Outline. A short version of a script in the present tense, third person, that gives the key story points, including the ending.

TURNING POINT

A dramatic step that changes the entire direction of a script.

V.O. (VOICE OVER)

Used for an unseen narrator, speaking from outside the story. This may be a character, for example recalling the events we're seeing on screen, or a quite separate commentator (not to be confused with O.S.).

Appendix 5: Resources

Useful software

Any recommendations for software can be out of date the moment they are written. But here are a few that I have found particularly useful when researching, planning and writing scripts. I've put links to all these on my website, www.charles-harris.co.uk

Celtx
Free. The most popular of many free screenwriting programs, Celtx will automatically ensure that your script is formatted correctly and helps with outlining and breaking down. However, don't expect all the features of a paid-for program such as Final Draft.

Evernote
Free and paid. A very flexible research tool. You can write and order notes on any subject, clip web pages and save a wide range of material, from pictures to sounds, all in one place for reference. It will synch with all your devices and also allow collaboration. The paid version adds extras such as the ability to search for text in pictures.

Final Draft
Free trial. The industry standard word-processor for screenwriting, with a range of useful features from formatting to suggesting names of locations and characters you've used before.

Movie Magic
Free trial. The other industry standard word-processor for scripts. Full of useful features and links well with production breakdown software.

Scrivener
Free trial. As well as making it easy to write in the correct format, Scrivener offers the best features for planning and editing. You arrange scenes and move them around as if on a corkboard, with powerful tools for storing research, saving pictures and sounds, developing ideas, exploring different versions of the same scene, and more.

Textpad
Free trial. Sometimes you need to be able to jot down or save a note very simply and quickly. Textpad is inexpensive, loads fast and is more flexible than the built-in notepad software that comes with your computer.

Whizfolders Organizer
Free trial. Whizfolders offers a simple yet powerful system of organizing your thoughts. Very useful for keeping and accessing research notes, as well as odd jottings, outlining diary writing, storing experimental scenes and outtakes, to name but a few.

Word screenplay format template
Free. If you want to stick with your favourite word processor, I've created a template on my website that will give you the correct screenplay formatting in Word and compatible programs. http://www.charles-harris.co.uk

Suggested reading

A great teacher once told me that, if you read 30 books on a subject, you own that subject. Books can't replace writing and reading scripts, but they can certainly supplement it.

A serious writer's bookshelf should include a number of reference volumes, including at least one good dictionary and thesaurus.

I also advise buying a reverse dictionary. This, as it sounds, works in reverse. Instead of looking up a word to find out what it means, you look up a definition to find the word you were trying to think of. This is remarkably useful. At least one visual dictionary or visual encyclopaedia is also recommended. This allows you to find the correct word for an item, style or detail – for example, the name for a specific kind of classical column or the different parts of a gun.

Other reference books to consider are a good slang dictionary, a slang thesaurus and books on style and grammar.

For further study

The 21st Century Screenplay – Linda Aronson (Allen & Unwin, 2010; Silman James, 2011). This highly insightful guide to how a screenplay works begins with the basics and then accelerates into a detailed analysis of the many variables of different narrative structures.

Alternative Scriptwriting: Beyond the Hollywood Formula – Ken Dancyger and Jeff Rush (Focal Press, 2013). One of the few books that deals with breaking the rules, it also offers rare but welcome coverage of genre.

The Art of Adaptation: Turning Fact and Fiction into Film – Linda Seger (Henry Holt & Co., 1992). One of the few books that concentrate specifically on adaptations. Excellent.

The Craft Art of Playmaking – Alan Ayckbourn (Faber & Faber, 2001). Specifically about writing for theatre, from a master dramatist, but highly relevant to screenwriters.

The Craft of the Screenwriter – John Brady (Simon and Schuster, 1981). In-depth interviews with six major screenwriters, from Paddy Chayefsky to Robert Towne.

The Devil's Guide to Hollywood – Joe Eszterhas (Gerald Duckworth & Co, 2007). Much wise (and worldly-wise) advice from one who's been to the Devil's lair and survived.

The Film Director's Intuition: Script Analysis and Rehearsal Techniques – Judith Weston (Michael Wiese Productions, 2003). Contains a wealth of powerful tools useful for screenwriters.

Getting Things Done – David Allen (Piatkus Books, 2002). Indispensable guide to organizing your life, for all who feel overwhelmed and want to manage their time.

The Guerilla Film-makers Handbook – Chris Jones and Genevieve Jolliffe (Continuum International, 2006). How to work at the micro-budget level, from the founder of the London Screenwriters' Festival.

Hitchcock's Secret Notebooks – Dan Auiler (Bloomsbury, 1999). Fascinating first-hand materials from one of the cinema greats at work with his screenwriters and other collaborators.

How to Make Money Scriptwriting – Julian Friedmann (Intellect Books, 2000). An agent's no-nonsense view of the industry and what it takes to survive and succeed.

How to Write a Movie in 21 Days – Viki King (HarperCollins, 2000). Good on first-draft writing.

Inside Story – Dara Marks (Three Mountain Press, 2007). Excellent analysis of how character journey connects with the outer story.

Made for Television: Euston Films Limited – Manuel Alvarado and John Stewart (BFI/Thames Methuen, 1985). Includes treatments for highly successful single dramas, series and serials. Not currently in print, but second-hand copies can be tracked down.

Making a Good Script Great – Linda Seger (Samuel French, 2010). One of the classic texts on editing and redrafting.

On Film-making – Alexander Mackendrick (Faber, 2006). Although aimed at the film director, Mackendrick's sections on scriptwriting are invaluable.

Raindance Writers' Lab: Write and Sell the Hot Screenplay – Elliot Grove (Focal Press, 2008). Direct and accessible, from the creator of the Raindance Film Festival.

Save the Cat! – Blake Snyder (Michael Wiese Productions, 2005). A favourite from the moment it came out. The Hollywood system made simple.

Screening the Novel – Gabriel Miller (Ungar, 1980). By comparing eight classic films in detail with the novels they were made from, Miller produces a unique insight into how films, and novels, work.

Seeing is Believing – Peter Biskind (Pluto Press, 1984). This is an engrossing analysis of how genres (from gangster and Western to melodrama) can be adapted to different political ends.

Selling Your Story in 60 Seconds – Michael Hauge (Michael Wiese Productions, 2006). Clear and practical advice on preparing the pitch and using it in action.

Story – Robert McKee (Methuen, 2010). The guru's guru. McKee's book is better than some of his critics would have it, and very strong on key elements of storytelling and scene construction.

Thinking in Pictures – John Sayles (Houghton Mifflin, 1987). A top indie writer-director on the writing and making of his movie *Matewan*, complete with the full screenplay.

Woody Allen on Location – Thierry de Navacelle (Sidgwick & Jackson, 1987). A detailed hour-by-hour diary of the shooting of Allen's classic *Radio Days*. The appendix includes a parallel breakdown of the film as it was planned and as it was actually filmed.

Writers' & Artists' Yearbook (A&C Black, annually). Reference work including TV and film companies, agents, publishers and magazines, together with useful advice sections.

Writing for Television: Series, Serials and Soaps – Yvonne Grace (Kamera Books, 2014). A very solid introduction to the world of the professional TV writer from a highly experienced award-winning screenwriter and producer.

Industry directories, print and online

Kays – www.kays.co.uk
KFTV – http://www.kftv.com/
The Knowledge – www.theknowledgeonline.com
Mandy – www.mandy.com

Trades

Hollywood Reporter – Cinema and TV: www.hollywoodreporter.com
Screen International – Cinema, UK based, global coverage:
    www.screeninternational.com/
Variety – Cinema and TV, US based: www.variety.com
Broadcast – UK TV and radio: www.broadcastnow.co.uk
Televisual – UK TV, radio and video: https://www.televisual.com/

Useful websites

BBC Writers Room – www.bbc.co.uk/writersroom – Strong resource for new writers
    looking to write for the BBC (or anyone else).
BFI – www.bfi.org.uk – British Film Institute, provides funds to support screenwriters
    and film-makers as well as other educational resources, films to watch online and in
    the BFI's own cinemas.
Cinando – www.cinando.com/ – Database of industry people, facts and figures,
    including festival delegates. Subscription based.
Drew's Script-O-Rama – www.script-o-rama.com/ – Best internet resource for
    downloading free scripts, mostly cinema, more limited for TV.
Euroscript – www.euroscript.co.uk – Originally London Screenwriters' Workshop, the
    first screenwriters' workshop in the world. Free networking events, screenwriting
    competitions, workshops, industry news and articles on many aspects of
    screenwriting.
The Internet Movie Database – www.imdb.com – Largest database for cinema and
    TV. Invest in the IMDb Pro version for fuller contact information on companies,
    producers, directors and cast.
Raindance – www.raindance.org – The biggest indie film festival in the world also runs
    workshops for film-makers internationally.
Shooting People – https://shootingpeople.org – Discussion lists for screenwriters and
    film-makers, with news of events and courses, low-budget work opportunities and a
    pitching forum.
Writers Guild of America, West and East – www.wga.org and www.wgaeast.org The
    screenwriters union for the US also offers script registration for international writers
    (no need to be a member), articles and other resources.
Writers' Guild of Great Britain – www.writersguild.org.uk – The primary screenwriters'
    union for the UK offers advice on contracts for members, together with an excellent
    supply of screenwriters' interviews as downloadable podcasts.

Further contact

If you found this book useful, you can find me at www.charles-harris.co.uk. Here you'll be able to join my mailing list for the latest information on screenwriting, read a large archive of articles, download templates and guides. It would be great to hear from you. Email me, ask questions and share your experiences and successes.

You can also find me on Twitter at @chasharris,

Facebook: https://www.facebook.com/charlesharris008

LinkedIn: uk.linkedin.com/in/charlesharris01

Finally, join JustWrite – the online community run by John Murray Learning for all creative writers, sharing news, exclusive content, writers' workshops and general literary musings: http://www.tyjustwrite.com/

Index